Donald Olding Hebb

Professor and Chairman
Department of Psychology
McGill University

psychology

To

Elizabeth

Preface

Aʙᴏᴜᴛ six years ago I took a new look at the introductory course in
psychology and finding no textbook that covered what I wanted in subject matter, was driven to write one. This book is the result. In it I
attempt to clarify and codify the ideas which make up the main structure
of psychological theory in ways that will be intelligible to the beginning
student and at the same time reasonably rigorous. In doing so I have
omitted (or treated very succinctly) matters that have traditionally made
up a good proportion of the introductory course; and have included
others that are, as far as I know, here stated formally for the first time.
My object has been to include the ideas and information needed for the
understanding of psychological problems, as far as this is feasible in an
introductory textbook, and to exclude the merely traditional.

The raison d'être of the content, the underlying philosophy of science,
will be found in Chapters 1 and 13. Psychology is fundamentally a biological science, not a social science, nor a profession; out of it have
grown social psychology and applied psychology, both of which now
exist in their own right as disciplines distinct from the parent stem—
and yet maintaining their organic relation with it. The relation exists
because both demand a solid understanding of the mechanisms of behavior in the individual subject. The student's approach to either social
or applied psychology, therefore, is through the ideas of "biological" psychology—the theories of learning, perception, emotion and so on which
are biological because they have always been profoundly influenced by
neurophysiology, neuroanatomy, and evolutionary and genetic theory.

This book is meant both for the student who will go on to further courses in the subject, and for the one who takes only one, the "terminal," course. Both pedagogically and professionally, it seems to me that the terminal course should be no less scientific than the one which is an introduction to further work.

If psychology is a science, it should be presented as a science; it is at least as interesting, intellectually, as its applications, and I surely do not need to argue here that basic science is in the long run a very practical training. We would not think at the graduate level of turning out practitioners without a thorough basic training; we insist instead that a critical understanding is vital to the professional psychologist. Training in methods only, it is agreed, is a mistake. But if we give a first course which is primarily concerned with personal adjustment and the like, we are making precisely that mistake. The function of the course instead should be to develop critical understanding, to prepare the student to evaluate his later reading in the field of method, and prepare him also to understand the new methods that will be developed after he has left his "terminal" course. Valuable as the practical methods of psychology now are, I believe that those of the future will be more valuable still; if so, the theoretical and academic course is—as I have said above—the most practical one in the long run.

In the references to be found in the *Notes* at the end of each chapter, I have chosen primarily to refer to textbooks (having in mind the difficulties that result when a large class is sent to read a journal article); and especially to the three handbooks of general experimental psychology (*General References,* p. 19). For the more advanced student who may wish to use the book, however, I have also given some references to the original literature.

My indebtedness to others is great. I have received invaluable assistance in having the whole manuscript read by Drs. F. A. Beach, D. Bindra, W. J. McKeachie, Helen Mahut, P. M. Milner, C. Pfaffman, Muriel Stern, and W. K. Stewart: they have improved the book in many respects, including some of its major features. Improvements have also been made by Drs. W. Heron, R. Melzack, and S. K. Sharpless, who read large parts of the manuscript. On the clerical side I am indebted to D. Kimura for most of the drawings, and to Doreen Hogg for bibliographical help; and I am particularly indebted to Helen Temple for preparation of the manuscript and for painstaking work with proofs. But I must not conclude here without adding that the staff of the W. B. Saunders Co. have given me assistance in many ways that go far beyond the call of a publisher's duty. It is a pleasure to acknowledge all this help, without which the book would not have been possible.

D. O. HEBB

Contents

Chapter 1

Behavioristics and the study
of mind

A_N introductory textbook in psychology must begin by showing what psychology is and how it goes about its business, for there is no other field in which the gap is so great between popular and scientific conceptions. Experimental psychology bears little relation to what is called psychology in the magazines and newspapers. This book of course will present the student with a good many facts, methods of experiment, and so forth, but it has a still more important purpose: namely, to teach the student to think in a new way about the living organism and the activity that we call behavior.

In this first chapter we shall try to see what the field of psychology is (though the student may find it hard to understand until he has mastered the following chapters, and then returns to this one). The word psychology literally means the study of mind. In this century, however, psychology has become known as the study of behavior. The term "behavioristics" refers to a combination of these approaches: we are trying to understand what people do (that is, behavior), but to do this we must understand what goes on in their heads (that is, mental processes or mind). Thus we study both behavior and mind—from somewhat different points of view, as we shall see.

Definitions

It is difficult to give a precise and unequivocal definition of psychology, partly because the terms which must be used in a definition are themselves equivocal, meaning different things to different people. To define it as the study of behavior is not quite satisfactory, because this includes a large segment of physiology. Mouth-watering is behavior, and so is clenching the fist; to find out how the parotid gland secretes saliva, or how muscle cells produce finger movements, is a problem for the physiologist. (The psychologist is more concerned with the way in which many such small single items of behavior combine to form complex actions over longer periods of time.) On the other hand, the older definition—that psychology is the study of mind—does not cover the full range of phenomena with which we are concerned. Psychologists for example have traditionally been students of learning, not only in higher species but also in the earthworm and the ant. These organisms do not have the complexity of function which is referred to by the terms "mind" and "mental," so when a psychologist studies learning in the ant he is not dealing with mental processes, in any reasonable use of the term.

With these considerations in mind, we can attempt some definitions, with commentary to avoid misunderstanding.

Psychology is the study of the more complex forms of organization in behavior, and of processes such as learning, perception or emotion which are involved in the organization. The focal problem is found in the patterns of behavior shown by the whole animal of a higher species over appreciable periods of time; to say the same thing in a different way, it is found in the mental processes of the higher animal.

Behavior is the publicly observable activity of muscles or glands of external secretion as manifested in movements of parts of the body or in the appearance of tears, sweat, saliva and so forth. Talking is behavior; so is a smile, a grimace, eye-watering, trembling, blushing (which is produced by muscular changes in blood vessels), changing one's posture, or following the words of a printed page with the eyes.

The *organization* of behavior is the pattern, or combination, of separate items in relation to each other and to environmental stimulation. A pattern may be either spatial or temporal, but usually is both. A spatial pattern is the combination of activity in different parts of the body; a temporal pattern is a sequence of activities. An example of a very simple spatial pattern is the simultaneous movement of thumb and forefinger, in opposition, when taking hold of a small object; an example of a spatial and temporal pattern is reaching forward, picking up the object with one hand and, having focussed the eyes on it, touching it or turning it over with the other hand. Far more complex patterns are produced when an animal is looking for food, or when a child plays with a toy.

It is more difficult to specify what behavior is well organized and what is not. Such distinctions are made in a rough sense only. We may say that behavior is judged as organized when the various muscle contractions seem to the observer to constitute a smooth flow of movement, or to have a coordinated effect; otherwise, as unorganized, or disorganized.

Most behavior is not a disjointed series of separate actions but a continuing process, a flow of activity which varies in smoothness or turbulence. For the purpose of analysis and recording it is often necessary to divide the flow into arbitrary units, but this is artificial and theoretical, like describing water as consisting of atoms of hydrogen and oxygen.

Mind and *mental* refer to the processes inside the head that determine the higher levels of organization in behavior. These are most evident in the higher mammals, and concern the activity of the whole body over periods of minutes, hours or days. In this book we shall assume that mind is an activity of the brain, and that our knowledge of it is chiefly theoretical, inferred from behavior rather than being obtained directly from self-observation (i.e., from *introspection,* "looking inward").

There are two theories of mind, speaking very generally. One is animistic, a theory that the body is inhabited by an entity—the mind or soul—that is quite different from it, having nothing in common with bodily processes. The second theory is physiological or mechanistic; it assumes that mind is a bodily process, an activity of the brain. Modern psychology works with this latter theory only. Both are intellectually respectable (that is, each has support from highly intelligent people, including scientists), and there is certainly no decisive means available of proving one to be right, the other wrong.

In these circumstances, we use the mechanistic set of ideas as we would a working assumption, because they are proving—at present, though not in the earlier history of psychology—to be more useful in analysis and research. The student should realize that scientific theories are never regarded as final truth but as subject to possible revision at any time. Working with a particular theory is often on an "as-if" basis, and does not require that the user should believe it.

Saying that our knowledge of mind is theoretical rather than observational means that we study mind in the same way as a chemist studies the atom. Atoms are not observed directly, but their properties can be inferred from observable events. The chemist says in effect, If the atom of hydrogen has such-and-such characteristics, then the gas should behave so-and-so when it is mixed with a certain other gas, let us say, at a particular temperature. He performs this experiment, and if the results agree with expectation his theory of the nature of the hydrogen atom can be retained; if not, the theory is modified and he tries again.

For psychology, our problem is to construct, in imagination, the complex machinery of mind that will account for the phenomena of behavior. This is the method of *behavioristics* (*behaviorism* is a related term, but is often used to mean a particular kind of theory, which when first formulated denied the existence of mental processes entirely; behavioristics refers to a method of studying mental processes. See the following paragraphs).

Finally, *public* or *objective evidence* is defined as evidence which might be obtained equally well by any of a number of observers: in most cases, evidence which two or more observers can record at the same time. *Private,* or *subjective,* or *introspective evidence* concerns events within the observer himself, and by the nature of things available to that one observer only. It may happen that there is only one observer of a public event, as for example when there is only one eye in the whole world that is applied to a telescope pointing in the right direction when some unique event occurs in the heavens; even more, there may be only one telescope strong enough, so that it is impossible for more than one person to make the observation; but the event is still public, for another observer could have seen it just as well—it is not peculiar to one person. On the other hand, if the reader gets a headache from this text his pain is a private event—no one else can experience it as he does.

But if he describes the pain, aloud or in writing, the description itself is a public event; and so are his facial expressions. That is, speech, writing and facial contortions are behavior, which others can observe. From such behavior they can infer, and have theoretical knowledge about, something inside the subject which he calls pain and which makes him behave as he does. As an objective science, therefore, modern psychology constructs its theory of mind from the public data of behavior.

Sometimes it may seem that private data are being used, especially when there is agreement among different persons concerning their private experiences. Visual after-images are a good example (p. 34). But the only agreement we know about is in the *reports* of these different persons: in certain conditions they behave in the same way. Speech, and introspective description, is not a sort of pipeline direct to the consciousness of another, giving us first-hand knowledge. It is behavior, from which we may infer, correctly or incorrectly, the nature of the underlying processes that determined what the subject has said. All that we can know about the conscious processes of another, or about what the psychiatrist calls the unconscious, is *an inference from behavior,* verbal or nonverbal.

Further, we shall see in Chapter 2 that a subject's reports may be a most unreliable source of information about what goes on in the mind of another, even though he is entirely honest. Just to ask the color-blind subject what colors he can see is likely to give most unsatisfactory results. Many subjects report having memory images at which they can "look" just as if a picture or a page of print were being held up before their eyes; but objective test methods show that the actual situation is very different. Where emotions are involved self-knowledge and introspective report become still less satisfactory. When therefore we make behavior the basis of psychology, and eschew reliance on introspective evidence, we are not necessarily throwing away a superior kind of information about the mind or refusing to take the most direct route to our goal. What we are really saying is that one kind of behavior, introspective report, is extremely difficult to interpret, and that it is a reasonable procedure to build in the first place on other forms of behavior in which perhaps we may find more reliable evidence.

This brings us to the large part that animal subjects play in modern psychology.

The place of animal studies in psychology

There are three reasons why scientists study animals, and all three apply in psychology. The first, as important for pure science as any other, is that animals are fascinating and may be studied for their own sakes. Their behavior presents some of the most engaging puzzles to be found anywhere, which is quite enough reason for trying to solve them.

The second reason is more crudely practical. One can do experiments on animals that one cannot do on men. If one is interested for example in knowing what would happen to intelligence if a particular part of the brain were destroyed, one's only hope of finding out with human subjects is to wait—perhaps forever—until a patient enters hospital with a brain injury in exactly the right place. But surgical operations can be done with animals, with the same anesthetics and the same care to prevent infections. It is experimental animal surgery that has led to the skill with which a surgeon can treat human illness, and in the psychological laboratory is now leading to a new understanding of man's behavioral problems, with humanitarian values whose future extent we can only guess at today.

Also, one cannot do breeding experiments with man, or rearing experiments. One cannot bring up children shut off from contacts with the rest of the world to see if the effect is to produce low intelligence, or abnormal behavior, but one can do the experiment with animals. Man is a poor animal for breeding and rearing experiments anyway, because it takes a child so long to grow; the experimenter would be dead before the experiment got well under way, unless the answer could be had from a single generation of experimental subjects. This difficulty applies to a number of higher animals, and not man alone. The great apes in particular take eight to ten years to grow up; and so nearly all breeding and rearing experiments in psychology have been done with laboratory rats and mice, with which one can readily get two or more generations a year for study.

The third reason for studying animals is less utilitarian, nearer the high philosophical plane of the first. It is the need of *comparative* study, to understand one animal better by setting his behavior against that of another and seeing how they are similar as well as how they differ. Only in this way does one see how remarkable some features of behavior are; paradoxically or not, it is only through working with animals that one is likely to gain a proper respect for man's intellectual capacities.

If we knew nothing about animal behavior, for example, we would never guess what a tremendous intellectual feat is performed by the two-year-old child who can make a sentence and use it to get something he wants. Language is picked up by the child without apparent effort. Even children we think very stupid can use it to good effect, and only the proud parents of a first child are much impressed when the feat is achieved.

But comparative psychology puts a different light on the matter. The rat's intellectual processes we know now are complex (too complex to be well understood yet, despite thirty or forty years of intensive effort); dogs are much more complex, more intelligent, than rats, and chimpanzees still more so—far beyond the rat in many ways; yet no chimpanzee, nor any other animal, is capable of using language as the child does. (The talking birds, as we shall see later, are no exception.) Only through such comparisons does it become possible to put the intelligence of man in proper perspective. The behavioristic approach, by applying similar methods to man and animal, does not degrade man but on the contrary dignifies him. It shows, as the introspective method never did, the true enormity of the problem of accounting for his mental processes.

No psychologist would dream of arguing that we should fully solve the problem of animal behavior before tackling man. But there are great advantages to studying both at the same time. One reason is to be able to use the comparative method, but there is also the hope that it may be easier to unravel the less complex behavior of lower animals and, in so doing, that we may find new leads to the study of human behavior. It is quite clear that the anatomical organization of the brains of all mammals is essentially the same; and it seems clear also that the principles of behavior, or of brain function, are the same in great part if not entirely. Psychology in the twentieth century is not the study of the human mind, but the study of *mind*—when mind is defined as at the beginning of this chapter. It is as proper an occupation for a psychologist to study the chimpanzee as it is to study man; and there is reason to think that the study of both, by similar methods, will be a more profitable enterprise than the study of either alone.

Problems of human behavior: abnormal personality

In abstract terms, we have seen what psychology is and what it tries to accomplish. Our definitions will have more meaning if we now begin the study of behavior by looking at some aspects of personality and, in the following section, of social behavior. Under these headings come the topics of mental health and mental illness, juvenile delinquency, racial and religious prejudice, and the causes of war (to name a few, but not at random). There is no need to emphasize the importance for human welfare of learning how to deal with such problems. Much of the money and time spent on research in psychology is spent in the hope that it will contribute to their solution. The hope is justified by the fact that a good deal has already been accomplished. But obviously there is much more to be learned than has been to date.

Does this mean, in view of the urgency of the problems, that all research should be concentrated on them directly? The answer certainly is No. A scientific problem is not always solved by attacking it head on, and the present discussion will try to show the student how experiments with learning in dogs, for example, form part of the whole process of understanding human problems. There are different levels of analysis of such complex structures as the nervous system; it is important to study mental illness directly, but if it is to be really understood we need to study normal mechanisms also, and—sometimes in man, sometimes in animals—the separate processes that are involved in the development of normal or abnormal personality.

Personality is a relatively vague term, not susceptible of very precise definition. It refers to the mental characteristics that determine the general pattern of behavior in a higher animal, especially as it makes the individual distinctive in his relations with others. Some psychologists use the term to include intellectual characteristics; others distinguish, roughly, between intelligence and personality, and use the latter term to refer to the total picture of such emotional, motivational and social characteristics as friendliness, selfishness, sluggishness, initiative, leadership, cheerfulness and so forth, excluding intelligence as far as possible.

In mental illness the whole personality is apt to be affected, in many different ways (it is not quite true that every patient thinks he is Einstein, or the Emperor Napoleon come back to life). Three cases are cited here to show some of the variety that is observed in the clinic.[1]

Mrs. X, 47 years old, had begun with an attack of depression lasting three days. Later the attacks became monthly and increased in length to about two weeks. Still later, these attacks were preceded by periods of exhilaration ("euphoria"). When she was depressed Mrs. X wanted to die (though she did not try to commit suicide), refused to see any visitor, would not speak, and did not eat or dress herself. In the periods of exhilaration she sang and danced, expected unreasonable things of other persons, and was angered by advice or any attempt to get her to behave in a reasonable way. Her behavior continued to deteriorate and after two years she had to be confined in hospital, for her own protection and that of others. No effective treatment had been found at the time the case was reported.

Dr. Y, 35 years old, was a dental officer in the army. Following an attack of laryngitis he continued to feel weak and tired, and lost all interest in his work. He developed a persistent indigestion, with heartburn, and thought he must have a stomach ulcer, but no evidence of this was found when he was examined medically. His ability to work was interfered with, and he lost his confidence in himself so that difficult cases were handed over to his colleagues to deal with. He did not of course have to be confined in hospital for such symptoms ("contact with reality" was maintained) but his emotional discomfort was severe and his working efficiency was greatly impaired. Psychotherapy (cf. p. 9) did not remove his fundamental emotional problems, which were connected with certain family relations, but did lessen their severity so he could tolerate them and permitted him to go on with his professional work.

Mr. Z, 30 years old, had been a medical student. He had done satisfactory work in his

---

[1]These cases are paraphrased from Strecker, Ebaugh and Ewalt: *see Notes*, p. 18

first year but began to have difficulty with the second. He had headaches, could not concentrate, and lost weight. He began to think that his teachers wanted him to fail, in the forthcoming examinations. Then, studying alone one night, he suddenly leaned out of his window and shouted obscene objections at some unknown persons who were, he said, shining a light in his eyes. In hospital, his illness progressed; he often refused to talk to anyone, but sometimes would speak about mysterious persons who were persecuting him. These persons were disarranging his thoughts (which prevented him from studying), calling him obscene names, and directing a mysterious penetrating ray at him which damaged him sexually. He had prolonged periods when he was totally unresponsive, even to pinprick, and had to be fed by stomach tube. In these periods his limbs could be moulded into any kind of bizarre posture and would remain so. No effective treatment was found.

What causes mental illnesses? How can they be cured, or better, prevented? We can go about finding answers in two ways. One is empirical and practical; working directly with mental patients, trying this procedure and that, finding out directly by trial and error which procedures help and which do not. The second approach is more or less theoretical; it sets out to understand the problem first, not to help anyone. The idea is that when we understand both normal and abnormal personality we will see new possibilities for treatment (and prevention) which would never be thought of otherwise.

Both aspects of research are essential. The first has produced immediately practical knowledge of great importance—for example, in the current use of tranquillizing drugs, which have benefited large numbers of patients though no one quite knows how they work nor why—and, in any case, when a patient is seriously in need of help the psychiatrist cannot say, We do not yet really understand your problem; come back in ten years' time and let us see what can be done for you then. He must help now, and in fact he can help a great deal. But for the great majority of cases the available treatments are palliative; they lessen the severity of illness rather than removing it; and the hope of better ones in the future lies mainly in the development of our theoretical understanding.

Fundamentally the question is, What *is* mental illness? At one extreme we have the possibility (1) that it is simply a set of bad habits, wrong ways of thinking, the result of special stresses, of having learned to fear things that need not be feared, or of not learning how to deal with the problems of adult life. This would mean that we are not really discussing an *illness;* it is not a medical problem but an educational one. If children are brought up right, so-called mental illness will not occur. At the other extreme we have the possibility (2) that it is truly an illness, a medical problem only, to be treated with drugs or the like (when we know what drugs to use). Some part of the machinery is out of order and repairs are needed before its functioning can return to normal.

Which of the two answers is correct? We do not know certainly, but the answer in all probability is Neither, or Both. Views on this question differ radically, and presumably will do so until we understand the human mind much better than we do now. But there are many indications that mental illness frequently is a combination of undesirable learning or ways of thinking, and some disorder or weakness of a part of the machinery.

Those who have attacked the problem directly have often settled in advance on one of the two answers. (1) Working with the first hypothesis, that the disorder is the result of childhood learning, one can explore the patients' histories to see what particular experiences or what kind of rearing they have had that normal subjects have not had. If this should be successful, one could then prevent mental illness in the future by showing parents how to rear children whose behavior at maturity will be normal and healthy. Or, with the same hypothesis, one can explore methods of changing what was learned in childhood and replacing it with something more satisfactory, thus correcting behavior that is already disturbed. *Psychotherapy* is the attempt to correct disordered behavior by talking to the patient, encouraging him to talk, and putting him into situations where relearning is possible, to change underlying attitudes of fear or hatred or whatever is the cause of trouble. The most widely known form of psychotherapy is *psychoanalysis,* which began with the brilliant speculations of Freud about 1890: it is both a theory and a form of treatment.

(2) Working with the second hypothesis, one searches for disease processes in the brain, or in an endocrine gland whose output, secreted into the blood stream, is necessary for brain function; for defects of nutrition (such as lack of some vitamin); or for injuries or inherited defects.

Each of these rather extreme approaches has had some success: the "childhood learning" or psychotherapy school mainly by advancing our knowledge of behavior, normal as well as abnormal; the "brain disease" school by actually producing some cures. Psychotherapy helps the patient to live with his problems, but the present evidence is that it does not abolish or shorten the disorder. The search for constitutional defect or disease has scored brilliant successes in the discovery, for example, of syphilis of the brain or the mental disorders of beriberi and pellagra (vitamin B deficiencies), for which prevention is fully possible (and cure as well, if the patient is caught in time, before lasting damage has been done). But this approach has added little to our understanding of behavior problems, and has left us with no clues to the prevention or cure of the large body of other mental illnesses. These include both the *psychoses* (the more extreme disorders of personality) and the *neuroses* (less extreme, but still the cause of a great deal of suffering).

Dogmatism flourishes in direct proportion to ignorance; we are very ignorant of the mechanisms of mental illness and are apt to be correspondingly dogmatic. The student will find that many writers choose one of the two alternatives discussed in the preceding paragraphs, and deny that the other is of any great importance. And this is hard to understand, because there is no reason why past experience and constitutional deficiency should not work together, jointly, as causes of mental illness, and much evidence to indicate that they do work jointly.

We know that brain processes affect what happens in other organs, and that these other organs in turn affect what happens in the brain. Anger or fear interrupts digestion, accelerates the heart, and steps up the production of some glandular substances. The brain of course cannot live in isolation; how it functions depends essentially on the chemical products delivered to it by the blood stream; and each of the changes referred to (digestive, circulatory, hormonal) affects the chemical environment of the brain. The brain both controls and depends on the rest of the body. This makes possible a vicious circle: A is upset in function, which upsets B, which further upsets A, and so on. Normally there are limits to such a cumulative process; the disturbance stays within bounds, and the whole system returns to an even keel fairly quickly when the original source of disturbance is removed. But one weak link in the chain might lead to a very different end result.

Consider the *psychosomatic* ailments (the name is supposed to remind physicians that body and mind form one total entity). These are the cases of stomach ulcer, asthma or skin disease in which the patient's attitudes and emotions are an important cause of the disorder, and the only cause according to some investigators. There is no doubt that the patient's mental state is a major factor in these and other illnesses; but there is real doubt that it is the only one. The difficulty for such a conclusion is always this: Why do other persons, under equal emotional pressure, fail to develop ulcers (or asthma, or heart disease)? The situation would be much easier to understand if, in addition to prolonged emotion, there were also some incipient disorder in the part that eventually shows disease. A man's stomach ulcers might begin with a mild digestive disorder, unimportant in itself until worry or the like sets up the vicious circle. Emotion increases indigestion; indigestion means a possibility, at least, of changes in blood chemistry that might increase emotional responsiveness (e.g., irritability), this in turn increasing or prolonging the indigestion.

It is clear, also, that a person who had learned in childhood to worry about his physical health would be particularly vulnerable to such a process; the first sign of pain from the stomach, or asthma, or irregularity of heart beat, would produce an excessive emotional response, exacerbating the process described. We do not know that this kind of interaction is in fact what happens in the psychosomatic illness; but if it is, it would account both for the role of the patient's emotional sensitivities, and for the disturbance of one particular organ of the body and not other organs.

Or consider this possibility with respect to the occurrence of neurosis or psychosis. A woman has some deficiency of the pituitary gland (let us say) such that some part of its output is sufficient in ordinary circumstances, but rapidly exhausted under pressure of emotion. Prolonged irritations, anger which must be suppressed and which thus tends to last, or repeated sexual arousal without satisfaction—any such continued emotional strain might deplete the pituitary output of some component which is necessary to normal brain function. This at once would mean aberrant mental processes: perhaps to a very slight degree, not noticeable to other persons. But if the abnormality should take the form of a further addition to emotional tension ("neurotic anxiety," for example) it would increase the load on the pituitary and tend thus to perpetuate itself. If something of the sort is what happens in some forms of mental illness (though this is a quite hypothetical example), there is an interesting corollary. It is known that heredity is one factor in mental illness, and the possibility just discussed would mean that what the patient had inherited, roughly speaking, was not an inadequate nervous system but an inadequate pituitary or adrenal cortex; the pathologist looking for an "organic" basis of mental illness (see p. 122) must not restrict his search to the brain, but must include other organs as well.

The brain and the rest of the body constitute one system. Disorders of behavior may originate in the glandular system, as we have just seen, but they can also originate in the subject's perceptions and thoughts. It is estimated that *any* human being will break down in the conditions of modern warfare if the strain, the conflict of duty and fear, is continued long enough. Such breakdown is known as "shell shock" or "battle fatigue," but could better be called battle psychosis. Mental strain, therefore, can lead to mental illness: if in the extreme case of battle psychosis this can happen without any predisposing factor of heredity, then in less extreme cases, where predisposing factors do operate, mental strain must often be the decisive cause of breakdown. When we recognize the importance of constitutional deficiencies in mental illness we must not begin to deny the importance of the factors of experience, as if one explanation precluded the other.

What are the features of childhood experience that shape adult personality so as to make the patient a "worrier," or short-tempered, or a trouble-maker who inevitably gets himself into trouble, or a perfectionist who is emotionally disturbed when little things go wrong? One man sloughs off his responsibilities when he is away from the job; another does not. One learns how to behave socially (in the broad sense) so as to minimize emotional conflict, another seems to maximize it. One learns easily to adapt himself to new and perhaps unpleasant conditions, another does not and so makes them worse.

How can we understand such differences of personality? They involve, among other things, differences of learning capacity which must to a considerable extent be rooted in the learning of childhood. Again and again such problems of human behavior bring us back to the fundamental problem of learning, which psychologists still do not clearly understand despite half a century or more of intensive study. A great deal has been learned about learning, but only too often the new information presents us with further riddles for our solution. We crack the outer shell of the nut, which is certainly progress; but within we find a second shell, harder than the outer one.

Consider an important example, which again is relevant to the problem of disordered personality. Pavlov, the great Russian physiologist, found that dogs given a problem too difficult for solution sometimes develop neurosis, or a state very like it. As with some other important discoveries (penicillin is a modern example), the original observation was an accident that occurred in the course of studying something else, but its importance was at once recognized. The experimenter was trying to find out how small a difference the dog could detect between two objects, using the method of conditioned reflexes (p. 21). He taught the dog that food would be given following the sight of one object, and not following that of another. No punishment was given if the dog failed to discriminate between them. The objects were made more and more alike until, after several days of failing to discriminate, the dog's behavior changed, suddenly. Instead of coming eagerly to the experimental room the dog struggled to avoid it; instead of standing quietly in the apparatus, waiting for the next signal to appear, he struggled and howled. Discrimination disappeared. The experimenter went back to easier forms of the problem which the dog had solved previously, but this had little effect on the changed behavior. The disturbance never completely disappeared; even after prolonged rest, there were signs of it when the dog was put back into the experimental apparatus.

Some irreversible learning process seems definitely to have taken place. The whole picture, including the emotional aspects as well as the persistence of symptoms for a long period, has direct relevance to the human problem. We cannot be certain that this "experimental neurosis" and neurosis as it is known in the clinic are really the same, until we understand both better than we do now. But it is of great importance to have demonstrated that a conflict of perceptions by itself, with no pain or other unpleasant consequence following failure to discriminate, can produce such an extensive disturbance of behavior. If such phenomena do occur in man, it would explain much that is otherwise puzzling.

But the other side of the picture is that we do not understand the breakdown, nor how the learning can be so persistent. We do not know just what kinds of situation would constitute a similar conflict for man. What is a difficult problem for a dog may be no problem at all for a child; and we cannot, obviously, get the answer experimentally. What we must hope instead is that we can discover the principles involved, both with respect to the breakdown and with respect to the learning that is involved. From the dog work alone, of course, we will not be able to generalize directly to man, even when we think we understand what is going on in the dog: the higher levels of man's intellectual processes may mean that other variables enter in and modify our conclusions. What we can do is apply the principles tentatively, and see whether in fact they do lead to better understanding of human phenomena; if they do, splendid; if not, we then search farther to see what other processes need to be taken into account, or whether we have perhaps misinterpreted the animal data.

For some time in psychology a concentrated attack has been directed at learning in the laboratory rat. When a clear-cut answer is achieved, concerning its nature and the specific conditions in which it occurs or does not occur, this will have an immense clarifying significance for other problems, involving higher species. One cannot tell in advance where a scientific breakthrough will occur. We will not solve human problems by the study of lower animals alone, but a combined attack, at different evolutionary levels and from different points of view, holds far greater promise than a narrower attack on a single species, man.

Personality and social problems

Our introductory look at the field of psychology, and at the connection between academic and practical problems, can be concluded by considering the relation of "normal" personality to certain social problems; specifically, the problem of group conflict and prejudice.

Suspicion, dislike and hatred of others who differ from him in appearance or beliefs are so common in the human adult as to be almost universal. Whether we like to face it or not, the fact is that persons without such attitudes are a small minority of mankind, and always have been in recorded history. War is not a psychological problem—there are limits to what psychology takes blame or credit for—but unreasoning attitudes, which help to make war possible, certainly are. What can be done about them?

As with mental illness, the first objective is to understand, before we can hope to cure or to prevent. And here too we find that the farther our investigations go the more complicated things become, but also, the more fascinating, considered purely as intellectual riddles posed by society for our solution. If Jew dislikes Gentile without apparent reason, or Protestant fears a Catholic domination of society, or White regards Negro as a potential threat to his own future, one naturally looks first to see whether such attitudes are determined by verbal learning—by the things that members of the one group have been told about the other. And, as we know, such learning does occur. Jewish children are told about the evil things that Gentiles have done, Gentiles are told bad things about Jews, and so forth. But is this the whole story? There are two points that raise some doubt: when one looks for them, one can find examples where such antagonisms seem to arise spontaneously, where prior learning does not seem to explain the attitudes; and secondly, if the attitudes are learned, how is one to explain their strength and persistence? The learning sometimes must have been on the basis of a few casual remarks; yet other things that we try to inculcate in children by verbal training are often achieved only with the greatest effort and then, too often, have little permanence. Such considerations are bound to raise some suspicion that more is involved in the problem.

Let us take a broader view. One is accustomed to think of man as a rational animal, and it is puzzling, consequently, when one finds him afraid or hostile with no good reason. We try therefore to find some special explanation for the social attitudes in question. But *is* man's behavior so controlled by reason? When we take a wider survey we find some very peculiar phenomena indeed, which suggest that group antipathy is only a special case, a manifestation of something more deep-seated. Fear does not occur only where injury is anticipated. Anger is not caused only by frustration. Man is indeed much more intelligent than any other animal so far studied by scientists, but it appears that the price paid for a higher level of intellect is a corresponding susceptibility to emotional disturbance. Development of *capacity* for rational thought may be paralleled by capacity for bigger and better irrationalities.

Comparative studies in this field have served two purposes. They allow us to study the development of emotions under controlled conditions, so that the animal's previous history is fully known (and verbal learning, of course, is not a complication). They also give us perspective, and draw our attention to significant relations that otherwise might not be seen, partly because the phenomena are so familiar. Fear of strangers—so-called shyness—is normally present in the 6-to-12 month infant; fear of darkness, or imaginary things in the darkness, occurs in a large fraction of children, who experience them at one time or another after the age of 3 years; fear of harmless as well as harmful snakes is very nearly universal after the age of 6 years or so; and this list could be greatly extended. But—perhaps because they are so well known, singly—we do not put these facts together and ask whether man is after all as reasonable as we think him, or, when we are concerned about social hostilities, whether man's attitude toward those who have a different skin color or different beliefs may not be part of the same broad picture of irrationality. But this is exactly what is suggested by a comparative approach to the problem.

As we go from rat to chimpanzee (from lower to higher animals), we find an increasing variety in the causes of fear. Pain, sudden loud noise and sudden loss of support are likely to cause fear in any mammal. For the laboratory rat we need add only strange surroundings, in order to have a list of things that disturb the animal under ordinary circumstances. With the dog, the list becomes longer: we must add strange persons, certain strange objects (a balloon being blown up, for example, or a large statue of an animal) or strange events (the owner in different clothing, a hat being moved across the floor by a thread which the dog does not see). Not every dog is equally affected, of course, but dogs as a species are affected by a much wider variety of things than rats. Monkeys and apes are affected by a still wider variety, and the degree of disturbance is greater. Causes of fear in the captive chimpanzee make up an almost endless list: a carrot of an unusual shape, a biscuit with a worm in it, a rope of a particular size and color, a doll or a toy animal, and so on. What one animal fears another may not, but some things, such as a toy animal or (as we shall see later) a sculptured head or a death mask of a chimpanzee (Fig. 1), will terrify nearly all adult chimpanzees.

Similarly, the causes of hostility are more numerous in the higher animal. The rat bites to escape being held or captured, to avoid pain, or in the course of fighting for food or to protect the young, but rarely for any other reason. There is no need, in discussing the rat's behavior, to make any reference to anger. In the dog causes of aggression are more complex; there are occasionally suggestions of sulking (in man a form of anger), and attacks based apparently on jealousy. In the chimpanzee anger is a frequent phenomenon, aggressions with no apparent cause are common, and the causes when they are evident are

Figure 1. A problem in the behavior of higher animals: why should such objects frighten chimpanzees? Left, a plaster of paris cast of a chimpanzee's face; right, a nearly life-size model of an infant's head in clay.

extremely varied. A young male had temper tantrums whenever a female, in heat, would not sit where he could watch the lovely creature. Another male was angered when he saw a sexual examination being made of a female in a separate cage. A female took food from a smaller male in the same cage and was then enraged because he had a temper tantrum, and gave him a beating. An offer of food, then withholding it, does not (as with a dog) make the chimpanzee more eager to get the food, but makes him angry—or produces sulking and refusal to accept the food that was originally desired. This list, like the list of chimpanzee fears, could be extended almost indefinitely.

So far, the data are consistent with the idea that the more complex machinery required for higher intellectual function is also capable of more complex aberrations—that is, susceptibility to irrational processes increases with the capacity for rational problem-solving. Furthermore, there are indications that this may be so as intelligence develops in the growing animal. It is certainly true of the dog and the chimpanzee that it is the older animal, rather than the younger, in which the more complex and hard-to-understand causes of fear and aggression are found. This is true as well of children up to the age of five or six. However, it seems not true of adult man in civilized societies: we regard ourselves instead as being free of baseless fears, and unlikely to injure someone else except in self-defense. Is this so?

Is it true that adult civilized man is sweet and reasonable? Or should we see him instead as a dangerous animal, with enough intelligence to try to bring his dangerous propensities under control by means of the social institutions he is able to set up—a process that has gone a long way, but has a long way yet to go? This social machinery would include the prolonged training of the growing child in customs, manners and morals, the elaborate rules of courtesy and propriety for the adult (enforced by ostracism or detention), the emphasis on religious belief and the social practices enjoined by religion, as well as all the apparatus of law and government.

The hostility toward other groups would certainly be an integral part of such a picture, if this is in fact a true account of the behavior of the human species. We do not know that it is true; but such an account as this deserves serious consideration when one asks how to deal with the problem of war. If man is by nature peaceable and friendly, and hostile to others only because he has learned to be hostile, all we need do to prevent the hostility is to make sure that the growing child is not taught bad ideas about other social or national groups. If man is by nature something else, what we must do is get busy and find out what kind of childhood environment produces the kind of adult personality that can live in friendliness with others who differ in appearance and beliefs. Such persons do exist, so this is by no means a hopeless task; but we do not know at present just what conditions are necessary if the child is to become an adult of this kind.

The questions that are involved include all the topics of psychology. The reader is reminded that we are not primarily concerned with social psychology (or clinical psychology) in this text, and that the present discussion is meant to show him why, when there are such pressing problems as mental illness or social conflict, many psychologists devote themselves to the academic study of emotion in chimpanzees, or the learning of nonsense syllables by college students, or the perception of simple diagrams by the rat or cat. If we are really to have a hope of transcending the rule-of-thumb procedures available at present for deal-ing with social problems, we must *understand* human thought and perception and emotions, and such academic studies are aimed at understanding. We know that the way in which a member of another social group is perceived is affected by beliefs about that group; we do not know precisely how. We know that purely intellectual ideas, such as that the earth moves about the sun instead of vice versa, or that man is descended from lower species, can arouse intense emotion and profound hostility. We do not know why, nor how it is that some persons are not so disturbed. We know that attitudes learned in childhood are sometimes permanent, but we do not know how this learning differs from other learning that is more subject to modification.

Psychology, as it will be presented in this text, is primarily an academic discipline, the study of the more complex aspects of be-havior—or of mind, which determines the behavior. We may hope, with reason, that it will continue to produce results of practical value in dealing with human problems, as it has done in the past. But in order to do so, it must be aimed primarily at the solution of the fundamental problems; and the student who studies psychology with the hope even-tually of contributing to human welfare must master it first as a purely academic discipline, just as much as the one whose interests are scientific instead of humanitarian. The purpose of this text, accordingly, is to make available to the student the fundamental ideas of psychology as a science. Before one can have applied science, one must have a science to apply.

Summary

Psychology used to be called the study of mind; today it is usually called the study of behavior. If however mind is that which deter-mines the complex behavior of higher animals, both definitions are approximately correct. In modern psychology mind is considered to be some part or aspect of brain activity—though this is held only as a working assumption—and is studied by objective methods. Mental events are known theoretically, being inferred from behavior. In such a framework the study of animals has a natural part, both for its own sake and for the light it casts on human behavior.

The most pressing problems of behavior are those of mental illness and social conflict. These must be attacked at more than one level. Practically, they must be dealt with here and now, by whatever means are available from current knowledge. The "pure-science" approach, the development of theoretical understanding, complements the practical approach by providing the only guarantee of better methods in the future. Mental illness involves perception, memory, emotion, thinking; so does the attitude of hostility to other peoples. But we do not fully understand perception, memory and so on; thus anything that tells us more about these processes, whether it is a study of the eyeblink in man or a study of the mating habits of the rat, is a potential addition to our understanding of mental illness or the causes of social conflict.

Notes

For a review of animal psychology the student may consult N. R. F. Maier and T. C. Schneirla, *Principles of Animal Psychology*, McGraw-Hill Book Co., 1935 (now somewhat out of date, but still valuable as a systematic account of the subject), or C. P. Stone (Ed.), *Comparative Psychology*, 3rd ed., Prentice-Hall, 1951 (more up-to-date, but rather uneven).

Two other books supplement the present text by giving an account of the work of ethologists (biologists engaged in the study of behavior, especially instinctive patterns in birds and fish). One is less technical: K. Lorenz, *King Solomon's Ring*, Methuen & Co., 1952. The other is a technically detailed account of much of this field: N. Tinbergen, *The Study of Instinct*, Oxford University Press, 1951.

On the abnormal personality: the three cases of mental illness are abstracted from E. A. Strecker, F. G. Ebaugh and J. R. Ewalt, *Practical Clinical Psychiatry*, 6th ed., The Blakiston Co., 1947. On psychoanalysis, see C. S. Hall, A *Primer of Freudian Psychology*, World Publishing Co., 1954. For animal experiments on abnormal behavior, see for example R. A. Patton's chapter in Stone (cited above).

On social problems: the argument relating the level of intellectual capacity to level of emotional aberration has been presented more fully in Hebb and Thompson, The Social Significance of Animal Studies, Chap. 15 in G. Lindzey (Ed.), *Handbook of Social Psychology*, vol. 1, Addison-Wesley Publishing Co., 1954.

General references

The following books will be generally valuable for reference purposes throughout this textbook; on most psychological topics, when more detailed information is desired, one of these is likely to prove useful:

C. E. Osgood, *Method and Theory in Experimental Psychology*, Oxford University Press, 1953, especially in respect to current treatments of learning theory.

S. S. Stevens (Ed.), *Handbook of Experimental Psychology*, John Wiley & Sons, 1951: the 36 chapters by different authors range from neuroanatomy and neurophysiology to the higher mental processes, and from behavior of newts to that of adult man.

R. S. Woodworth and H. Schlosberg, *Experimental Psychology*, 2nd ed., Henry Holt & Co., 1954: based originally on the older approach to psychology, this book is particularly useful in its combination of a treatment of such classical topics as imagery and imageless thought with a fully up-to-date treatment of theoretical problems.

Chapter 2

Mental processes: the inference from behavior

THE preceding chapter proposed that constructing a sound theory of behavior—which we expect to lead to better and better ways of dealing with practical problems—requires the use of objective data only. Instead of trying to observe mental processes directly, by introspection, we must study them as inferred from behavior. How is this to be done? Also, it was proposed that verbal report by the subject concerning his own processes, though it is behavior and can be used quite objectively, tends to be an unreliable form of evidence, so that we depend primarily on other and simpler behavior for theory construction. The reason for this statement must be given in greater detail.

Accordingly, in this chapter we shall consider the inference from behavior to mental processes, which is not as difficult or strange as it may sound at first. In fact, it is thoroughly familiar in everyday life. The scientific problem is to improve it, make it more rigorous and reliable. We shall look at some examples which show how straightforward the inference can be in simple cases, as well as the pitfalls to be met in others; and equally important, how similar it is in principle with animal and with human subjects.

These examples also will introduce the student to the topics of learning and perception, which are of first importance for the study of behavior, and the topic of attitude and emotion, equally important in the higher animal. The chapter consequently should be read as dealing

20

both with questions of method and with behavioral data that are important in their own right.

Perception: training and test methods

Learning is a fundamental tool for the study of perception. What we try to find out, essentially, is what things are alike for the subject, and what things are different. To find out how fine a difference he can detect between two objects, we train him to respond in a specific way to one but not to the other. If he is capable of making such differential responses, he is clearly able to discriminate between the objects. If they are not perceived as being alike, training should be quickly established; if they are alike, but still discriminable, training will take longer but will succeed; if no amount of training is successful, we may conclude that he cannot discriminate between them. Further, after an animal has been trained to respond to one object, we can now test him by presenting other objects, more or less similar from our own point of view, and see which of them are also able to elicit that response: which of these seem similar to the subject?

In this way we can discover how the world looks, sounds, feels and smells for the animal subject. With man, special training is usually not needed, because we can make use of all the responses the subject has learned, from infancy on, and especially his verbal learning. The subject has learned to give names to common objects; all we need do is ask him to name the objects we show him, and when he calls one a square, the other a circle, for example, we know at least that he perceives some difference between these objects. We can also find out that perceptions of circles differing in size, color or distance from the eye still have something in common, since human subjects spontaneously make the same response to these different objects, calling them all circles. For this reason—because no special training is needed—man is a very convenient subject to use in the study of perception. There is however one drawback. We do not know all the details of the past learning of the human subject and (as we shall see below) this can produce error.

Two forms of training have been used for the study of perception. The conditioning method presents the subject with one stimulus-object at a time, the discrimination method with two.

1. *The conditioned-reflex method* was developed by the great Russian physiologist, Pavlov. It is extensively used as a research tool, with respect to various aspects of behavior, and it is important that the student should understand it. Pavlov's own work was with dogs, and with salivary secretion as the response to be conditioned (Fig. 2), but subsequent work has been done with many species, including man, and almost every form of response (Fig. 3).

The essence of Pavlov's procedure is this. A neutral object or event

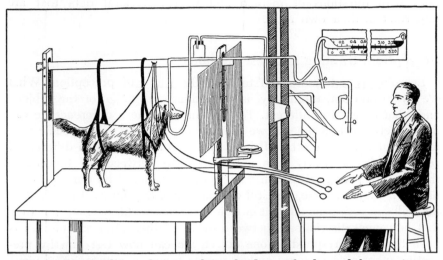

Figure 2.   Studying salivary conditioned reflexes. The dog and the experimenter are in separate rooms; before the experimenter's hands are the controls for the CS (tactile: note the attachments on the dog's shoulder and thigh) and UCS (the food dish swings round into the dog's reach). Attached to the dog's cheek by cement is a tube that leads to the manometer at upper right, by which the amount of salivary secretion is measured. (From Pavlov: *Lectures on Conditioned Reflexes*, trans. by W. H. Gantt, International Publishers, Inc.)

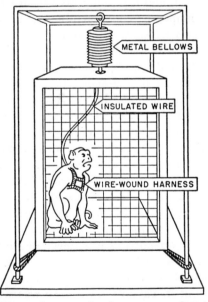

Figure 3.   Conditioning the generalized response to electric shock. The monkey is in a "stabilimeter," in which any movement he makes is transmitted through the bellows to a recording device. An auditory CS is used, followed by electric shock delivered through the wire attached to the monkey's harness. (From Harlow, H. F., Primate Learning, in *Comparative Psychology*, Calvin P. Stone, Editor, 3rd Ed., Prentice-Hall, Inc.)

is presented to the animal: one that is not especially exciting, and does not tend to evoke any specific response. This is followed by an object or event that does excite a specific response, such as giving the animal food when he is hungry, which produces salivary secretion and eating movements, or electric shock to a foot, which produces flexion of the leg. With repetition of this sequence the first, neutral, stimulus itself begins to elicit a response, more or less similar to the one elicited by the second stimulus. The animal secretes saliva before food appears, or lifts his foot before it is shocked. This response is said to be conditioned; the originally neutral event is now a *conditioned stimulus* (CS), the response to it a *conditioned response* (CR). The original exciting stimulus event is called the *unconditioned stimulus* (UCS), and the response to it the *unconditioned response* (UCR). The essence of the procedure is in the sequence of CS–UCS, eventually producing a CR.

Also, other neutral stimulus-objects may be presented to the animal, but are not followed by a UCS. Does the animal discriminate these negative CS's from the positive—can his response become conditioned only to the positive CS (followed by food or by shock)?

For example: in Chapter 1 an experiment was described in which a dog was conditioned to respond to one object, not to another, but suffered a severe breakdown ("experimental neurosis") when the two objects were made very similar. The positive CS was a circle projected on the wall in front of the dog, the UCS was food; the negative CS was an oval. The CR was salivary secretion, a minor operation having been done on the dog's cheek to enable the experimenter to collect and measure the output of one salivary gland. At first the circle and oval were quite different, the ratio of length to breadth in the oval being 2:1. A clear differentiation was established. The dog secreted saliva to the circle, not to the oval. Then the ratio was decreased. When it became 9:8 (the oval was now nearly a circle) there was at first imperfect differentiation—more saliva was secreted to circle than to oval, but not with the earlier clear-cut difference—and then the breakdown occurred (p. 12). For the dog, perceptually, the 2:1 oval was clearly distinct from the circle, the 9:8 oval was not; as we say in everyday terminology, the 9:8 oval "looked like" a circle.

The conditioned-reflex procedure is particularly suited to the study of auditory perceptions. We may use a buzzer, for example, as CS. A CR is readily formed. Now we can go on to find out something about how the buzzer is perceived by the dog. We sound a bell instead of a buzzer, or use a buzzer of higher or lower pitch. At first the dog secretes saliva to almost any noise in the experimental room. Does this mean that all noises sound alike to him? No; as we shall see in a moment, the dog's ability to distinguish between different sounds is very good. What is found in all such experiments is that the dog, like other animals (including man) *generalizes;* he is capable of responding either to a general class of noises, or to a specific noise; and what he is likely to learn first is the generalized response.

We can now make the conditioning more specific by the use of a number of negative CS's, sounds which are not followed by food, as well as the positive one. The dog will rapidly reach a stage where he secretes saliva for the buzzer of a particular pitch only (within the limits of his capacity to discriminate). Or we may use a pure tone (vibrations of a single frequency) as positive CS with other pure tones negative. By this means Pavlov obtained in one dog a remarkable discrimination between tones of 1000 and 1012 cycles per second. Or we may go on to condition a response to a pattern of sounds: a series such as 500 cycles—600 cycles—300 cycles; and we find that the dog readily discriminates this sequence from other sequences involving the same frequencies, just as man can distinguish two tunes which use the same notes in different order. Also, the dog will respond to the same pattern using different frequencies (e.g., 750—900—450), just as man does when a tune is played in a higher key. Such results tell us how things sound to a dog; what sounds are alike, and what are different.

2. *The discrimination method* requires the animal to make a choice, nearly always between two objects though more can be used. Let us see now how it has been shown that the rat is, in effect, color-blind, along with other mammals apart from the primates (monkeys, apes and man). Dogs, cats and rats—and presumably bulls, to whom a green rag may be just as exciting as a red one—appear to have a low-grade ability to distinguish clearly marked differences of hue; but it probably is not great enough to play any important part in the animal's day-to-day discriminations.

The procedure is simple in principle. A rat is put in a Yerkes box with two doors that lead to food (Fig. 4). The one door is locked, the other unlocked. The unlocked door may be the right or the left door, on different trials; it is always marked with a blue card, the locked door with a green card. We want to know whether the rat can learn to look at the two cards and always go to the blue one. If the unlocked door were always on the same side, the rat would simply learn to go always to that side without looking at the cards; if alternated regularly, left, right, left, right, and so on, the rat might learn this as well; so the position of the unlocked door and the blue card must alternate irregularly. This is an essential feature of method in all such discrimination experiments.

When in these circumstances the rat learns always to go to the door bearing the blue card, we know at least that he sees some difference between the two cards. But this does not mean that he sees green and blue as we do. If now we change the green card, trying lighter and darker greens, we find that the rat must have perceived the difference between the cards as a difference of brightness, not of hue; for when the green is made lighter, or darker, a point will be found at which the rat begins to choose the green card in preference to the blue, and with a green of just the proper brightness one may find that the rat never learns to distinguish it from the blue. With extreme care to avoid any misleading difference of brightness between the two cards one may be able to get what appear to be genuine discriminations of hue; but it seems clear that brightness differences dominate in the rat's perception, making hue of little significance. (The meaning of this statement may be clearer if Figs. 6 and 7 are consulted: in Fig. 6, certain form characteristics *can* be detected, but brightness predominates in determining which of two numbers is perceived.) The situation is quite different with a monkey or chimpanzee. Discrimination of hues is easy to establish in the first place, and rather great changes of brightness do not disturb it once established. The primates have clearly marked color vision, along with many birds, fish, reptiles and insects; for some reason, this is not true of the lower mammals.

All this seems very roundabout compared to working with human beings who can look at the cards and tell the experimenter just what they see. At least, one would think so. But as it happens they cannot always tell us how things look to them, and for reliable results the

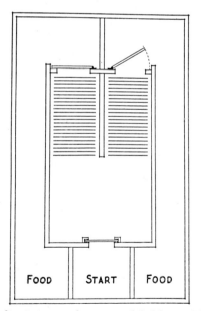

Figure 4. Yerkes discrimination box, as modified by Lashley. A trial begins when the sliding door of the starting compartment is raised by the experimenter. On each trial one of the two swinging doors is unlocked, one locked. In front of each door is an electric grid (horizontal lines) by which the animal can be "punished" for the choice of the wrong door. (From Lashley: *Comparative Psychology Monographs,* 1935, vol. 11.)

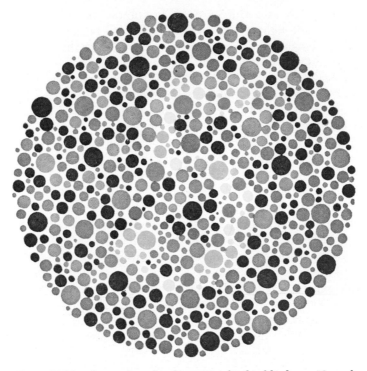

Figure 5.   Hidden-figure chart for detection of color blindness. Normal eye sees figure 5, color blind eye sees figure 2. (Copied by permission from Ishihara's Series of plates designed as tests for color blindness, Tokyo, Kanehara & Co., 1920.)

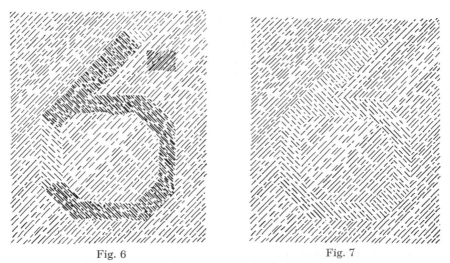

Fig. 6   Fig. 7

Figure 6.   What number is shown here? Cf. Fig. 7.
Figure 7.   A "6" can be found here, on the basis of form characteristics: i.e., the slope of the hatching lines. *The same form characteristics are present also in Fig. 6,* but there the eye is distracted by the addition of differential brightness cues. The effect is analogous to the difficulty of the color-blind in the Ishihara test, where brightness cues lead them to perceive one number, while the normal subject sees a different number on the basis of hue.

subject must be tested by objective methods. The color-blind subject for example sometimes does not know that he is color-blind. He has learned to use color names, perhaps on the basis of relative brightness, perhaps on the basis of other cues such as the shape of an object or its surroundings. He sees a drop of blood and knows that such juice oozing from the flesh is called red, or that the leaves on a tree in June are green, and may not have found out until he is tested that "red" and "green" mean something else to other persons. Just as with the rat, one must see what the subject does when the help of all other cues (shape, size, brightness, context) has been removed and greenness or redness alone is left to guide him. Instead of having to set up a testing compartment with green and red doors, however, we can just give the subject a bundle of pieces of yarn dyed in different colors, varying in brightness,[1] and ask him to sort out the different colors. The completely color-blind subject is lost in this task, though he may not realize it.

Figure 8.   Cards bearing diagrams for studying the perception of horizontality in the apparatus of Fig. 9. Top pair, training diagrams; below, two pairs of test diagrams.

[1] That is, different brightnesses for each color, confusing the color-blind but not the normal subject.

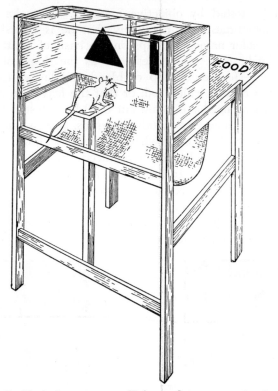

Figure 9.   Lashley's "jumping stand" for studying perception in rats (having to jump makes the rat pay better attention to the stimulus object). There are two windows, each closed with a piece of light cardboard bearing the positive or negative diagram (on the left a triangle; on the right, partly hidden, a square). When the rat jumps to the positive diagram the card falls away and he reaches the food platform. The negative card is locked in place; if the rat jumps to it he falls into the net below. (After Lashley, from Munn: *Handbook of Psychological Research*, Houghton Mifflin Co.)

Others (there are different kinds and degrees of color-blindness) will mix up colors that normal persons do not.

Another test is to show the subject a number made up of a lot of small circles of one color against a background of circles of another color (Fig. 5). For the normal eye the color predominates so the number is seen; but the circles vary in brightness too, and the color-blind may see an altogether different number. Figures 6 and 7 may help a person of normal vision to realize how such diagrams appear to the color-blind. In Fig. 6 a "5" appears; but this is only on the basis of the brightness relations. There is also a "6" in the figure, on the basis of pattern (i.e., the slope of the hatching lines), as the reader will see if he looks at Fig. 7, in which the brightness differential has been eliminated. Brightness relations can dominate normal vision, making the subject see one pattern and concealing another, as they do for the color-blind and the lower mammals.

The two tests of color-blindness, the Holmgren wools and the Ishihara color plates, are not infallible and it is not always easy to determine the presence or degree of defect. But both tests are usually effective, when simply asking for a subjective report is not; and the point here is the similarity, in principle, of the human and animal test methods.

This appears also in the perception of visual form and pattern. The method with an animal begins by training him to discriminate between two patterns, as in Figs. 8 and 9. After the laboratory rat has learned to choose always the card bearing horizontal striations, he will choose the horizontal bar when the second pair of cards (Fig. 8) is presented to him. However, he also shows that he perceives the difference between the training cards (with striations) and the test cards (each with a single bar), for on the first test trial the rat hesitates long before responding, though with the training diagrams he was choosing promptly. We can therefore conclude that he perceives both similarity and difference between the test cards and the training cards. The similarity is not merely in the horizontal edges and the vertical edges, but something more generalized, for now he will transfer his response also to the horizontal pair of circles though they do not even contain a horizontal line. As far as we know at present, the rat's perception of the horizontal is very like man's.

In his response to "triangularity," the rat still shows some similarity

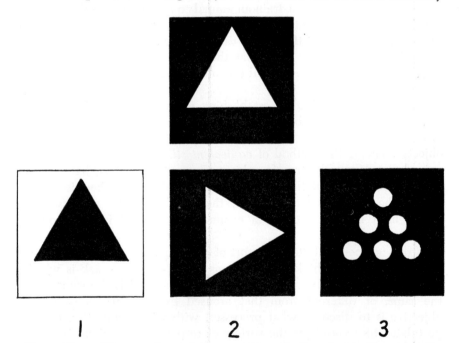

1   **2**   **3**

Figure 10.   Diagrams for studying perception of triangularity. Above, training diagram. Test diagrams 1 and 2 are perceived by chimpanzees as similar to the training diagram; diagram 3 is not, though a two-year-old child perceives it as such.

to man, but this is evidently a more complex process and the rat's limitations become clear. If we train a rat to discriminate a triangle from a square, for example, we can make the diagrams bigger or smaller and still get the discrimination; but if we rotate both through 45 degrees the discrimination breaks down—that is, the rat does not perceive a rotated triangle as the same. Or if we train the rat to discriminate an erect triangle from an inverted one, we find that he does not transfer to black triangles after training with white, nor does he transfer to triangular masses of small circles (Fig. 10). In other words, his perception of the original triangles was not as generalized as man's, and it seems clear that the rat does not see a triangle as a triangle, as one of a distinctive, unified class of figures, separate from squares, circles, rectangles and so on. The chimpanzee's perception is closer to ours, since he responds selectively to the triangle after it is rotated, and also when brightness relations are reversed; but he still does not transfer to the triangular arrangement of circles, though a two-year-old human child does so.

The meaning and limitations of verbal report

To summarize up to this point: in such analysis we make use, fundamentally, of only two kinds of evidence—discrimination, and generalization or transfer. We first train an animal to make a particular response to one object, a different response to another (or no response). If this succeeds, we know that the animal can perceive some difference between the objects. To find out just what the difference is, one method is to make changes in the objects until the animal cannot learn to discriminate between them.

The second method, after establishing a discrimination, is to present the animal with other objects (test objects) to see whether he responds to these, without further training, as he did to the original ones (training objects). This is the method of *equivalent stimuli*, or of *transfer*. If the animal spontaneously transfers his response to B after having been trained with A, and if this response is not made to B otherwise, A and B must be similar for the animal: that is, the mental processes they arouse must have something in common, to account for the common response.

We do not penetrate to some sort of esoteric awareness in the animal, nor do we need to think in such terms at all. What we ask is whether the *process* aroused by stimulus A inside the animal is the same, partly the same, or different from that aroused by stimulus B. Our grand objective is to discover what processes, with what properties, must be postulated to account for the variety of responses the animal is capable of making to the varied stimulation of his environment.

And the objective with man is not different. When we ask the human subject to tell us what something looks like, we are no more able by means of his answer to penetrate directly to the processes making up his perceptions. His verbal report, as he tells us how an object appears to him, is behavior that functions in principle like that of the laboratory rat seeking food behind one of two differently marked doors. They tell us what things arouse similar processes in the human brain, or different processes.

For example: a child has learned to say "round" when he sees a ball; when he encounters a sea urchin on the beach for the first time, and calls it round also, he shows us that the two objects arouse processes in the brain that have something in common. They must have something in common if the response transfers spontaneously from one stimulus to the other. By responding differently in other circumstances—for example, by using different names for the two objects, or freely picking up one and handling the other gingerly—he also shows us that the two perceptual processes are not completely identical. In the same way, the rat which hesitated before transferring his response to a solid bar after training with striations (p. 29) showed that the new pattern did not produce exactly the same process in his brain, though it had enough in common to produce, after some delay, the same response.

We must of course still be on guard against the danger of mistaken inference. The conclusion that two perceptual processes have something in common does not apply if the subject has been separately trained to make the same response to each object. For example: with a laboratory animal it could happen that another experimenter had previously taught him to expect food where he sees a square; not knowing this, I now teach him the same thing about a circle, and then test him with a square. He goes at once to the square, and I draw the erroneous conclusion that squares and circles look alike to him.

This may not be very likely in the animal laboratory (one always keeps careful records of what an animal has been exposed to), but it does happen with man. Before they come into the laboratory, human subjects have done a great deal of learning about which we know little, especially in their use of language. This is a particular reason for caution in the interpretation of a subject's reports about his own mental processes. We have already seen that the color-blind person may tell us, with perfect honesty, that grass looks green to him, that blood looks red or lemons yellow. We must conclude that such a response as "green" has been separately learned by the color-blind person, for grass, leaves, the color of a particular house, and so on, for he does not spontaneously transfer this response to other objects which the normal person calls green also.

What a verbal description does is to classify the object described with other objects previously experienced. Saying that an object is green, sharp and cold is saying that it has sensory effects partly the same as those produced by looking at leaves or grass, partly the same as those produced by touching the point of a needle, partly the same as those produced by touching ice.

But this is all it does, and if there is no past experience that corresponds to the present one a description of the present event is not possible (a "strange" object can usually be described, but only because most strange perceptions are new combinations of familiar elements). The congenitally blind, operated on after they are old enough to talk, are never able to describe to us how the world looks to one seeing for the first time: they lack the terms in which to do it. When they have begun to learn to name what they see, they seem at first to perceive the world much as the rest of us do. But here again language is deceptive, because it is not based on the same past experience. The patient names objects on the basis of color (and probably size) rather than form. But as long as he is tested only with the particular objects he has been taught to name, this does not appear, and it may come as a surprise, to both the patient and the clinician who is doing the training, to find how different from the normal is the patient's perception. A subject was taught to name, among other things, a cube of sugar, and then could not name it when he saw it in colored light. Having learned to name a matchbox, he could not name it when it was turned over to show the bottom, with a different color. The similarity to the method used with animals is clear: first train the subject to produce a specific response to the stimulus object, then test him with other related objects to discover whether there is transfer.

In the same way, there is great difficulty in the interpretation of verbal report from the congenitally blind concerning space and form perception. The blind subject uses the same words as a seeing person, but this does not mean that both have the same tactual perceptions. For some congenitally blind persons, "round" means only "lacking sharp corners," and this may not be discovered unless the subject is tested, for example, with an egg-shaped object—which he also says is round. Words such as "high" or "distant" seem to be used as the seeing subject uses them, but the ideas, the underlying mental processes, are not the same. The congenitally blind person may only discover this fact when he is operated on and obtains vision—he may then report, for example, that he has just discovered that a tree is really much taller than a man. (These things do not apply to the person who has had vision for some years before becoming blind; in this case, reports of spatial perceptions correspond well to those of the normally seeing.)

Imagery

In the topic of imagery we find something that, it may seem, has to be dealt with subjectively. But this is not so; and in seeing how it is to be treated behavioristically we can also see another example of the way in which objective analysis may correct the untrustworthiness of subjective report.

What does it mean when I say that I have an image of some childhood scene, that I can "see" the face of an absent friend, or that I can still "hear" some piece of music after the musician has stopped playing? It means, simply, that some process is occurring in my head which is the same, in part, as the process that occurred earlier as I looked at a visual object, or heard actual music. How this can happen, what the nature of the process is, constitutes one of the great problems of psychology (i.e., the problem of ideation, p. 48); but though we have a great deal still to learn about the details, there is no great philosophic problem involved. For some reason, in some way or other, a process that occurred earlier is occurring again. When it is excited via stimulation of a sense organ it is perception; when it is excited in some other way, it is an image (or memory, or idea). Looking at a scene produces complicated activities in the nervous system; the problem of imagery is to find out how the same activities (or partly the same) can be aroused in other ways than by sensory stimulation, and also to find out of course what these activities are.

Now let us see how much farther the subject's report can take us reliably, with respect to the nature of the process. Some people with good memories seem to have a sort of photographic record of what they have looked at. In exceptional cases, after reading a page they say they can close their eyes and still "see" the page with the words on it. These people tend to explain their memories for verbal material by saying that they simply call up an image of the page and read it off. Not many people report this for whole pages; but many report having memory images of single words which help them with spelling or, in memorizing verse, report that they have images of whole lines or stanzas. It seems to such persons that a picture (this is what "image" implies) can appear in one part of the mind at which another part can look, just as one can look at an actual picture held up before the face.

In spite of what the subject may think, however, we can show that things are not quite like this. If the subject were looking at a picture of a word he could read off its letters backward about as fast as forward. So we ask him to think of a long word such as "university" or "Louisiana" and form a clear image of it. When he has done this, we ask him to look at his image and read off the letters backward. We find that he cannot do so nearly as fast as forward; and we usually observe too that the subject himself is rather surprised at what he finds, when he tries this for the first time. The person with the "photographic memory" of a stanza from a familiar poem cannot repeat the last words of each line, going from bottom to top, without first thinking of most of the rest of the stanza; if he really had an image that was like a picture at which

Figure 11.   Demonstrating the negative after-image. In a good light, stare at the dot in the center of the letter E at the left while slowly counting to 35, without moving the eyes. Then look directly at the dot in the center of the gray square, right, and the negative after-image will appear.

he could look he would not have to look at all of each line in order to give the last word, and would not have to run through the first lines in order to read the last, but this is what the subject usually has to do, to greater or less extent, in order to get the last word of each line in his "image."

A memory image, then, is not what it seems. In spelling a word or repeating a verse there is some sort of visual process going on, when the person says he has visual imagery, but it is not really the equivalent of something within the mind which one can simply look at. Calling it an image is a misleading analogy with looking at a painting or a reflection in a mirror.

There is a case in which the analogy is less misleading. This is the after-image, positive or negative. If the student will stare for 30 or 40 seconds at one corner of a brightly lighted window or a piece of white paper on a darker background, without moving his eyes, and then immediately afterward look at a plain, moderately dark surface, he will see a dark pattern surrounded by a lighter area, of exactly the same shape as the window or white paper: the *negative after-image.* Another example: stare fixedly at a piece of colored paper or any brightly colored object on a background of a different color, then look at a plain surface (as in Fig. 11). Something will appear that has exactly the same pattern but in complementary colors (green instead of red, yellow instead of blue, and so on). *Positive after-images* can also be demonstrated; they are most impressive if one has been in a dark room for half an hour or more (or if one wakes up in the middle of the night in complete darkness) and switches on the room lights for an instant only, moving the switch on and off as quickly as one's fingers can move. Immediately afterward one will have a detailed and faithful reproduction of the scene at the moment when the light was on. One cannot look from one part of this "picture" to another, because it moves as one's eyes move, but it is still astonishingly like looking at the original scene. Calling it an image is not a bad analogy.

The memory image of very simple objects may be in the same class: it seems possible that one may be able to "look" freely at different parts of an imagined line, or even a square or a circle. But the memory image for complex scenes is something else.

Whatever it may seem subjectively, the memory of a familiar scene or a page of print is not equivalent to having something before one's eyes, any part of which can be looked at freely, in any order. Objective analysis thus indicates that the "image" of "memory image" is a misleading term when applied to the memory of a complex object. The objection may not apply, however, to simpler memories such as that of a line or of a simple geometrical figure, and it is possible therefore that the more complex memory may include a series of part-images, one after another.

Attitudes: the use of repeated tests

The next point to make explicit is that more than one test may be needed to identify a mental process. As examples, "interest" and "fear" have been chosen, to show what kind of elementary detective work may be involved in identifying attitudes in an animal. If what we call fear always produced the same behavior, varying only in strength or persistence, the problem would be simple. Fear in general tends to produce withdrawal or avoidance; but mild fear may be interfered with by other mental processes, so that withdrawal does not occur, and stronger fears may produce immobility. Also, an animal may move away from an object for some other reason. In these circumstances, a single observation is often not enough to permit identification of the attitude, or attitudes, underlying a response.

Let us see first what it means to say that some object, such as a photograph of a man's face, interests a caged chimpanzee. The first necessary requirement is that it should have some effect on his behavior. If the animal is quiet at the moment of testing, interest is shown by an increased activity as he moves closer to the picture. If the interest happens to take the form of fear, however, the response will be to move farther away. If instead the animal is active when the picture is presented, the effect may be to *decrease* activity; he stops what he was doing and simply directs his gaze toward the picture. There may be an increased activity inside the animal, but its outward manifestation is an arrest of movement. The behavior that shows interest is not a particular response, but a change of response. Thus the detection of interest must depend upon a comparison of behavior as it occurs at two different instants in time at least.

Next, to be sure that it is the photograph itself that has interested the animal, one would have to make other tests. The observed change in behavior might have been caused by something else happening at the same moment. One could go on to present the photograph in different ways, and on different occasions, or one might offer it to the chimpanzee to see if he takes it and examines it. In practice, the experienced person would only need two or three such observations before reaching a conclusion. But this would be because he already knows chimpanzees in general, and possibly this one in particular. He would have already made a great many observations in other circumstances which would tell him whether the animal was more responsive than if the observer had simply held out an empty hand, and whether the behavior in general was of the kind shown by this animal when a desirable object was in sight, or a frightening object, and so on.

As a matter of fact, the cage-reared chimpanzee usually shows only a slight and transient interest in pictures (unlike one home-reared chimpanzee). The points we are discussing may be illustrated better by the reactions of chimpanzees to some of the fear-producing objects already mentioned (p. 15, and Fig. 1; these are discussed in more detail later).

Such objects produced little reaction in one- and two-year-old infants, marked interest in the five- and six-year-olds, and gross fear in most adults (i.e., over 9 years old or thereabouts). When the experimenter approached one of the youngest group, test object in hand, interest and excitement was evident—but the effect was evidently produced by the experimenter himself, because the infant's gaze was not directed at the test object and the behavior was the same when the experimenter approached with empty hands. The five-year-olds were more excited when the test object was shown than when it was not, and they stared at it rather than at the experimenter. This is also an essential point about the recognition of interest: the behavior is oriented by the exciting object. As we shall see farther on, an animal may be interested in an object and not show the orientation clearly, but if so the detection of his interest becomes less direct, more a matter of inference, and in such cases we assume that some other process is interfering with—suppressing or distorting—the behavior that interest alone would produce.

As for some of the adults, a single glance at one of the more horrifying test objects was enough: the animal screamed and ran out of sight. Others vocalized (screamed, barked, whimpered) with hair erect—common signs of emotional disturbance in any mammal—and moved to a safer distance. A few showed none of these overt signs of fear, but still stopped what they had been doing and kept their eyes fixed on the test object. They could not be induced in further tests to come closer than a certain distance from it, and any sudden movement when the animal was close would make him move back abruptly. It was evident that the object had produced fear in these animals, though not as strongly as in the rest of the group.

This illustrates two points. First, no single observation could establish this inference about one of the apparently unexcited animals: it took a number of observations with the individual animal, and was greatly reinforced by observation of the kind of behavior shown by others. Secondly, we have here a case of identifying a mental state in the absence of the behavioral signs which are regarded as typical of that state.

One does not assume that a mental state or process—even one such as fear, which tends to have strong effects—is always manifested in behavior whenever it occurs, and for as long as it occurs. We do assume that it tends to be so manifested. "Fear" by definition is a process that tends to result in avoidance or flight, "anger" a process tending to produce attack. We can define "liking" as a process that tends to produce approach toward the object liked, or some other behavior that maintains the sensory stimulation received from it. But the actions that one of these states would determine by itself may be interfered with by some other, concurrent, process, distorting or suppressing it. As a matter of fact this sort of suppression must be occurring all the time in the higher animal's behavior; in ordinary circumstances when there is not one strongly developed action tendency which is dominant over others, it may be a matter of chance which particular form of behavior emerges.

Limens and the summation method

At other times, an action tendency may be on the verge of becoming dominant over others, and yet not become so. Some other process is strong enough to prevent this one from producing overt behavior, but barely strong enough. In these circumstances it may be possible to demonstrate the presence of the "hidden" process directly, by—so to speak—giving it a little nudge, a slight increase in strength. The subject may be irritated and show no clear sign of it; a slight further irritant is added, not in itself enough to produce a strong response, and a burst of anger appears. We can then safely infer the presence of some process related to anger *before* the second, precipitating, stimulus was applied. In other words, a mental state is later identified as existing at a time when it was not producing behavioral signs of its presence.

This is the method of *summation.* Summation is said to occur when two excitations achieve a reaction that neither is strong enough to achieve alone. The excitation that is not strong enough to produce a reaction is said to be below the *limen* or *threshold.* The term limen refers to the point at which an excitation becomes capable of producing a reaction. A light that is too weak to be seen is subliminal, a strong light is supraliminal.

These terms were originally developed in the study of sensation, and are mainly used there and in the field of physiology; but the conceptions

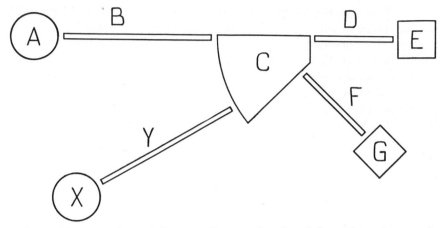

Figure 12.   Mechanical device to illustrate the idea of the subliminal versus the liminal process, and of summation. A, X, light-sensitive units ("eyes"); B, Y, connectors ("optic nerves"); C, central integrating and controlling unit ("brain"). See text.

to which they refer are fully applicable to our present problem of identifying mental processes. In fact, this problem has aspects which cannot be dealt with otherwise.

To clarify the way in which these ideas are employed, consider Fig. 12, representing a mechanical device with certain correspondences to the human visual system and structures connected therewith. If a very weak light stimulus falls on A, a light-sensitive unit, no activity is induced, and thus none is transmitted to the rest of the system. The stimulus is therefore subliminal either for a part (A) or for the whole. Next, a stronger stimulus excites A but not strongly enough to excite B; now the stimulus is liminal for part of the system, subliminal for the rest. Logically, it is also possible to find a strength of stimulation which excites A, B and C at a time when the limens of D and F are high, so that D, E, F and G remain unexcited. E and G are "effectors" in this scheme, corresponding to human muscles, so what we have is analogous to stimulation arousing a central activity which is not manifested externally.

Now consider that A and X represent the two eyes of a human subject, C his brain, E the muscles moving the eyes and G the muscles used in speech. We stimulate one eye with a very weak light for a brief instant, and obtain no response from the subject. Next, we stimulate both eyes in exactly the same way and observe an eye movement directing the subject's gaze to the spot where the faint flash occurred; there may or may not be a verbal response also. In these circumstances one usually says that the flash of light is subliminal to one eye, but liminal when both eyes are stimulated. The evidence shows, however, that the statement should be qualified somewhat. The summation that occurred could only have been in the brain, at the point C in the diagram, since the eyes are connected separately with the brain; therefore the flash to a single eye must be liminal for exciting A and B (or X and Y), though it is subliminal for C.

Further, suppose that the subject is just sitting between tests, when one of the experimenters strikes a match to light a cigarette. This is a common event and the subject happens not to respond either by looking in the direction of the lighted match or speaking of it. The stimulation is subliminal for overt response, but it is not necessarily subliminal for central processes of perception. That is, the subject may have *perceived* the lighted match without showing it. One can apply a further stimulation by saying immediately after lighting the match, "Did you see what I just did?" and unless there is something unusual going on we now obtain a verbal response, and probably also a movement of the eyes toward where the match was lighted.

The principle here is that of summation, even though we cannot be specific about details. One stimulus had an effect which was not evident in behavior, but which, in part at least, became so as the result of a further stimulation. As long as it is clearly realized that we are far from understanding exactly how this came about (our knowledge of perception, thinking, emotion and so forth being so incomplete) the notion of subliminal processes which may become liminal with further stimulation is very valuable. In fact, we cannot begin to understand behavior without it.

Now we can return to our analysis of fear as distinct from overt fear behavior. We must be able to deal with (1) the mild fear that produces no avoidance, (2) the stronger fear that has some behavioral manifestation such as trembling and sweating but still no avoidance, as well as (3) the fully expressed fear. In the following observations, the behavior that was observed was not intelligible in and of itself, but became interpretable (though still unusual) by means of the summation procedure—informally applied, it is true, but still effective.

During some preliminary observations in a study of fear in chimpanzees, a painted wax model of a snake was shown to a large male, Shorty. He looked away from it at once and moved, with no other evidence of excitation, to the other end of the cage. Chimpanzees in general fear snakes (or dislike them strongly), and the fact that the movement coincided exactly with seeing the snake made it unlikely that the movement was accidental. However, considered as avoidance of a fear-provoking object, the quiet, leisurely change of position was most remarkable. Was it only coincidence after all? The experimenter carried the snake over to where Shorty was sitting and held it up before him a second time. He screamed, sprang up with hair erect, seized a balk of timber lying near and hurled it at the test object or the experimenter, or both. Whether this was anger or fear, or anger resulting from fear, need not concern us now; these conceptions are not very precise in any case. The important point is that there were two similar stimulations which had cumulative effect. The response to the first was moderate in strength and not clearly interpretable; only summation, from the second stimulation, showed what sort of internal process one was dealing with.

Another example: during a later stage of the same experiment the procedure was more formalized. A presentation box was set up before the cage. The animal was brought near it by the offer of a piece of food; as he took the food, a compartment of the box was opened to expose the first test object. Most of the objects were found to produce fear behavior in most of the animals. In Soda, the female chimpanzee with whom we are now concerned, a strong disturbance was produced on the first few trials. But Soda was also eager for food, and instead of staying away from the presentation apparatus altogether (as one or two others did) she developed another mode of behavior. She came for the food each time and at once, without haste or apparent disturbance and without seeming to look at the apparatus, moved away for a few feet and sat down facing away from it at a 90-degree angle while she ate the food. On any one trial her behavior was fully consistent with a total lack of interest in anything but the food.

However, it seemed very unlikely that Soda had suddenly lost her fear of objects that were still very disturbing to other animals, and the stereotyped pattern of behavior, appearing without change trial after trial, was certainly unusual. Then on one trial, just as this peculiarity had become evident, the experimenter's hand slipped in lowering the top of the exposure apparatus. It dropped with a slight clatter. Soda jumped back, her behavior for the moment showing all the evidences of fear. By itself the noise was definitely not enough to produce startle in ordinary conditions.

Here again we have a summation process. We may conclude that a state of fear existed in Soda, prior to the sudden noise, but that this process was not strong enough (in the presence of other processes such as a desire for food) to produce a clear pattern of fear behavior. In this respect it was subliminal, but it became liminal with rather slight reinforcement.

Other cases of inferences from behavior

The cases so far considered have come from the study of perception and of attitude or emotion. Other examples, of the inference from behavior to unobserved states or processes inside the head, will be seen later. The behavioristic method of course implies that such inferences are part of the analysis of any behavior in the higher animal, and it would not be possible to list them all here—they are instead an integral part of the following chapters—but some idea of their variety can be given by listing a few of them.

"Memory" for example is inferred from behavior. We usually think we can find out what the human subject remembers just by asking him. Often enough this is true; but even here, when he tells us what he remembers, his speech is behavior, from which we infer the existence of some lasting effect of an earlier experience. But the "savings method" (p. 246) generally shows again that verbal report in such cases may be inaccurate. When for example a subject says he has completely forgotten something he learned earlier, we have him learn it again. He does not take as long to learn it the second time. Hence, by the objective method of relearning, we can show that the subject had retained some of the effects of the earlier learning though he could not tell us so.

A very interesting point related to this example is the fact that the skilled typist very often has "forgotten" where some of the keys are on the typewriter. If you ask her, when she is away from the typewriter, what finger she uses to type the letter *s* or just where it is on the keyboard, she may not be able to tell you though she could have done so at once when she was just a beginner. But set her down at the typewriter and ask her to type the word "Mississippi" without looking at the keys, and she types it easily and accurately. The objective test once more shows that, in another sense, she has not forgotten where the letter is at all. Her other behavior is more reliable, more diagnostic, than her verbal report.

Another example of the inference from behavior is the detection of "expectancy" in animals (p. 54). A monkey has seen a slice of banana put in a food-cup, where he has been allowed to obtain food in the past; now he opens the food-cup and finds, not banana, but lettuce, and has a temper tantrum—though if he had seen lettuce being put in he would have quietly taken it out and eaten it. Here the inference is rather complex, and cannot be based on a single observation; it involves the comparison of what the monkey does when he has seen banana put in and finds lettuce, and what he does when he sees lettuce put in and finds lettuce. Like many of these inferences, it requires repeated observation; but when it has been found in every such test that the monkey does have the capacity for anticipating a future event on the basis of past experience, and when we find that his other behavior is fully consistent with the presence of such expectancies, we do not have to demonstrate them on every occasion but assume that in certain circumstances they are present and take part in the determination of his behavior.

A final example is the occurrence of "insight" (p. 204). The course of solving a difficult problem may involve a long learning process, with slow improvement until finally the subject performs the task well. With a higher animal, however, a different course of events is sometimes observed. The animal tries the task repeatedly and fails, or achieves it in an inefficient and indirect manner. Suddenly, however, the animal's behavior changes, and a direct solution appears with little previous warning. In brief, a "flash" of insight has occurred, the animal has perceived the problem situation in a new way, and behavior has changed accordingly. This sort of thing is a common phenomenon in doing crossword puzzles, solving geometry problems, and the like.

It should be said at once that "flash of insight" is purely a figure of speech. The student must not take it seriously. What he can take seriously is the conclusion that some reorganization of thought processes, or of perception, took place and that the effect of the change was evident in behavior. The conclusion, of course, is an inference from behavior. Also, the conception of insight is not a precise one, referring only in a very rough way to a reorganization of mental processes. (Psychiatrists use it in a different sense, however: meaning—again roughly—the ability to see oneself objectively, as others would.)

Note on terminology

In this chapter terms have been used which would be out of place if we were dealing with precise conceptions. "Memory image" and "flash of insight" are figures of speech which have a good deal of value for communication, when precision is not necessary. Terms such as "interest" and "liking" have a similar value. At the same time, they are quite out of place when one is attempting to analyze the mechanisms of behavior, because they are not precise. Psychologists sometimes—very often, in fact—feel that they should be avoided entirely, as popular terms which have no place in scientific discussion. It seems to be thought that science demands complete precision at all times, but this is a misinterpretation.

Exactitude in terminology has a nice parallel with exactitude of measurement. To demand a complete avoidance of everyday language in describing behavior would be like keeping track of time to the nearest second in all circumstances. It is as if a physicist, having learned to measure in angstrom units, then felt that the use of a foot rule was unscientific. To measure a piece of land in millimeters is at best inefficient; and describing it in such terms is apt to be scientifically dishonest, for it implies a degree of accuracy that one's measurements do not have. This is especially true when one uses a foot rule to measure, and translates the answer into millimeters carried to too many significant figures. It is very easy in psychology, in describing or interpreting some piece of behavior, to use language which is unnecessarily cumbersome as communication and which, only too often, implies a precision that neither the data nor our theoretical knowledge can justify.

What one must aim at is a degree of precision, in reporting data or conveying an idea, that is warranted by the circumstances. We have more precise conceptions than those referred to by such terms as "anger" or "desire" or (as we shall see in later chapters) "intelligence" or "emotion," for use when exactness is needed. There is, year by year, an increasingly difficult technical jargon in psychology which has a real function; it differs from everyday language because it refers to conceptions that are steadily developing in complexity and moving farther and farther from everyday ideas about mental processes. Where precision is needed, the use of this technical terminology is quite essential. But there are different levels of analysis, with respect to the degree of precision, and one's terminology varies accordingly.

There is nothing wrong in saying that a dog "likes" food, except that this is not a very exact statement. When one wishes to be more exact, for example in dealing with mechanisms of learning, one would say that food in the mouth is an unconditioned stimulus or, as we shall see later, a "reinforcing" agent; the sight and smell of food provides "secondary reinforcement"; and so on. "Learning" itself is not a very exact term, and one often needs to qualify it ("motor learning," for example) or to use the term conditioning instead.

This makes two points: (1) simple, direct terminology is always preferable where it meets the case; and (2) the more complex technical terminology is necessary for finer analysis, and was not invented—as some persons have thought—simply to impress the layman and make the subject-matter appear more esoteric than it really is.

Summary

The main purpose of this chapter is to show how mental processes are identified from behavior; that verbal report of one's own mental processes is sometimes quite erroneous; and that identifying a mental process in an animal is much like doing so in man. The main difference is that human speech is, for many of these inferences, a flexible and complex form of behavior in which the subject has received long training before he comes to the experiment; thus it is usually very efficient as an indicator, though errors of inference must always be guarded against.

In the course of making these points, the chapter introduces important topics to which we shall return in later discussion: learning, perception, generalization of response, and emotion; and with these, the method of conditioned reflexes and the discrimination method. Two other topics of some importance, color-blindness and imagery, are dealt with in this chapter only and will not be returned to.

The main problem in the inference from behavior is that a mental process is not always strong enough to express itself in behavior, or the expression is distorted by other processes which are present at the same time. In this case many different tests may be necessary. An important conception is that of the limen; and of summation, which may strengthen a mental activity to the point at which it can surmount the limen and have its effect on behavior.

Notes

Pavlov's *Lectures on Conditioned Reflexes* (International, 1928) is still a readable and stimulating book. For the method of studying color vision in animals, see N. L. Munn, *Handbook of Psychological Research on the Rat*, Houghton Mifflin Co., 1950. For pattern perception in the rat, see Munn also (the rat data cited in the text are Lashley's: the chimpanzee and child data Gellerman's, *J. Genet. Psychol.*, 1933, 42, 3–27). On the space perception of the blind, see *Notes* for Chapter 6; on chimpanzee fears, *Notes* for Chapter 8. On imagery and objective testing thereof, an excellent reference is Woodworth and Schlosberg (General References, p. 19).

Chapter 3

Modes of sensory control:
reflex and mediating process

W_E now begin a closer examination of the mechanisms of behavior, with a fundamental question: How do sensory events guide behavior, and how close is their control? The influence they exert is by means of the nervous system, which is essentially a transmitter of excitations from *receptors* (sensory cells) to *effectors* (muscles and glands). But this transmission may be complicated by a number of factors. In this chapter we shall see how the complications, in principle, determine the level of behavior. When transmission is relatively direct, we are dealing with *reflexive* or *sense-dominated* behavior; when certain complications are involved, we are dealing with behavior that is under the control of both sensory events and *mediating processes* (ideas, thinking). Behaviorally, our question is: How do we distinguish between the two forms of response to the environment?

What is the difference between the behavior of a spider building a web, and that of a man ploughing a field to plant potatoes? Both organisms will obtain food as the result of the preliminary action; are the two forms of behavior to be seen in the same light, or on what principles is the difference to be defined? A dog is cold; he shivers reflexively, which produces heat, or he goes to the door and barks to be let in where it is warmer. What difference is there in the mechanism of response?

Behavior is primarily an adaptation to the environment under sensory

44

guidance. It takes the organism away from harmful events and toward favorable ones, or introduces changes in the immediate environment that make survival more likely. Not all behavior is adaptive in such a narrow sense; sex and maternal behavior are not necessary to the behaver's survival, nor is play. But with these forms of behavior also (for example, in finding the mate, avoiding obstacles in moving to and from the nest, or maintaining bodily orientation in play), sensory guidance is always an essential factor. No organized behavior is possible without it.

A simple one-celled organism such as an ameba does not have the specialization of parts, sensory and motor, found in higher animals. In obtaining nourishment, for example, the same tissue must act to detect the presence of food, move the animal toward it, ingest and absorb it, and excrete wastes: a single cell must be nose, mouth, legs and alimentary canal. As a result, the ameba has very limited ability in capturing food and avoiding destruction. Only events in its immediate vicinity, at the present moment, affect its behavior. In a higher animal, specialization of parts permits an extraordinary sensitivity of some cells (the receptors) to environmental events, so that food or danger is detected at a distance, and an equally extraordinary speed and precision of movement in others (the muscles). But specialization means that the receptors and effectors are spatially separated, and there must be some means of communication from one to the other. This is the first function of the nervous system: a *spatial integration* or coordination of parts. The specialization of effectors also means that they must be active in a definite sequence or at just the proper time, in order to have their effect; this *temporal integration* is also achieved by the nervous system.

For example: when a mosquito alights on the forehead and begins operations, the skin of the forehead has no adequate means of self-defense. Nerve fibers in the skin transmit the excitation, originating in the skin, to the central nervous system, whence it is relayed to effectors at a distance, the muscles of a hand and arm. The mosquito is swatted. For successful defense, cells at a distance must be called upon, and they must be called upon in the proper order; the muscular contractions involved in a swift, accurate movement must have a very precise timing or the hand will reach the wrong place. Another example: the nose of a hungry animal smells food but, though it is just as dependent on nutrition as the rest of the body, it cannot obtain the food directly; what it must do is initiate a complex series of activities in other parts of the body, in definite order. The end effect is that food gets into the stomach and the blood stream delivers to the olfactory cells of the nose (and of course to other parts) the proteins, salts, sugar and so forth that they need in order to keep on serving their function.

The role of sensation is clear, not only in initiating the activity but in continuing to guide it throughout. In swatting a mosquito the muscular contractions to be made depend on the initial position of the hand, so they are determined by the sensory processes which, coming from muscle and joint (p. 58), "tell" us where our limbs are at any moment. The predatory animal seeking food must change the course of his movements as the prey changes position; and so forth. This is true of any form of adaptation to the environment, simple or complex, and we must recognize sensory control as a first principle of behavior.

Classifying behavior by means of the S-R formula

The next step is to see how the directness of sensory control varies. This brings us to the *stimulus-response* (*S-R*) *formula,* and its importance in classifying behavior.

The S-R formula is a fundamental tool for theoretical analysis. It treats each movement or glandular secretion as a reaction to an immediately prior sensory stimulation. Temporarily integrated behavior, extending over a period of time, is treated as a series of reactions to a series of stimulations. As we shall see, any reaction must produce a new stimulation ("feed-back"), so a single sensory event could readily initiate such a series of motor events. Stimulus followed directly by response is the archetype of behavior, the fundamental pattern from which other patterns must have developed.

Accordingly, behavior is classified by its relation to the S-R formula. In one broad class are those actions that begin at the same time as the stimulus (assuming there is no interference from other processes) and end at the same time. These actions, under direct sensory control, fit the formula. Another broad class of actions, loosely described as voluntary, lack the close temporal relation with the stimulus. They do not fit the formula, and they present us with a problem which is at the heart of understanding behavior in the higher animal. This is the problem of thinking (which of course underlies voluntary behavior). But though actions of the voluntary class may involve more complexity than those that are sensorily controlled, with respect to underlying mechanisms, the same fundamental principles of function in the nervous system are concerned in both cases. The question is how we are to extend the ideas incorporated in the S-R formula to cover voluntary behavior as well.

There is no hard-and-fast distinction between actions in the two broad classes. In fact, they seem to form a continuum, and separating them into classes is arbitrary. This is a further reason for not thinking of two or more kinds of behavior involving quite different principles. The extremes of the continuum show very clear differences, but these are a matter of degree.

Now let us see what the reasons are for distinguishing between classes of behavior. It has already been said that the nervous system is essentially a transmitter of excitations. In a classical analogy, we may think of the brain and spinal cord as a sort of automatic switchboard, with lines coming in from the receptors and going out to the effectors. Some of the connections are built in, others are acquired (in learning). Some are very direct; these function promptly and reliably, as an automatic switchboard should, and the reflexive responses they produce are the ones that fit the S-R formula. We can think of such responses as produced by through lines from receptor to effector; and for these the switchboard analogy is good. But other connections must be indirect, and perhaps involve a different kind of circuit. The responses concerned are much less reliable or less predictable, and may involve long delays in transmission.

Conduction by nerve fibers is swift; when we are dealing with through lines in the switchboard, a stimulus should have its effect on behavior within a second or so. In its simplest form, the problem of understanding behavior of the second (non-S-R) form occurs when there is a clear delay between sensory input and response. The switchboard, it appears, is not merely a connector of incoming lines directly with outgoing; some more complicated operations go on within, and it is these that we have to unravel theoretically. How can the brain "hold" an excitation fed into it, and then deliver it at some later time to the muscles?

With these considerations in mind, we may extend our classification of behavior to four headings—two comprising S-R-type actions, under direct sensory control, and two in which sensory control is indirect.

1. *Reflex:* when the connection from sense organ to muscle or gland is direct, and determined by growth processes, without learning (Chap. 6), we are dealing with the unconditioned reflex. Such connections show a close correspondence in time between stimulus and response, and function with high reliability; except when fatigue occurs because of excessive stimulation or when there is clearly marked interference from some other activity (e.g., a competing reflex), the stimulus always elicits the response.

2. *Conditioned reflex:* when the connection functions in much the same way, but only as the result of certain prior stimulations, we have a conditioned reflex or acquired S-R connection. Usually the functioning of such connections is less reliable, presumably because they follow a longer, less anatomically direct path in the nervous system, and are thus more subject to interference from other activity. The formation of such new connections is *learning*, which can be defined in general as the formation of new neural connections, or the lasting modification of old ones, as the result of sensory stimulation and the excitation of the pathways concerned.

3. When an S-R connection operates or not according to whether the animal has first been prepared to act that way, we have the phenomenon of *set*. In this case, the S-R connection acts as if there were a switch in the line which must be closed before the response can be obtained. As we shall see, the switch may be controlled chemically (by hormones in the blood stream, for example) or neurally. The problem of "holding" and

delay appears with neural set: there is a first stimulation which need not evoke any response but which has effects that are clearly seen when a second stimulation is given. The first stimulus closes the switch (or "sets" the animal to respond in a certain way), the second one elicits the response. As long as the switch remains closed the animal's behavior is under sensory control, and corresponds well to the S-R formula; the problem presented by this class of behavior is in the nature of the switching mechanism.

4. Finally, there is a large class of actions, characteristic of the higher animal, which cannot be predicted from knowledge of the immediate stimulation alone; the behavior is partly controlled by sensory input to the switchboard, partly by some autonomous activity of the switchboard itself—events going on within it which are not at that moment under sensory control. These autonomous central processes are referred to as *ideation* or *mediating processes*.

The meaning of these terms will be clear with the later discussion, but a preliminary explanation can be given here. Sensory stimulation arouses a central process, which at first occurs only when that stimulation occurs; but with repetition the central process changes, becomes internally organized, so that it is capable of an independent existence. Now it may continue after the sensory input stops; or it may be aroused, in the complete absence of the originally necessary input, by connections with another central process. The process is autonomous in that it can be detached from the original sensory event (for example, in the so-called memory image).

"Ideation" is the classical term for such activities. We may use it in a rather general sense, defining it as (1) the occurrence of processes in the brain in the absence of the sensory events which originally produced them, or (2) new combinations or developments of such processes. "Mediating process" is a more modern term with essentially the same meaning, and has the advantage that it lacks the varied connotations of the earlier term. ("Mediating" refers to the possibility that the process may act as a link between a sensory input and a response not directly connected with it—one main function of such a process.)

There is a long history in psychology of skepticism about the existence of ideation, and opposition between this conception and that of the S-R formula. The reason for the skepticism, which was a healthy one, was that ideation is much more theoretical, more inferentially complex, than S-R connections. We have seen, however, that ideation or mediating process is not an alternative to S-R connections but an attempt to extend the same kind of thinking to cover certain behavior that otherwise would make trouble theoretically. There is no opposition between the two, provided we are quite clear about the nature of the behavior that makes the inference to ideation necessary, and the criteria that distinguish sense-dominated from other behavior.

Sense-dominated behavior: UCR and CR

In psychology as in other fields of scientific thought one is compelled to accept the simpler explanation rather than the more complex, as long as the facts permit it. We must prefer the S-R connection to ideation, as involving fewer steps of inference and thus more nearly factual. But in doing this, we must ask what properties of behavior are implied by S-R connections if the explanation is to be satisfactory. For example, it was suggested in the preceding section that the conditioned reflex fits into the S-R formula. When we apply our criteria, however, we find that while some CR's fit, others are doubtful cases.

The behavioral indications, or criteria, of the operation of a path running from receptor to effector are (1) immediacy and (2) constancy of response to the adequate stimulus. The speed of neural conduction ranges from about a meter per second, in small nerve fibers, to 120 m./sec. in the largest. Even though there is the possibility of some slight delay at the *synapses* on the pathway (junction points, where excitation passes from one fiber to the next), a second or so should be enough time for almost any response; thus any greater delay raises some doubt that we are dealing with an S-R pathway. Also, if the direction taken by the excitation as it leaves the sense organ is determined solely by through routes in the nervous system we should not find a given stimulus combination now producing one response, now another (this would be class 3, above: set-determined behavior). Any stimulation should produce a constant response in the absence of interference from other stimulation.

The UCR meets these requirements, except when it is interfered with by another process. If stimulation for two incompatible reflexes is given simultaneously, of course, only one of the two can occur. A pinprick in the foot of a newborn infant produces a flexion (withdrawal) response of the leg, mild pressure on the sole of the foot produces an extensor thrust; if both stimuli occur at the same time, only one response can be made: it is usually the flexion. Also, especially in older subjects, the higher centers of the brain are capable of interfering with reflex processes. The reflex response to a pain stimulus in the fingers, for example, is to pull back the hand; but if one is holding a valuable teacup which becomes too hot, the pain reflex is usually inhibited long enough for one to set the cup down before letting go of it.

Otherwise, however, the UCR is highly constant and predictable. There is a long list of separate reflexes: the pupillary response to increased light in the eye, producing contraction of the pupil; salivary reflexes produced by stimulation of the mouth; sucking reflexes, produced by stimulation of the lips; sneezing, coughing, eye-watering, produced by irritations of nose, throat or eyeball; reflexes of heart and arteries, regulating the flow of blood to different parts of the body; reflexes of the stomach and gut, controlling digestion and the movement of food through the alimentary canal; a large number of postural reflexes, producing main-

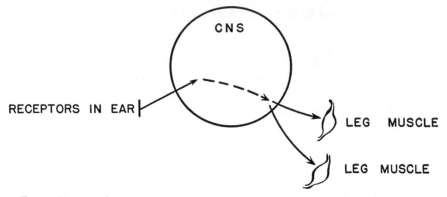

Figure 13.   Schematizing the possible S-R pathway in a conditioned response, the excitation being conducted from the receptors of the ear to the muscles of the leg which is flexed when a buzzer is sounded. *CNS*, central nervous system.

tenance of orientation of the body in space; and so on. All these UCR's are highly consistent in their action; there is no doubt that the responses are controlled sensorily, and depend on straight-through S-R connections.

Now let us see how these considerations apply to the learned reflex-like responses, the CR's or acquired S-R connections.

In our first example, the CS is a buzzer; the UCS is an electric shock to the foot, delivered two seconds after the buzzer begins. After a few trials, the animal raises his foot off the grid immediately when the buzzer sounds, and continues to do so on almost every trial. We may then think of a pathway as being set up from certain cells in the ear to the muscles of the leg (Fig. 13). If the connection does not work every time, we need not reject this conclusion; any path through the nervous system must thread its way through a tangle of other paths, and is exposed to possible interference from other processes, especially *inhibition* (see Chap. 5). What we can ask is whether a given stimulus combination *tends* to arouse always the same response (any deviations from this being referable to interference or fatigue); or whether, on the other hand, the same total pattern of stimulation produces systematically different responses on different occasions.

Thinking not of single stimuli but of combinations of stimuli, as in the preceding paragraph, helps us deal with another possible difficulty. Having established a CR to the buzzer, we take the animal out of the apparatus and sound the buzzer again. The CR does not appear. This does not necessarily mean that the response is not controlled by S-R pathways, but shows that a pathway from ear to leg muscles is not enough, by itself, to account for the response; but we can assume that the path is supported by others (Fig. 14) from eye, nose and skin—i.e., by sight, smell and touch of the apparatus. The S-R formula may have seemed overly simple to the student at first glance, but when we begin to deal with actual behavior it involves us in complexity enough. But the principle still remains clear. In the apparatus, at least, the experimenter can elicit the CR whenever he wishes by manipulating the animal's environment: there is an effective sensory control of behavior.

Next example: with another animal, the CS (buzzer) is presented for 10 seconds before the UCS (shock). After a few repetitions, the CR appears, immediately following the beginning of the CS. After few more trials, however, the CR is delayed, and eventually a time comes when the animal does not respond until 7, 8 or 9 seconds after presentation of the CS. How is the delay to be accounted for? The S-R formula may still be applied if we assume that the CS arouses also an inhibitory process, lasting 7 or 8 seconds, after which the CR can occur. This assumption is a quite possible one, in view of what we know about the nervous system. (A possible alternative is that we are dealing with some sort of mediating process which changes, or develops, with time; when it reaches a liminal stage after 7 or 8 seconds, it produces the response. At this point however such an inference, though possible, is not required.)

But now we change the experimental conditions further, and obtain a conditioned response which must depend on a mediating process. Instead of presenting the CS for the whole delay period of 10 seconds, we present it for 1 second, and give the UCS 9 seconds later. Once again we obtain a 7 or 8 second delay in response. What produces the CR, when it does occur—8 seconds after cessation of the CS? In some manner the brain holds the activity aroused by the CS, instead of transmitting it at once to the effectors. What is held we may refer to as a *trace activity,* which by definition is a mediating process. How it is to be understood we shall consider shortly.

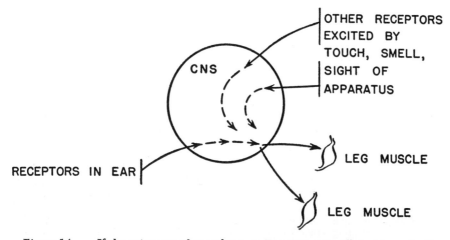

Figure 14.   If the primary pathway shown in Fig. 13 is not sufficient to evoke the response outside the apparatus, this may mean only that in the apparatus it is supported by other pathways, from different receptors. The S-R formula can still hold.

Humoral and neural sets

It has already been suggested that the problem of set may be approached via the analogy of closing a switch in an S-R path, making it functional. There are two ways in which this switching mechanism is controlled: (1) a *humoral* mechanism (referring to the "humors" or body fluids, not to joke-making); and (2) a neural mechanism, involving prior sensory stimulation.

1. First, the humoral mechanism. Instead of a CR involving electric shock, let us take Pavlov's classical procedure with feeding as the UCS. We have given a dog some 40 trials, in each of which the sound of a metronome was followed by presentation of food, and we have developed a reliable CR of salivation on presentation of the metronome. To do this, however, the dog must be hungry. After establishing the CR, we feed the dog as much as he wants to eat, put him in the apparatus, and start the metronome clicking. There is little or no salivation. If the conditioning procedure really amounts to forming an uninterrupted pathway from ear to salivary glands, and if this is all that is involved, then the sound of the metronome should result in salivation whether the dog's stomach is full or not.

It may be suggested that sensory excitation from a full stomach inhibits the salivary glands; but this is not so, as we discover if we now introduce a mild acid into the mouth—salivary secretion is prompt. The answer instead appears to be that some of the cells involved in the ear-to-gland pathway are more active, better transmitters, in the humoral conditions of hunger: figuratively, a switch is closed.

There is a similar situation with respect to sexual reflexes. When a female dog is in estrus (heat), stimulation of the vulva produces reflexively a movement of the tail to one side and the adoption of a particular posture (as the breeders say, the bitch in heat will "stand" for the dog), both of which are such as to permit mounting and copulation by the male. At other times, exactly the same stimulation results in very different behavior—the bitch may turn and attack the dog, or run away, or simply clamp the tail tight over the vulva and refuse to stand. These reactions can be shown to be related directly to the chemical contents of the blood stream and extracellular fluids bathing the nervous system, by testing a spayed dog (with ovaries removed) before and after injection of estrogens. Other behavior is of course affected also; but we have here a perfect example of an unconditioned reflex, in which the functioning of the neural pathway is fully controlled by a humoral factor. There is much that remains to learn about the mechanism,[1] and just which neural cells

[1]One possibility is worth mentioning here. In Fig. 41, p. 99, sensory fibers A and B are capable of exciting either X or Y. Which is excited may depend on the frequency of activity in AB, and on the "preferences" of X and Y for different frequencies (X responding most readily to one frequency, Y to another). When Y is active it inhibits activity in X (and X similarly prevents activity in Y, though this is not shown in Fig. 41). In such a situation, the humoral set would be accounted for if estrogens in the blood

are affected by the estrogens, but in principle the humoral set presents us with no real deviation from the S-R formula.

2. It is otherwise with neural sets. Let us take as experimental subject an intelligent student, for whom simple arithmetical operations are automatic. We seat him before a screen, tell him that pairs of numbers will be projected on the screen, and instruct him to give their sums as quickly as possible. We present then a series which is made up of combinations such as $\frac{8}{2}$. To each we obtain a correct and rapid response. A given stimulus combination always gives the same answer, and the reaction time is of the order of a second. This is a highly practiced form of behavior, no thought appears to be involved, and we might conclude that the behavior meets the criteria of the S-R connection—that is, promptness and reliability.

But the reliability depends on the subject's being *set* to add. The 8,2 combination produces the response "10" every time—until we say to the subject, "Now subtract" (or divide, or multiply); whereupon the same stimulus pattern produces, with equal reliability, the response "6" (or 4, or 16). There may be a path from receptors to effectors which operates in the addition; but if so, there must also be other paths for subtraction, division and multiplication. Which one is operant depends on the prior stimulation of the instruction.

This is the paradigm of set: stimulus A is presented, then at some later time stimulus B; the response is triggered by B, but its nature is determined by both A and B, and the problem we are concerned with is to understand how A has its effect when there is a considerable lapse of time before the response occurs. With humoral set there is no such difficulty: the chemical in the blood stream is continuously present. The problem of neural set arises because the switchboard appears to hold the effects of the first stimulus until the second is available, and then deliver both to the muscles. "Closing a switch" is a figure of speech; there are no grounds for thinking that a gap in the pathway is literally opened or closed by the first stimulation. It seems that the set must somehow depend on a trace activity, set up within the switchboard itself.

The adding-versus-subtracting example, just considered, is the classical laboratory demonstration of set in human beings. Another example is equally significant as a classical demonstration of both *expectancy* (a form of ideation) and neural set in animals. A monkey is trained in the *delayed-response* procedure. (The preceding discussion has referred to delay in responding, but the term "delayed response" is used technically

---

stream changed the frequency of the incoming sensory fibers AB, so that instead of exciting X only, they now excited Y only. Or a low blood sugar level might change the "preferences" of X and Y so that an excitation in AB is now conducted over the other path. In this way, the same sensory event would excite a different path in the nervous system—produce a different response—when the chemical content of the blood is changed.

to refer to the method about to be described; it was developed by Hunter in 1913 especially to test ideation in animals.) First, the monkey is allowed to see food put in one of two containers out of reach. A screen is then put between him and the containers, so that he cannot later find the food simply by keeping his eyes fixed on the correct container. After a delay of 5 seconds, 10 seconds, or more, the screen is removed, the two containers are brought within reach, and the monkey is permitted to choose between them.

The monkey is quite capable of success with this task, in a way that provides some evidence of the presence of mediating processes. In one experiment, particularly, the evidence was decisive. In it the experimenter sometimes used lettuce as the food reward, which the monkeys liked, or banana, which they liked better. When the monkey saw lettuce put into one of the containers, chose the right one, and found lettuce in it, he took it and ate it. But when he saw banana put in, and then found lettuce—the experimenter having deceitfully made a change during the delay period —the monkey did not take the lettuce, but showed surprise and searched in and around the container (looking apparently for the missing piece of banana). On occasion the animal simply had a temper tantrum instead.

Here is our trace activity again. Seeing banana put into the food container had some lasting effect, as shown by the conflict that appeared when lettuce was found instead. We know that when the monkey found lettuce without having an expectancy of banana he reached for it and ate it. This is consistent with a direct sensory control of response. But the temper tantrum, and failure to take the lettuce, is not: this behavior must be jointly determined by a mediating process resulting from the earlier stimulation, and by the effects of the present stimulation.

The problem of holding does not always arise when there appears to be a delay of response. For example, a lower animal may succeed in delayed-response tests by making a postural adjustment immediately and maintaining it. Specifically, when the animal sees food put into the right-hand container he may move over to that side of the cage and wait there until the screen is raised; then he simply chooses the near container. Monkeys and chimpanzees do not usually solve the problem in this way, but are capable of moving around in the delay period. It would be possible however, if we did not have any other data, to suppose that the monkey might tense the muscles of the hand nearest the food and keep them tensed while moving around; when the screen is raised and he turns back to face the containers, he could then choose the correct one by using the hand whose muscles are contracted.

However, there is usually no sign at all of the monkey's "remembering" the place of food in this way; and the lettuce-versus-banana experiment has a special importance in ruling such an explanation out as far as the higher animal is concerned. It might be suggested, perhaps, that in this experiment the monkey not only remembered the place of food posturally, but also the kind of food, using another set of muscles. But this is not plausible. The postural mechanism for right-left discrimination appears only after many trials and must be the result of a slow learning process. The conflict we are now considering, however, appears on the first trial in which lettuce is substituted for banana. This fact, and other details of the original experiment into which we shall not go here, make it necessary to conclude that the monkey is capable of a genuine expectancy: a mediating process or trace activity which continues to exist after the stimulating conditions which aroused it have ceased.

The holding mechanism

Our behavioral evidence therefore indicates that an apparent delay between stimulus and response is, in some circumstances, produced by some sort of holding process in the nervous system; a lasting activity is set up within the switchboard, and has its motor effect only when a second sensory input occurs, with which it acts to produce an output to the muscles.

What is the nature of this activity? It is important for the student to realize that we do not know certainly, and that the answers given here are quite theoretical. What is established certainly is that a block of brain tissue, cut off completely from incoming and outgoing lines, can still maintain an excitation fed into it for upwards of an hour—that is, the holding referred to above has been demonstrated physiologically; and secondly, that the holding has been demonstrated in the control of behavior. As to how the process occurs, only one theoretical explanation is available to us at present.

This mechanism is represented schematically in Fig. 15. The brain and spinal cord are known to include everywhere throughout their extent closed pathways, reverberatory or re-entrant circuits. In one of these, an

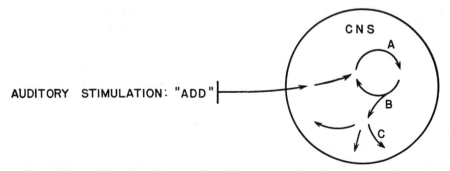

Figure 15. Diagrammatic representation of a reverberatory pathway: incoming stimulation excites *A*, which excites *B*, which re-excites *A* and so on. It is suggested that this is the mechanism of holding or trace activity, in principle. *C* represents other paths which may be excited by collateral fibers (branches) from *B*, which might be excited each time the excitation travels round the closed pathway.

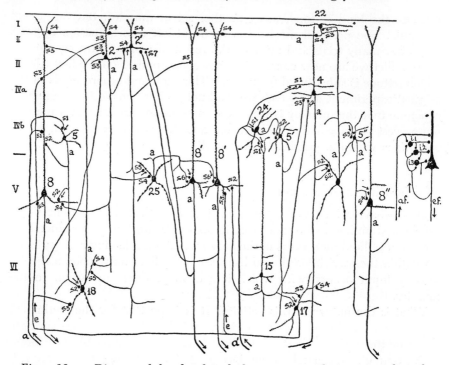

Figure 16.   Diagram of closed path in the human cortex. This is more realistic than Fig. 15 but still diagrammatic since it shows only about one one-thousandth of the connections that would actually be found in a block of cortex. The small diagram at the right is a simplification of the larger one. Arrows show the direction of transmission in different cells. (From Lorente de Nó, in Fulton: *Physiology of the Nervous System,* 3rd ed., Oxford University Press.)

excitation might theoretically continue for an indefinite period, "chasing its tail," and not leave the circuit until some other excitation came along with which it might combine to produce a motor effect that neither could produce alone.

The student must of course remember that the circuits in question, as they are known from anatomical study of the brain, are far more complex than the schematizing of Fig. 15; Fig. 16, which is itself simplified, and Fig. 17 give a somewhat better idea of what is involved. There is reason to believe that a two-link pathway could not hold an excitation for more than a small fraction of a second because of fatigue in the two cells. For longer periods, there would have to be a larger number of links in the circuit, and probably more than one closed circuit. This problem is discussed in more detail in Chapter 5. In principle, however, though the systems involved are complex, we can regard Fig. 15 as representing the mechanism of a mediating or ideational process. Figure 18 then shows schematically how we can treat the process as a trace activity which selectively reinforces one motor response and not another. With one activity going on in the brain, a particular stimulus arouses one response; with another central activity, exactly the same stimulus arouses a different

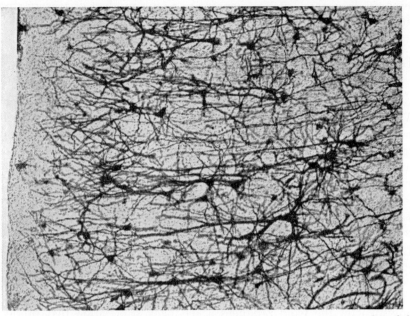

Figure 17.   Photomicrograph of a section of cat cortex, giving a better idea of the complexity of connections—but still only about one neuron in 60 is shown here, stained by the Golgi-Cox method which for some unknown reason is selective. If all were stained, no detail could be observed, only a solid mass of stained tissue. The outer layer of the cortex is at left. (From Sholl: *Organization of the Cerebral Cortex,* Methuen and Co. Ltd.)

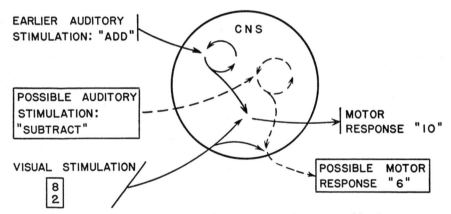

Figure 18.   Diagramming a possible mechanism of a set to add. The excitation from the prior stimulus, "add," is held in a reverberatory loop. The second stimulus, (8,2), is connected with two motor paths, and can evoke "10" or "6"; but the reverberatory activity supports only one of these, and the response is "10." If the prior stimulation had been "subtract," a different reverberatory circuit would have been active and would have determined the response "6." Needless to say, this diagram is entirely schematic (any resemblance to neural tissue is entirely coincidental).

response. In general, such responses are a joint product of sensory stimulation and of activity already going on in the central nervous system.

Temporal integration in behavior

We turn now to the way in which such theoretical considerations are to be applied to a series of actions, combined in an organized sequence. We have seen that a single action which involves a neural set is determined by two separate factors, sensory and central: the set is a central process that characteristically does not determine the response by itself, but instead collaborates with a later stimulation. This applies equally to serially ordered behavior.

The role of the sensory guidance is referred to by a principle known as the *motor theory of thought,* which embodies a conception of the greatest importance for understanding behavior. In brief, the original theory was devised to see whether it was possible to avoid postulating ideation to explain thinking. It proposed that, when a man is thinking, what is really going on is that he is talking to himself, or making movements with his hands and fingers that are too small to be seen. Each word or movement of the hand produces a feedback stimulation that produces the next one, in a chain reaction: instead of ideation, therefore, what we have is a series of S-R reactions. The theory is no longer entertained as a complete explanation because of the data, on trace activities and set, discussed in the preceding pages; but the conceptions which it developed concerning sensory feedback remain valid and important for the understanding of serial behavior.

Sensory feedback is usually of two kinds: *exteroceptive,* and *proprioceptive* or *kinesthetic.* The exteroceptors are the sensory cells (of the eye, ear, mouth, nose, skin) which are excited by events external to the body. The proprioceptors are those which, embedded in muscle or joint or in the labyrinth of the inner ear, are excited by movements of the body. Moving a limb involves a change of tension in the muscles, to which receptors buried in the muscle are sensitive; they are of course excited also when two sets of opposing muscles tense without producing movement of the limb. The *labyrinth* of the inner ear has three fluid-filled semicircular canals, approximately at right angles to each other; any movement of the head will cause a movement of fluid (by inertia) in one or more canals, and this movement produces an excitation of sense organs in the canals involved.

Any behavioral response to a single stimulation thus produces a sensory feedback which can act as the initiator of a second response, whose feedback initiates a third response, and so on. The student should keep in mind both exteroceptive and proprioceptive components here. When a hand is moved, there is (1) proprioception from muscle and joint, but there is often (2) a visual stimulation as well (sight of the moving hand)

and usually (3) a tactual stimulation, since the action is apt to involve contact with some object or surface. In the periphery of the visual field, again, some movement of an object excites a contraction of eye muscles which produces fixation on that part of the environment: the feedback is dual, consisting of (1) proprioception from the eye muscles and (2) the change of retinal stimulation.

Now apply this to the problem of thinking. The problem is to explain the delay that characteristically intervenes between stimulus and response. Ask someone what the product of 21 and 14 is, or how many angels can stand on the point of a pin, and (if you get any answer at all) there is apt to be a delay between the stimulation (the question) and the subject's response (the answer)—a delay too long to be consistent with the operation of an S-R path. The motor theory of thinking said that this delay is only apparent; it proposed that instead of a single stimulus and single response, there is a chain reaction, with the intermediate links consisting of *implicit responses of the musculature:* movements for example of the speech apparatus, too small to produce any sound, but each one providing a feedback stimulation which evokes the next, until finally an answer to the question is arrived at which is spoken out loud. The process is equivalent to talking to one's self without being heard. Or if one is thinking about some mechanical operation, the thinking would consist according to the theory of a series of slight movements, or merely changes of tension, in the muscles of the arm and hand; it would probably be accompanied by movements of the eyes, and perhaps of the speech apparatus too. Deaf-mutes of course would do their verbal thinking with their fingers.

There is clear evidence that this kind of activity goes on in thinking, and it is probably not merely a sort of overflow but really does contribute to finding answers in problem-solving. The student might find it profitable to observe another student who is working with a difficult problem. He will certainly observe some elaborate eye movements, and movements of the lips, jaws and throat—not uncommonly, he will hear speech and see movements of the hands. The "doodling" that many persons engage in if a pencil is handy is another form of the same thing; for the confirmed doodler, problem-solving is more difficult (less likely to be achieved in the same time) if no pencil and paper are available. Records taken of lip and tongue movements during thinking show patterns that correspond partly to the movements made when actually talking, and there are similar indications of hand and finger movements in the deaf-mute who uses sign language instead of speech. In difficult problems the human animal uses sensory aids wherever he can, making pictures or models of the things thought about, moving his eyes as if he were looking at such pictures, talking to himself (out loud or sotto voce) and so on. It seems evident that some of this behavior, especially the model-making form, plays a real part in problem-solving. In practice, the thought process that extends for

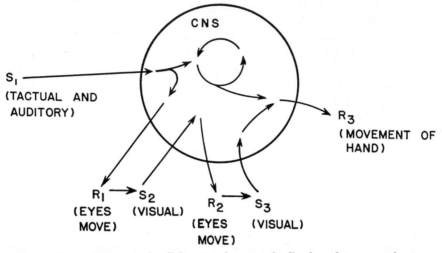

Figure 19. Diagram of collaboration between feedback and trace mechanisms. A visitor to a laboratory feels his hand touch something and hears something topple over. R_1 is directing his eyes to the approximate part of the bench where his hand was; S_2 is the visual stimulation that results. R_2 is a second movement of the eyes, to an object lying on its side. Seeing the object in this position would not be enough to make the visitor set it upright (R_3); but the effect of the earlier stimulation (hearing an object fall, thus "knowing" that it is not in its right place), combined with seeing it, does so.

more than a second or so is far from being an exclusively intracranial process.

On the other hand, it has not been possible to explain the whole process in such terms. Though activity can always be detected in the musculature during thought, if sensitive instruments are employed, and though overt activity is common during thought and must often make an essential contribution to the process, this does not dispose of certain difficulties. In short, we must not suppose that thinking, and serially ordered behavior, are to be accounted for *either* by central processes alone *or* by muscular feedback alone: both mechanisms are involved. No one for example has succeeded in explaining a speaker's sentence construction, during the course of ordinary speech, as a series of CR's linked together by feedback alone, and there are strong indications that his thought processes run well ahead of his actual articulations. The thought, then, is not identical with the speech. Also, in some cases of aphasia (loss or disturbance of speech due to brain injury, p. 84f.), thought is not impaired in the way or to the degree that one would expect if it consisted only of muscular reaction plus feedback. But the evidence concerning speech is complex, and may not be decisive, so it will not be considered in further detail.

The relevant considerations here may be summarized as follows. (1) Other evidence, considered earlier in this chapter, has established the existence of mediating processes; (2) it is unlikely that these take no part in an extended thought process, or in speech, especially since we can find no signs of a satisfactory explanation as yet for sentence construction, unless reference is made to mediating processes; and (3) certain high-speed skilled movements, such as the violin-player's arpeggios to be discussed in a moment, occur too rapidly to be accounted for in terms of feedback alone.

Our conclusion therefore is that serial order in behavior is determined both by sensory feedback and by mediating processes which may themselves contain serial order. In some cases one of these two components may play the larger part in thinking, in some the other. As to how they collaborate, a relatively simple case is schematized in Fig. 19. A stimulus S_1 arouses both an activity trace and an overt response, R_1; feedback stimulation from this, S_2, arouses a second response, R_2, with further feedback, S_3. The sensory event S_3 by itself might or might not arouse R_3; but the activity trace is such as to support R_3, which accordingly is the end response to S_1. The behavior is jointly determined by central and peripheral processes.

Another example is represented in Fig. 20. This concerns a timing problem to be found in the control of high-speed skilled movements. A violinist, for example, may make as many as 16 finger movements per second. How is the timing of each movement controlled? It cannot be the feedback from the immediately preceding movement, for there is not enough time. At most there is 60 ms (milliseconds)—less than this if some

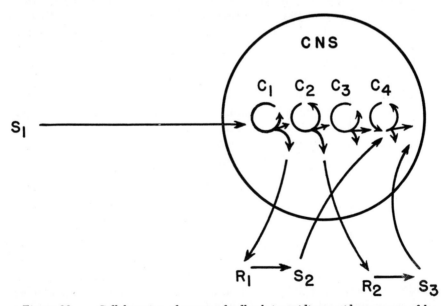

Figure 20. Collaboration of sensory feedback in guiding rapid sequences of behavior. The feedback from one movement is too slow to influence the one that follows immediately, but still may do so with a later response. Sensory feedback is not a sufficient explanation of the guidance of high-speed skilled movement, but it must always be an essential component.

movements are faster than others. But the *reaction time* for tactual stim-ulation is much longer, being of the order of 140 ms. If it is the auditory instead of the tactual feedback that is involved, the problem is the same, for auditory reaction time is still about 140 ms (visual reaction time is longer: 180 ms).

Reaction time is the interval between the onset of a stimulus and the onset of response, measured under laboratory conditions in which the subject makes a simple response to a simple stimulus as rapidly as he can. The values given above are well established, so there appears to be no doubt that the arpeggio playing of the violinist cannot be dealt with as a chain reaction in which the sensory effects of one response initiate the next. But we need not go to the other extreme and forget feedback as a factor in such behavior, as Fig. 20 shows: if the feedback from the first response does not get back in time to arouse the second response, it may well play a part in controlling the fourth or fifth.

There is a good deal of evidence to show that sensory input is continu-ously important for integrated behavior. As we shall see in later chapters, the normal variety of sensory stimulation has the function of maintaining *arousal:* the alertness, responsiveness or "vigilance" of the waking subject. When the stimulation is made drastically monotonous, mental function is significantly affected. In addition to such generalized functions, however, sensory feedback has specific guiding functions that are not always ob-vious. One is not usually aware, for example, of the part that sensations from the legs and feet play in normal standing or walking. But there is a disease in which this feedback is impaired, and the walk then becomes heavy-footed and grossly abnormal. The patient also becomes dependent on visual feedback to maintain his position in space, so that with his eyes closed he may be unable to stand alone or even to keep an arm or a leg in a given position. Without the normal feedback, the limbs "wander."

In talking, a constant accompaniment of course is the sound of one's own voice. This seems irrelevant, but is not. A deaf person is apt to have trouble regulating the pitch and flow of his speech. In an experiment, college students with a sharp hearing loss, produced by blocking the external passage of the ear for three days, complained that they found it impossible to continue speaking with normal loudness. In another ex-periment it was possible to delay the speaker's hearing of his own voice by a fraction of a second, and this produced a marked disorder of speech. Some subjects were able to speak if they did so very slowly but others were unable to speak at all, simply because they heard themselves saying one syllable while actually producing the next. This can hardly be a simple interference, or distraction, because there are no such effects when the speaker hears other material, or in fact his own speech if the sounds are delayed by more than a second or so. Together with the fact that the experimentally deafened subjects had great difficulty in maintaining a normal loudness, it suggests, at least, that in normal conditions the sound of one's own voice plays an important part in the course of speech production.

This part of the discussion may be summed up: (1) we recognize the existence of mediating processes and their role in higher behavior, but (2) we must not think of them as operating in a vacuum, independent of sensation. In a single rapid series of skilled movements, highly practiced, it is possible that behavior may be momentarily without sensory guidance—but only momentarily. With this possible exception, it is clear that sensory guidance is essential to any organized series of actions. Mediating processes are fundamentally a means of modifying the way in which sensory control acts, not an absence of it. The phrase "sensory dominance" is used here to refer to a particular form of sensory guidance, in which environmental events have their effects immediately and inevitably; by permitting a delay of response, the mediating process allows the organism to escape such close control. But in a broader sense all behavior is subject to sensory dominance, and the mediating process is simply another form of it, less direct and more elaborate.

Sensory dominance and voluntary behavior

"Volition" represents an old and troublesome philosophic problem, chiefly because the nature of the underlying psychological issue was not clearly formulated. The problem does not arise with the behavior of lower organisms such as the ant, in which there is no clear departure from direct sensory control; nor when the behavior of higher organisms remains under such control. It does arise at other times, and it is in short the problem of understanding how mediating processes are involved in response.

In an earlier day the nervous system was thought of as a collection of direct S-R connections. As we have seen, this would imply a direct sensory control; so whenever the control was absent, the behavior became a mysterious business, to be explained only by a mind or soul which was *not* a part of the brain's activity, but separate. Volition or will was a power of this separate agency, which somehow could be exerted on the brain to make it behave in a way that it would not otherwise. "Willpower" thus was something that one might have a lot of, or little. "Free will" for many workers meant that voluntary behavior was not subject to scientific law, not determined by cause and effect.

But all this was related to a very crude idea of how the bodily machinery operates, and especially the machinery of the brain. If the higher animal responds in two different ways to the same total pattern of stimulation, it is because the activity of the central switchboard is not the same on the two occasions, but "set" differently; as a result the sensory input is routed to different muscles. It is evident that we are as yet far from understanding these problems in detail, and must not be dogmatic about their eventual explanation in terms of brain processes; but at the same time there is no fundamental philosophic problem about voluntary behavior as such.

Consequently, in modern psychology the terms "volition" and "will" or "will-power" have disappeared. "Voluntary behavior" still has a certain usefulness, as a rough classification; it is, in short, behavior that cannot be predicted from a knowledge of the present environmental stimulation alone because a systematic variability is introduced by mediating processes.

Summary

All behavior is under sensory guidance, through the switchboard of the central nervous system. Reflexive or sense-dominated behavior is controlled by direct connections; higher behavior involves mediating processes (roughly, ideas or images). The mediating process is an activity of the switchboard itself, not a straight-through transmission. It can hold a sensory input for an appreciable time before transmitting it; it may also be excited by other central activities (i.e., other mediating processes), instead of by sensory input.

Set is analogous to closing a switch, preparing the switchboard for a particular kind of response. Humoral set depends on the chemical content of the blood stream; neural set depends on mediating processes.

The chief problem is to understand how mediating processes can hold an excitation. Existing theory (which may or may not be right) proposes that this is mainly done by closed circuits, in which excitation can travel round and round without dying out immediately.

Such processes explain in part the delayed response that is characteristic of thought, intervening between presentation of a problem and the solution. But, in part, the delay is illusory: the motor theory of thought shows us the possibility that in this period there may be many small responses, perhaps not great enough to be seen, each of which causes a fresh "feedback" stimulation which in turn gives rise to the next response. Thus thinking consists of (1) an internal series of mediating processes, accompanied by (2) a constant feedback from responses in muscle, which presumably helps to guide the internal series. Serial order in overt behavior is controlled in the same way.

Notes

For an extended treatment of mediating processes, see Osgood; on set in man (Ach) and monkey (Tinklepaugh), see Leeper, Chap. 10 in Stevens; on the motor theory of thought, Woodworth and Schlosberg, Chap. 26; and on the role of the semicircular canals in proprioception, Wendt, Chap. 31 in Stevens (for all these, see General References, Chap. 1, p. 19).

For the experiments showing that a block of isolated brain tissue can hold an excitation for long periods, see B. D. Burns, *J. Physiol.*, 1951, 112, 156–175. The problem of the violin-player's arpeggio (high-speed skilled movement) is discussed by K. S. Lashley in L. A. Jeffress (Ed.), *Cerebral Mechanisms in Behavior: The Hixon Symposium,* John Wiley and Sons, 1951.

For a report of the effect of delayed auditory feedback, see B. S. Lee, *J. Acoust. Soc. Amer.,* 1950, 22, 639; the report on 3-day experimental deafness in man is in *Canad. J. Psychol.,* 1954, 8, 152–156.

Chapter 4

The nervous system

W_E have seen that the nervous system is a collection of cells specialized for transmission, direct or indirect, from receptor to effector: some leading into the switchboard, some leading out, and others connecting between points within it. In this chapter we shall consider the way in which the switchboard is built, and how its major parts function; the following chapter will deal with the functioning of its finer parts, the individual cells of which the nervous system is composed.

The cells are microscopic in cross-section, but vary in length from a fraction of a millimeter to a meter or more. In higher animals their number is enormous (some 10 billion, or 10^{10}, in the human nervous system), closely packed in clumps and bundles to form the macroscopic, easily seen structures of nerves, spinal cord and brain. The general plan on which the cells are laid down is the same for all vertebrates; differences from one species to another are almost entirely a matter of how big the various segments are, not of the way in which they are connected. In mammals especially, the design is the same. Man's brain differs from the rat's in size (it is about 700 times as big), and in the relatively greater size of some centers, but the same structures are present in both, connected in the same way. Accordingly, we shall be concerned with the structure of the mammalian brain in general, referring to man in particular only when some question arises concerning one of his special abilities such as speech.

The central nervous system, or CNS, consists of the brain and spinal

66

cord, as distinct from the connections with the outlying receptors and effectors. Any individual nerve cell is a *neuron,* consisting of a cell-body and its "processes," the elongated fibers along which transmission occurs (Fig. 34, p. 89). A nerve (which must not be confused with a neuron) is a bundle of nerve-fibers outside the CNS, a cable containing hundreds or thousands of incoming and outgoing lines.

Inside the CNS, such bundles of connecting fibers form the white matter. The gray matter consists of masses of cell-bodies. The largest of these masses is the *cerebral cortex,* the outer layer or "bark" of the main part of the brain, but there are also many smaller clumps ("nuclei") found throughout the whole system. Junction points in transmission, the synapses between cells at which the direction of transmission is determined, mostly occur close to cell-bodies and therefore in the gray matter of the CNS. Thus the gray matter is the switchboard proper, the organizing and routing part, while the white matter and nerves are the closely packed conducting cables from one part of the switchboard to another or between switchboard and periphery.

Gross structure

Figure 21 shows man's nervous system as it is: the large mass of the brain at the top of the long narrow spinal cord, and the spinal nerves emerging from the latter. Its basic plan, however, can be better understood if it is thought of as simply a hollow tube which has some bulges in it (which make up most of the brain) and some tiny branches growing out of it (the nerves). It starts out its career, early in the life of the embryo, as a quite simple tube running the length of the organism (parallel to another great tube running from mouth to anus, the alimentary canal). The only complication at first is that the forward end is larger than the after end (Fig. 22). In the course of development the neural tube becomes very complex, but it remains a hollow structure whose walls have thickened more in some parts than others, with bulges here and constrictions there, and the nerves sprouting out of it like thin branches. The hollow of the tube is so small in the spinal cord that it can hardly be seen; but in the brain it is enlarged in four places (the "ventricles"), which are filled with the fluid which also surrounds the brain and cushions it within the bony box of the skull (Figs. 23, 24).

The brain consists of the *brain stem,* the anterior part of the original tube inside the skull, and three main outgrowths or swellings, the *cerebellum* and the *cerebral hemispheres.* The cerebellum is concerned with the coordination of muscular movement, but we have no adequate knowledge of its function (such a mass of tissue must play a larger part in behavior than our present information would suggest) and we shall not be concerned with it in this book. The cerebral hemispheres are another matter. They are essential to higher behavior; their development makes

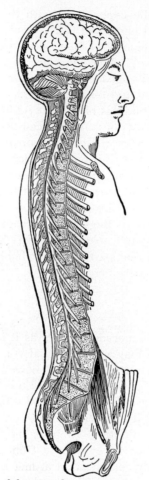

Figure 21.   General view of the central nervous system, showing the brain and spinal
cord in situ. (Bourgery, Schwalbe, van Gehuchten.)

the difference between lower and higher animals, and when they are
removed anything that can be referred to as thought or intelligence
vanishes. But the student should not gain the impression that thought can
occur in these hemispheres alone, or that they can function by themselves
or that intelligence is localized in their outer layer, the cortex. They
operate as a unit with the forward end of the brain stem, and intellectual
function can be impaired as easily by a small destruction in the stem as by
a large destruction of cortex.

As the student will see from the schematic diagrams of Figs. 23 and 24,
the hemispheres are attached to a quite small part of the brain stem,
at the very forward end. They enlarge tremendously with growth, and
this occurs within a limited space (inside the skull), so they are forced
up over the top of the brain stem, and backward and forward, concealing

most of the tube to which they are attached. In higher mammals, this growth also produces a wrinkling and infolding of the cortex (Figs. 25, 27).

The forward end of the brain stem is the *diencephalon,* of which the upper half is the *thalamus,* the lower half the *hypothalamus* (Figs. 24, 25). This is where the cerebral hemispheres are attached to the stem, and all their complex connections funnel through this region. The thalamus is a way-station for incoming paths; all sensory input to the cortex (with the single exception of olfactory excitations) is relayed here. The hypothalamus has motor functions rather than sensory. It is closely connected to the hemispheres, but may be considered as the highest level of reflex organization in the brain stem; here, for example, are controlled the water

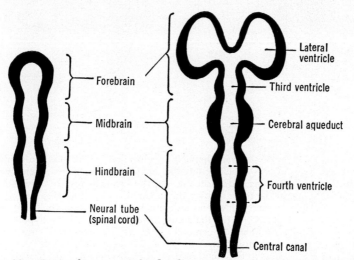

Figure 22. Two early stages in the development of the brain. Left, the tubular form is still evident. Right, at a later stage, the two swellings are the beginning of the cerebral hemispheres; the spinal cord, of which only the end is shown, remains tubular. (Gardner.)

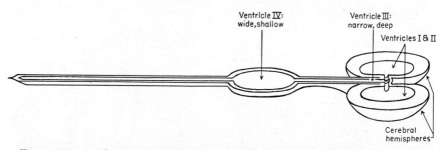

Figure 23. Schematic representation of the adult brain, with top half cut away to show the ventricles. Inside the skull the hollow of the tube widens out to form ventricle IV (beneath the cerebellum, not shown), narrows again to form the "aqueduct" and then deepens in the narrow ventricle III at the forward end of the tube. Ventricles I and II open off from III. This is the shape the brain might have if it had plenty of room to grow in, but with limited space in the skull the parts are crowded together, as shown in the following figures.

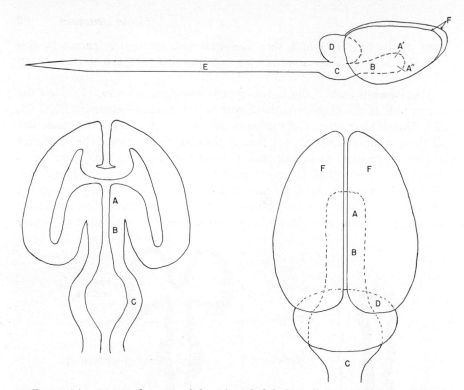

Figure 24.   Main divisions of the CNS, slightly less schematic, in an animal such as the rat. Above, side view; below, left, horizontal section; below, right, view from above. Instead of ballooning out, as in Fig. 23, the hemispheres are crowded together around the front end of the tube, up over the top, and back so that they hide the central tube completely except from below, and hide much of the cerebellum. *A,* diencephalon, of which the upper half (*A'*) is the thalamus, lower half (*A"*) is the hypothalamus; *B,* midbrain; *C,* medulla and pons; *D,* cerebellum; *E,* cord; *F,* cerebral hemispheres. *A, B* and *C* together form the brain stem.

    The human CNS differs in two main respects: because man is built to walk erect, the brain stem is bent downwards at *B;* and the cortex is deeply wrinkled (as shown in Figs. 25 and 27).

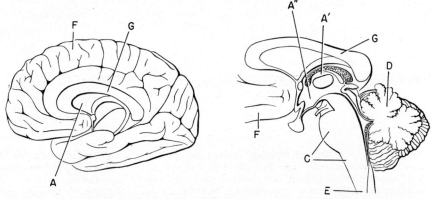

Figure 25.   Sections through the midline of the human brain (the frontal lobe is to the left). In the left-hand diagram the lower part of the brain stem has been cut off; at the right, it is shown in full, with the cerebellum attached. Labels as in Fig. 24; *G,* corpus callosum.

70

balance of the body, temperature regulation and appetite. We have seen that reflex activity is subject to some control from thought processes, so this does not mean that the hypothalamus is unaffected by the cortex— quite the contrary—but for much of its activity the cortex does not appear to be necessary.

The brain stem with its subdivisions has a complex structure but it is not necessary to go into this for our purposes. If the student will think of it in principle as simply being the forward end of the spinal cord, where it projects into the skull, he will see the situation more clearly. The cord and stem are thought of as having reflex functions only, and the cerebral hemispheres as the seat of higher processes and learning. This probably oversimplifies things; some learning may occur in the cord and stem, though whether to any important extent is debatable, and parts of the hemispheres may well be the basis of some reflex activities. However, on our present knowledge we can regard the brain stem (and cerebellum) as the highest level of reflex function, and the cerebral hemispheres as the still higher level at which learning occurs. The cord and stem represent the built-in S-R connections, the rigid part of the switchboard; the hemispheres a collection of unallocated lines which are available to form new connections and to make mediating processes possible.

Figure 26 shows this diagrammatically. A-X and A-Y are two built-in

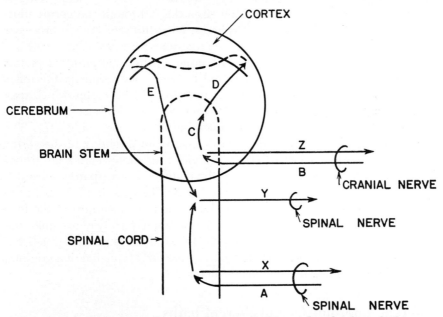

Figure 26.   Illustrating the "long-circuiting" of learned paths through the cerebrum, as distinct from the more direct but less modifiable reflex paths. *A, B*, afferents; *X, Y, Z*, efferents. The broken-line connection, top, between *D* and *E* would not likely be a straight-through connection, but would involve some of the loops discussed in Chapter 3.

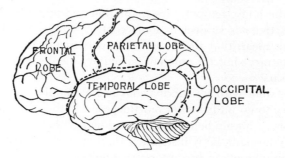

Figure 27.   The human brain seen from the left side, showing the four lobes. The central fissure is the one separating the frontal from the parietal lobe; the Sylvian fissure is the one that first runs upward, then horizontally to the right, separating frontal from temporal lobe, and partly separating temporal from parietal lobe. (From Herrick: *An Introduction to Neurology.* 5th ed.)

connections in the cord, ones that are provided for by growth processes without (as far as we can determine at present) any dependence on learning. These are, therefore, the pathways of unconditioned reflexes (see also Fig. 32). *B-Z* is another such pathway; though *A, X* and *Y* lie in spinal nerves (*A* and *X* in one, *Y* in another) and *B* and *Z* in a cranial nerve, their operations are in the same class. But that of the pathway *B-C-D . . . E-Y* is not. *B-C-D* is provided for innately, and so is *E-Y*; but the connection between *D* and *E* is established only by some form of conditioning or learning. This "long-circuiting" through the cortex illustrates the special role of the hemispheres. Heredity and growth processes lay down the reflex circuits, providing an automatic and unchanging form of adaptation to the immediate environment; when modification of this behavior is called for, it is not effected by new connections in the reflex circuits themselves, but by a long circuit through the cortex which may or may not include the closed circuits of mediating processes.

Each cerebral hemisphere is divided into four lobes (Fig. 27). The frontal lobe extends back to the central fissure, an infolding of the cortex that is an important landmark since it divides the motor cortex (in front) from the somesthetic cortex. Again, the Sylvian fissure partly separates the temporal lobe from the rest of the brain. The occipital lobe is at the back of the hemisphere. The parietal lobe, the most arbitrary of the four subdivisions (the least clearly marked off anatomically), occupies the space between the frontal and occipital lobes (front and back), and between the temporal lobe (below) and the great medial longitudinal fissure that separates the two hemispheres.

Afferent, internuncial and efferent paths

Conduction paths in the nervous system are classified as *afferent, efferent* and *internuncial.* Afferent neurons conduct toward the CNS ("sensory nerve fibers") and, within the CNS, from lower to higher centers. Efferent neurons conduct from higher centers to lower centers, and from these to effectors. Internuncial neurons are those that conduct between two points in the CNS without being clearly upstream or downstream. This distinction is not absolute, and the same set of cells in the cerebrum may be called internuncial at one time, afferent (or efferent) at another, depending on what larger set of activities they are part of at the moment.

A receptor proper is not part of the nervous system but a cell outside it, specialized for amplifying weak disturbances to a degree that excites the neuron and allows it to perform its own special task of transmission. Effectors of course are also separate from the nervous system. With the more highly developed senses which have such specialized receptors, an S-R path thus consists of five steps: (1) receptors, (2) afferent neurons, (3) internuncial neurons, (4) efferent neurons, and (5) effectors. The primitive free nerve endings in the skin and the olfactory paths from the nose do not have separate receptors: a neuron itself does both the receiving and the conducting. Also, some unconditioned reflex paths have no internuncial link—the afferent neuron makes connection directly with an efferent neuron; so (1) and (3) in the above list are sometimes missing. In Fig. 26, *A, B, C* and *D* are afferent; *E, X, Y* and *Z* are efferent; and whatever path connects *D* and *E* is internuncial.

Excitation from sense organs reaches the cortex in two ways (Fig. 28). One is by a set of trunk lines, the *specific sensory projection systems,* direct to the cortex; the other, branching off the trunk lines in the brain stem, goes through the *nonspecific projection system.* The function of the specific afferents is to guide behavior; of the nonspecific, to regulate the level of action of the cortex, or prime it so it can respond effectively to the specific afferent excitations.

Similarly, there are two main types of efferent conduction from the cortex: one via trunk lines from cortex to the motor centers of the cord and stem, through which a direct control is exerted over behavior, and one via the nonspecific projection system and related structures. Here again, the nonspecific system appears to have a sort of regulatory function, determining the level of responsiveness of motor centers in the cord rather than determining which response shall be made at any one moment.

Internuncial paths are found at all levels of the CNS. The nervous system is constructed in general in two symmetrical halves, and throughout are found tracts, large or small, which connect corresponding parts on each side and permit coordination of their activities. The largest of these is the corpus callosum—a great bridge, crossing just above the thalamus, between the two cerebral cortices (Fig. 25).

SPECIFIC AFFERENTS. Each of the incoming trunk lines runs directly

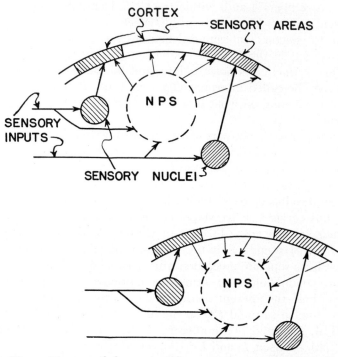

Figure 28.   Diagram of the nonspecific projection system (NPS). Two specific sensory paths are shown, the hatched circles representing two thalamic sensory nuclei, each connected with its own special cortical area. Each sensory input also sends branches into the NPS, which mixes up excitations from these different sources and transmits them indiscriminately to the cortex (upper diagram). The cortex also sends excitations to the NPS (below), so cortical processes can contribute to the level of arousal.

from its sensory zone through a thalamic relay nucleus to its own sensory projection area (Fig. 29)—the visual cortex or visual area, auditory cortex or area, and so on. In mammalian evolution the olfactory system may not have specialized its development as far as the others; at any rate, its input to the brain is not gathered together but dispersed through a number of structures, and since little is known about the way in which these structures interact in the process of smelling we shall not devote much discussion to it. Similarly with taste: though it appears to have a well marked cortical projection area, an extension of the somesthetic area which in man runs down into the Sylvian fissure, and though as we shall see (p. 99f.) there is valuable information about the way in which its afferents function physiologically, there is not a large body of information about its relation to behavior, and it may perhaps be regarded as a more primitive sense.

For vision, audition and somesthesis, however, the situation is different. Each of these is highly organized, for rapid conduction to the cortex and for keeping distinct the separate excitations produced by even slightly different stimulations at the periphery. This is quite unlike the nonspecific system, where conduction is slow and the connections seem such as to achieve a thorough intermingling of the effects of separate stimuli.

An important fact to be kept in mind is that more highly developed senses are "lateralized," and that conduction is primarily to the opposite side of the brain. The left side of the body is represented in the somesthetic area of the right hemisphere (and the motor area of the right side controls muscular contraction on the left side). There is some ipsilateral conduction (i.e., to the same side), but it is not extensive or efficient. In audition, both ears connect effectively with both sides of the brain, but the contralateral conduction (from the right ear to the left auditory cortex, for example) is the quicker. In lower vertebrates, the right eye is connected solely with the left hemisphere and vice versa; in mammals, there is a peculiar departure from this picture which reaches its highest

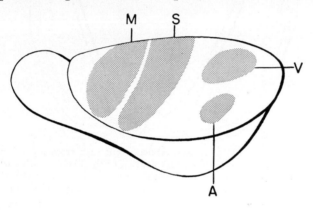

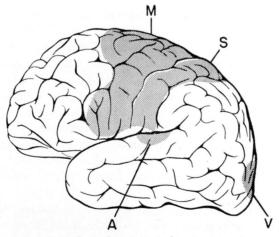

Figure 29.   Approximate loci of sensory and motor areas in rat and man. Man's visual area is pushed round into the cleft between the two hemispheres, so it can hardly be seen. The auditory area proper is buried in the Sylvian fissure. *M,* motor; *S,* somesthetic; *A,* auditory; *V,* visual.

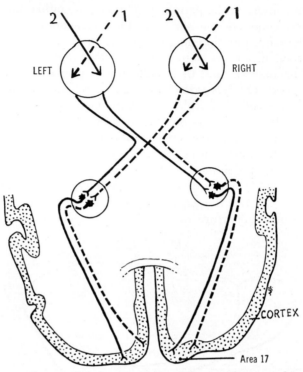

Figure 30.   The visual pathways. Above, light rays from an object (1) in the right visual field and (2) in the left visual field enter the two eyeballs, crossing as they pass through the lens. The left part of both retinas then connect with the left visual cortex at the back of the brain ("area 17"), and the right retina with right visual cortex. Thus an object in the right visual field excites the left visual cortical area only. (After Gardner: *Fundamentals of Neurology,* 3rd ed.)

development in man. The outer (temporal) side of each eye is connected with the ipsilateral visual area, the inner (nasal) side with the contralateral visual area. In the lower mammals the ipsilateral connections are not extensive; but in man a full half of the retina is connected with the same side of the brain (Fig. 30). The right half of each retina is thus connected with the right occipital lobe; and this means that the left visual field is perceived via the right side of the brain.

If one occipital lobe is damaged (as for example by gunshot wound at the back of the head, or by a tumor), the patient becomes blind in corresponding parts of both eyes. A common condition, produced by large destruction, is "homonymous hemianopia" (meaning, literally, "corresponding half-lack of vision"), in which the patient can see nothing to one side of the point in space at which he is looking; his visual field is cut in half vertically, in both eyes. Similarly, if one whole cerebral cortex is destroyed, the patient becomes anesthetic ("without sensation") on the opposite side of the body (nearly so: the ipsilateral connections with the undamaged cortex permit crude and poorly localized sensation with a high limen). The effective duplication of the auditory connections, however, means that loss of one auditory cortex has comparatively little effect on hearing.

A final point to be observed is the internal arrangement of the cortical connections of the three more highly developed specific sensory systems. There is a point-to-point projection of the sensory regions. Each sensory point conducts to a particular cortical point, and these are arranged in such a way that the spatial pattern of sensory stimulation is reproduced in the cortex (Fig. 31). It does not retain the same orientation in space and there are distortions of size. The legs are at the top, the head at the bottom, in the somesthetic cortex, and "up" becomes "down" in the visual cortex; the face and hand representations in the somesthetic cortex are enlarged, and so is the representation of the central retina. But points that are side by side in the periphery remain side by side in the cortex, and the patterns are recognizable despite the distortions.

This is related to an old problem in psychology (which is really no problem at all). On the retina the image of an object looked at is upside down, being inverted by the lens at the front of the eyeball. How then do we see it right-side up—especially since the projection of the retinal pattern of excitation in the cortex is also inverted? But in stimulus-response terms the upside-down-ness *within the system* has no signifi-

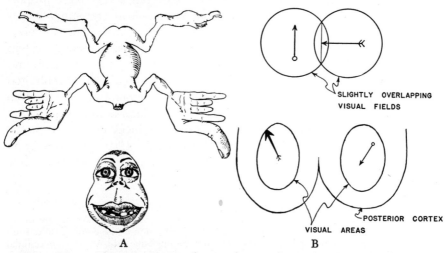

A   **B**

Figure 31.   The organization of somesthetic and visual cortex. A, showing the way in which the different parts of the body are represented in the cortex (legs at the top, head at the bottom) and the relative amount of cortex devoted to the different parts (mouth area and thumb well represented, top of the head and trunk with small representation). (From Penfield, W., and Boldrey, E.: *Brain,* 1937, vol. 60.) B, showing how a horizontal and a vertical arrow in the visual field of a rat (above) are projected on the cortex (below). (After Lashley, K. S.: *J. Comp. Neurol.,* 1934, vol. 60.)

cance; the significant question is, What is connected with what? The problem, it seems, exists only if one is thinking of a little man inside the skull, some sort of independent observer who looks at the back of the retina or the pattern of excitation on the cortex and, being upright in space himself, is puzzled when the pictures are upside down.

Once the "little man inside" is eliminated from one's thinking (as it should be from the student's by now) one simply asks, What does "up" mean, physiologically? It means the processes that produce movement against gravity, focusing the eyeballs toward the ceiling instead of the floor, moving a hand toward the head and away from the feet, bending the body erect from a stooping position, and so forth. "Up" has a behavioral meaning, referring to a class of responses, as well as the connections and mediating processes (or ideas) which relate to such responses. At a reflex level, the lower part of the retina is connected, via the brain stem, with muscles that roll the eyeball upward. A flash of light in the upper part of the field of vision excites the lower part of the retinal surface, and the reflex connections make one look upward, toward the source of light. It does not matter whether this pathway is above the pathway that makes one look downward, or beside it, or below it; all that matters is what is connected with what. The problem vanishes if one thinks consistently in S-R and behavioristic terms.

Specific efferents.   Efferent paths to motor centers of cord and brain stem originate in most parts of the cortex, but a very large proportion of the total is concentrated in what is known as the *motor cortex* (Fig. 29), immediately anterior to the somesthetic cortex. The organization parallels that of the somesthetic cortex. Efferent paths leading to legs and lower trunk leave from the top of the motor area, those to hand and arm from the middle (with thumb and finger areas on an enlarged scale), and those to the muscles of the head region from the bottom (mouth area large). Conduction is to the contralateral side; stimulation of the middle region of the left motor cortex produces movement of the right hand, and when a tumor or a hemorrhage ("stroke") results in destruction of right motor cortex it is the left side of the body which is paralyzed.

Just as the specific afferents are organized for rapid conduction and for keeping different excitations distinct from each other, so are the specific efferents from the motor cortex. Fibers are laid down in parallel. Two cells side by side in the cortex deliver their excitations to neighboring points in the cord on the opposite side, via the "pyramidal tract," a large band of white matter connecting cortex with all levels of the spinal cord. In general, the ventral half of the neural tube (next the belly) has motor functions, the dorsal half (toward the back) afferent functions. Thus the pyramidal tract conducts to the ventral horns of the cord (Fig. 32), from which arise the *ventral roots* of the spinal nerves containing the motor neurons. (Incoming paths to the cord are by way of the *dorsal roots* and the dorsal horn.)

A special feature of the motor outflow from the stem and cord is found in the *auto-*

nomic nervous system (part of the peripheral nervous connections), but consideration of this is postponed for a moment.

The direct control of spinal cord by the cortex is supposed to be exercised through the pyramidal tract, containing the specific efferents. However, there may be some question about this.

NONSPECIFIC FUNCTIONS.   Reference has already been made to a non-specific projection system, or arousal system. Here the word "system" may be misleading; perhaps it should be "systems" to indicate that we may not be dealing with one set of structures that have the same functions throughout. Anatomically the structures in question are highly organized, clearly marked and distinct from each other (though of course with inter-connecting paths), and it may not be long before the account offered here will have to be changed. This probability is increased by the fact that there appear to be qualitatively different kinds of arousal, as seen in the effects on behavior (p. 159f.). At present however we cannot correlate the behavioral effects with particular structures, and as a group these structures do appear to have a global action upon the general level of behavior. We may therefore speak of them as the arousal system, with the understanding that this is likely to turn out to be an oversimplification.

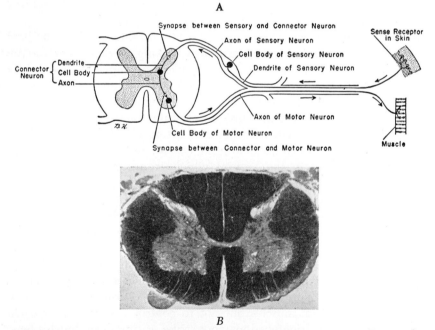

Figure 32.   The spinal cord. *A,* diagram of a reflex arc. (From Villee: *Biology,* 3rd ed.) *B,* photomicrograph of cross-section of human spinal cord; here the white matter is stained black, the gray matter remains gray, forming the dorsal horns (toward the top) and the ventral horns (toward the bottom). (From Gardner: *Fundamentals of Neurology,* 3rd ed.)

Closely related to this afferent system, in part at least identical with it, is a set of structures with similar efferent function: that is, they serve not to arouse or control specific motor movements, but to raise or lower the excitability of motor centers in the cord. These are separate from the pyramidal pathways, and thus known as "extra-pyramidal." It appears (though this too may be oversimplified) that the direct control from the cortex, determining specific responses, is exercised entirely through the trunk lines of the pyramidal system. Not much is known of the behavioral significance of the extrapyramidal paths, but it may well be that they are among other things the primary agency in control of the autonomic nervous system.

The afferent function of the nonspecific structures involves branches from fibers in the trunk-line specific projection systems. Conduction within the nonspecific system is to widely separated points, pooling the excitation from different senses, and the rate of conduction is slow. The cortical bombardment from the nonspecific system therefore derives from all the senses indiscriminately.

This bombardment is completely necessary if the specific paths are to have their proper function of arousing ideation or overt response. It has a tonic or priming action; without it, a specific sensory path can still deliver excitation to its sensory projection area, but the excitation goes no farther and cannot affect behavior. Thus S-R paths involving the cortex do not function unless the cortex is in the state of arousal which is shown by a flattened EEG record (electroencephalograph: p. 95), and this state in turn depends on the nonspecific bombardment.

In deep sleep the arousal system is at a low level of activity; the peak of this activity is reached only in the fully waking, attentive (or actively thinking) subject. The level of activity does not depend alone on the sensory input; otherwise we should promptly go to sleep whenever environmental stimuli are decreased, and be unable to sleep in a noisy, lighted room. One important source of continual activity, when sensory input is lowered, is a feedback from the cortex. This forms a closed circuit: arousal system to cortex to arousal system, and so on. Thus thought processes contribute to the arousal which is necessary to their own existence (Fig. 28, lower).

AUTONOMIC NERVOUS SYSTEM.   The autonomic nervous system, part of the peripheral nervous system, consists of motor fibers to the visceral (or smooth) muscles and the glands. It is a primitive motor system of which much of the action is very diffuse and not well controlled by cortical mechanisms. The result, in emotional situations in which there is a high level of neural activity (especially in the nonspecific system of the brain stem), is that ideational processes may continue to control the activity of the skeletal muscles but not to control visceral activity. The man who is angry or frightened may not strike or run away; but his heart beat increases, blood pressure rises, there is sweating and pallor or flushing of the skin, the orderly processes of stomach and gut are disturbed, and so on.

Most controlled studies of emotion are made in the laboratory with human subjects from the introductory course in psychology, who want to make a passing grade in the course, and who consequently restrain themselves from striking the experimenter when he makes them angry; but though their ideational processes can inhibit the muscles of arms or legs, they cannot inhibit the action of the autonomic system. Thus the chief effect of emotion-provoking situations *seems* to be autonomic, and psychologists have tended to identify autonomic activity with emotion. But this is a misleading conclusion. The autonomic nervous system may reflect the general level of arousal in the CNS, but this includes activity which we do not classify as emotional; and when emotional disturbance is present it tends to excite the skeletal musculature just as much as the viscera. Trembling and incoordination of skeletal movement are excellent indicators of emotional disturbance.

The autonomic nervous system is best regarded, not as a special indicator of emotion, but as a primitive part of the motor system, which is not subject to the same degree of cortical control as the rest. It has two main divisions (Fig. 33): the sympathetic nervous system, which has connections with the middle regions of the cord; and the parasympathetic, in two subdivisions, one connected with the posterior end of the spinal cord, one with the brain stem. Most visceral organs receive both sympathetic and parasympathetic fibers; their actions are, in general, opposed to each other. What the sympathetic facilitates the parasympathetic inhibits, and vice versa. The sympathetic has been regarded as designed for action in emergency situations, mobilizing the resources of the body for maximal expenditure—a spendthrift, while the parasympathetic is the skinflint that builds them up and conserves them. This is an oversimplification—the sympathetic for example has its role in ordinary situations, in the normal economy of the body—but useful to keep in mind, with reservations. Thus the sympathetic increases the heart rate, increasing the blood flow to the muscles and making more energy available for their action; it also inhibits the digestive processes that cannot contribute here and now to behavioral efficiency. The parasympathetic on the other hand slows down the heart and promotes digestion, adding to the future resources of the body.

An important link in the action of the sympathetic is the adrenal glands, whose inner portion (or medulla, as distinct from the adrenal cortex) secretes a hormone, epinephrine ("adrenalin"), into the blood stream when the sympathetic system is active. The effects in general are the same as those of the sympathetic fibers themselves,[1] and contribute

---

[1] In fact, the glandular cells which make up the adrenal medulla are modified neural cells which have become specialized for secretion instead of conduction, but which continue to cooperate closely with the sympathetic nervous system almost as if they were still neurons.

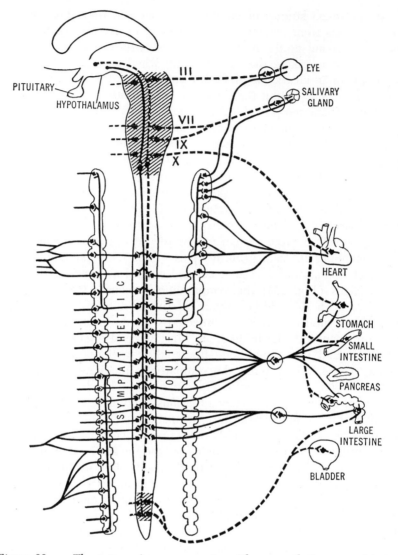

Figure 33.   The autonomic nervous system. The sympathetic segment is in the middle region, its connections shown in solid lines; the parasympathetic has two divisions, the cranial (above) and the sacral (below), its connections being shown in broken lines. (From Gardner: *Fundamentals of Neurology,* 3rd. ed.)

to the general picture of sympathetic action discussed above. Also, epinephrine excites the arousal system of the brain stem, this constituting another closed circuit: from arousal system to sympathetic system to adrenals and thence, via the blood stream, to the arousal system again. This circuit must contribute to the slowness with which a generalized excitation in the CNS dies down.

Localization of cortical function

We have already seen that the different sense organs connect with different parts of the cortex (Figs. 29, 31). These parts consequently have special services to perform in the control of behavior, just as the motor area has a special role in maintaining the control of the cortex over efferent fibers from the CNS. This fact, that a given process may depend on a particular part and not on others in the same way, is known as the *localization of function* in the cortex.

There is a trap here, however, that the student must be warned about. No psychological function can exist within a segment of cortex by itself. We commonly say that vision is localized in the visual area, a part of the occipital lobe; but this does not mean that the whole process of seeing (or even of visual imagery) can occur in the occipital lobe. What it means is that an essential part of the process occurs there, and only there. As we shall see shortly, speech is "localized" in the cerebral cortex on the left side (for most persons). This again does not mean that the mediating processes of speech can occur in that tissue alone; it does mean that their organization depends on it. Injury to this area of cortex can abolish speech (and certain other abilities to some extent), whereas larger destructions in other areas have no such effect.

Another important point can be mentioned briefly. Elsewhere in this text reference is made to "cortical processes," but usually as a brief way of saying "higher processes in which the cortex is essentially involved." The student should not think of the cortex as being able to function by itself, independent of other structures. In the first place, we have seen that arousal—activity in the nonspecific projection system—is fully necessary to these higher processes. Also, apart from this kind of input, the cortex itself is organized in neural circuits which involve the thalamus (and probably other structures as well). "Cortical" activity characteristically includes transmission from cortex to thalamus to cortex to thalamus, and so on, as well as from cortex to cortex. The cortex, in other words, is not a functional system in itself; and when we speak of cortical processes, what we mean is cortico-thalamic processes (or cortico-subcortical, since there are probably other subcortical structures involved).

The primary localizations are those of the sensory and motor areas. The rest of the cortex is known as *association cortex*. This name was first used by earlier students of the brain who thought of the association areas as providing a set of simple bridges from one of the specialized (sensory or motor) areas to another, and we know now that this is too simple a picture. The mediating processes discussed in Chapter 3 do not consist merely of linking together a series of images as relayed from the sense organs, and separately hooking these up with motor paths. Also, there is no reason to be sure that association—the establishment of new paths, in learning—occurs only in cortical association areas. Somesthetic-motor paths, for example, could be added without involving association cortex (since the two areas lie side by side), and it is likely that new paths involve the thalamus and other subcortical structures as well as cortex. "Localization of function" and "association cortex" are survivals from an earlier day, but they are well established terms in current use and may still be employed, if handled with reasonable care.

There are two great islands of association cortex: the prefrontal area, anterior to the motor area in the frontal lobe, and a posterior area comprising part of the parietal, occipital and temporal lobes (Fig. 29).

The prefrontal cortex presents us with a major puzzle because it appears to play no essential part in man's normal behavior. It is a large area, and must be important; also, its importance has been clearly shown in other animals' behavior. The monkey's capacity to perform delayed response under normal conditions is seriously impaired after clean surgical removal of the frontal poles of the brain, but man's is not. It is true that disease processes in man's frontal lobe usually cause marked changes of behavior, but disease does not merely involve destruction of neurons; it also changes the function of other neurons, and this abnormal function can be transmitted to the rest of the brain. With the whole brain functioning abnormally, the changes in behavior can be very great. If the diseased frontal lobe is removed surgically, and if the rest of the brain has not been damaged, the patient's behavior returns to normal and as far as can be ascertained his intelligence is unaffected.

We must assume however that the region is important. Our failure to show this is presumably because we have not yet made the right tests.

This conclusion is reinforced by another set of facts. If a patient is suffering from anxiety or depression, the emotional state is often much improved by a deep cut in each frontal lobe, severing many of its connections with the rest of the brain. The mental change, of course, means changes in behavior. This operation is frontal lobotomy ("-otomy" means "an incision into"; prefrontal lobectomy means removing the whole anterior part of the frontal lobe).

Historically the frontal association area has been regarded as the seat of higher mental functions, and all that is good and great about man. There is a much better case for the special importance of the posterior association area; the development of this area in man (as contrasted with lower animals) is at least as great as that of the frontal area, and damage to it is more likely to produce serious impairment of higher functions.

But the student is reminded that mental function is the function of the whole brain, not a special part; what we are saying here is that the posterior association area (particularly the temporal lobe segment) is especially important in the over-all integration of the activities of different parts of the brain. Mental function, or mind, is not resident in cortex alone; we have already seen that mental function is not possible if the arousal system is prevented from functioning. On the other hand, if all cortex is removed, but the arousal system left untouched, mental functioning is again reduced to the vanishing point, so we cannot make the brain stem the seat of mind either. Mind is the complex interaction of the various parts of the brain, not to be localized in one of them.

The most dramatic and well known effect of damage to the posterior association area is *aphasia,* of which the chief indication is loss of speech, but which is inherently a disturbance of the thought processes that are necessary to using language in any way. The disturbance takes different forms; in some writing and speaking are more affected, in others reading and understanding spoken language. In practically all cases, however, all four aspects of language show serious defects. Also, there is a considerable effect upon the scores made in some nonverbal intelligence tests, such as recognition of absurdities in pictures, and little or no effect upon others. The disturbance of "intelligence" is therefore very unequal, which of course is what would be expected if intelligence is not a unitary power but a collection of skills of different kinds (Chap. 12).

The lesions (damage to tissue) which produce aphasia are usually in the middle regions of the left cerebral cortex, close to the Sylvian fissure: more often somewhat posterior, but sometimes slightly anterior. A few left-handed persons may get aphasia with lesions of the right hemisphere, but these are rare, except in cases in which there was damage to the left hemisphere before the age of two years; then, at maturity, damage to the right hemisphere may produce aphasia. There appears also to be a group of persons, mostly left-handed, for whom damage to both sides is necessary to cause aphasia. In these persons, that is, "speech localization" is bilateral.

The relation of speech area and handedness bears on the topic of *cerebral dominance:* the conception that one hemisphere controls the other, or is more important in behavior. Thus a large majority of the human race are right-handed, with a higher level of skill for most tasks in the hand which is controlled by the left hemisphere: the same hemisphere which, as we have just seen, is usually involved in speech. For most persons therefore, the left hemisphere is dominant. However, older ideas of dominance implied that hand-control and speech-control would necessarily be localized together, and this appears not to be true (since left hemisphere lesions can produce aphasia in left-handed persons). Also, it was thought that "eyedness"—preference for the use of one eye over the other—was also an indication of the dominance of one hemisphere over the other. This idea has the difficulty that the "dominant" eye is connected equally with both hemispheres and cannot be preferred for the same reason that a hand is preferred—that is, one eye is not dominant because it alone is connected with the dominant hemisphere. It has not been shown that eyedness is more than a preference for one eye over the other, or that, when both eyes are normal (with equal acuity, etc.), the preferred eye has any higher level of "skill"—or perceptual development—than the other. Finally, eye preference does not correlate very highly with handedness.

The facts of cerebral dominance then are: in most persons the left hemisphere is dominant in handedness and speech control, but some persons (the ambidextrous ones) do not show handedness (or show it to a less than usual degree), and speech sometimes has a bilateral localization.

Summary

The nervous system is a hollow tube with three big swellings at the front end, this front end being the brain; two of the swellings, farther forward than the third, are the cerebral hemispheres and their outer layer is the cerebral cortex. Learning and higher behavior involve circuits passing through the cortex. Other circuits are the basis of reflexes.

There are two main kinds of input to the system: specific and nonspecific. Each sense organ in each side of the body has a trunk line to its own area in the cortex on the opposite side, specific to that sense organ. But it also sends connections to a common pool, the nonspecific projection system or arousal system, which mixes up these excitations and sends them on to the cortex; the effect is to tone up the cortex and allow it to carry out its functions. The arousal system is less active in sleep; damage to it produces unconsciousness.

Output from the brain to lower centers also is both specific and nonspecific: there are trunk lines from the cortex to lower centers, but some of the output goes through the nonspecific system and seems to affect the general level of motor activity instead of a particular activity. The autonomic nervous system, in control of glands, heart, blood vessels, and the viscera generally, acts like part of the nonspecific output. Its activity is not peculiar to emotion.

"Localization of function" is a dangerous term. Localizing vision in the visual area of the cortex, for example, does not mean that vision occurs in this area alone, but that the area is necessary to vision and not to other functions. The clear-cut localizations in the cortex are the special sensory and motor areas, each bilateral; and the speech area, in almost all cases on the left side. The prefrontal cortex is puzzling, since it seems to have little importance for man's behavior (it has much more in monkeys'). Intellectual processes are more closely related to parietal and temporal lobes.

Notes

A convenient guide to the nervous system, reliable but not so overloaded with detail that it is hard for the student in psychology to use, is E. Gardner, *Fundamentals of Neurology*, 3rd ed., W. B. Saunders Co., 1958. For an account of the arousal system from a psychological point of view, see Lindsley, Chap. 14 in Stevens (General References, Chap. 1, p. 19).

The definitive account of aphasia is T. Weisenburg and Katharine E.

McBride, *Aphasia,* Commonwealth, 1935. The question of localization has however been clarified since that book was published, particularly by Penfield and his co-workers: see W. Penfield and H. Jasper, *Epilepsy and the Functional Anatomy of the Human Brain,* Little, Brown & Co., 1954, pp. 109–111; and H. L. Roberts, *Trans. Amer. Neurol. Ass.,* 1955, 80, 143–147.

Chapter 5

Neural transmission

W_E may turn now to the way in which the transmission of excitation achieves the functions which have been ascribed to the various parts of the central nervous system. The basic problem of behavior, as we have seen, is to discover how the stimulation of receptor areas determines what is done by the effectors. In principle, the problem is to know what paths will be followed by a given excitation. The choice of paths is determined at the junction points between neurons: let us then consider the individual actor on this stage, the neuron, and the contact one actor makes with another, at the synapse.

Neuron and synapse

Examples of the different forms taken by neurons are given in Fig. 34 (see also Fig. 16). What these have in common is that they are all one-way streets, each with a receiving and a sending end. The *dendrites* are fibrils at the receiving end; the neuron may have more than one of these. There is only one *axon*, the fibril that conducts away from the cell-body and toward the next cell, but it usually has a number of branches or collaterals. Though the dendrites have the function of receiving excitation from other cells, the cell-body itself also receives excitation direct, by-passing the dendrites (Fig. 35). Conduction by the dendrite may be slow and inefficient; it has been suggested this is the primitive arrangement, and that direct excitation of the cell-body is an evolutionary development which permits more efficient conduction.

The *synapse* is the point at which an axon makes contact with the dendrite or cell-body of another neuron (Fig. 35). The enlargement of the axon fibril at the point of contact is known as a *synaptic knob.* One possible basis of the improvement of transmission at the synapse involved in learning is that this consists of an enlargement of the knob. So far, however, this is a purely theoretical explanation, and not a necessary one, for the change might be in the chemical functioning of the knob rather than its size.

Both dendrite and axon are conductors, but it appears that in general their properties are quite different. The axon (like the cell-body itself) works on the *all-or-none principle,* the dendrite does not. The all-or-none principle means that the axon, when it fires, expends all its accumulated energy. It is like a shotgun that either fires or does not fire, with no half-way measures; pulling the trigger gently does not produce a gentler explosion. The dendrite is more like a bow-and-arrow system, in which a weak pull produces a weak effect, a strong pull a strong effect.

The axon conducts "without decrement": since it burns all of whatever fuel is available at each point, the electrochemical disturbance does not decrease with distance as it travels along the fiber. In this respect the axon is like a train of gunpowder; the dendrite like a damp match in

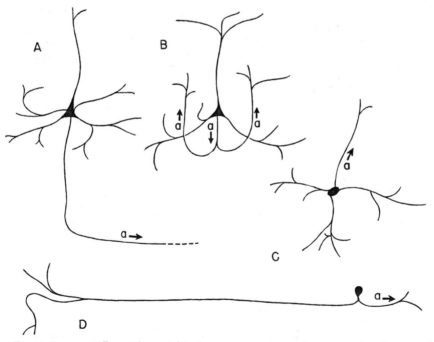

Figure 34.   Different forms taken by neurons. *a,* axon. In neuron *A,* only part of the axon is shown; in *B, C, D* the whole cell is shown. *B* and *C* are short-axon cells from the CNS (note how the axon in *B* comes back toward the dendrites of the same cell, as if to form a closed loop). *D* is an afferent neuron, from a spinal-cord nerve; here we find a very long dendrite and a short axon.

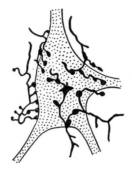

Figure 35.   Synapses: synaptic knobs (black) making contact with a cell body (stippled). Only a few knobs are shown; the cell-body and its dendrites may be completely covered by them. (From Gardner, E., *Fundamentals of Neurology,* 3rd ed.)

which the flame gets smaller and smaller as it moves along, so that it may go out before the end of the match is reached. The dendrite conducts "decrementally." Often, therefore, a dendrite may be excited at some distance from the cell-body and not excite the latter; the greater the disturbance in the dendrite, the greater the probability that the disturbance will reach the cell-body and fire it. The cell-body and the axon tend to act as a unit, both all-or-none in action; so that, if the cell-body is excited, the excitation sweeps over it and on over the axon, including all its branches.

This event, the *nerve impulse,* is the fundamental process of neural transmission. The important facts for our present purposes are summarized as follows. (1) The impulse is a change, both electrical and chemical, that moves across the neuron at a fast but limited speed,[1] the rate varying with the diameter of the fiber (up to 120 meters per second in large fibers, less than 1 m./sec. in the smallest); (2) this disturbance can set off a similar one in a second neuron, across the synapse, or when it reaches a gland or muscle cell can cause it to secrete or contract; (3) the neuron needs a definite time to "recharge" itself after firing in this way; (4) immediately after firing nothing can fire the neuron again, but a little later, before recharging is complete, the neuron can be fired by a supraliminal stimulation; and (5) when the neuron fires, its cell-body and axon fire completely—the all-or-none principle.

The *absolute refractory period* is the first stage of recharging, when the cell's limen is infinitely high and no stimulation can produce a second

[1] Students are sometimes confused about the speed of an "electrical" nerve impulse, and think that it must travel at the same rate as electrical current. Instead, the impulse is an electrical (and chemical) *disturbance* which travels much more slowly. It may be thought of as like a thunderstorm which moves across the countryside; electrical currents, in the form of lightning flashes, may travel at the speed of light, but the storm itself moves, perhaps, at a rate of only 10 or 15 miles per hour, just as a hurricane does though it consists of 120-mile-per-hour winds. The current flow in and around the nerve impulse may be at the speed of light, but the locus of disturbance, the impulse, moves in a relatively slow way along the nerve fiber.

discharge. The *relative refractory period* follows, in which the limen is high, but a strong stimulation can fire the cell again. For large cells the refractory period is shorter, and the resting limen is lower.

Next, we can look at some of the elementary consequences of these facts. Any nerve or tract is made up of neurons varying in size, and hence in speed of conduction. If therefore a strong stimulus fires all the neurons in a given bundle, the *volley* of impulses starts out at the same time but is dispersed, in time of arrival, at the other end. A short sharp stimulation of the foot, for example, does not produce an equally brief excitation at the level of the cord, but a scattering of impulses extending over an appreciable part of a second. (The dispersion in time is still greater at the level of the cerebrum.) Next, the absolute refractory time means that the fastest frequency of firing in a single fiber is of the order of 1000 per second.

The logical consequences of the all-or-none principle are quite clear, though students usually have some trouble with it. A strong stimulation does not produce bigger impulses in a fiber. It can however fire the cell more frequently, by catching it earlier in the relative refractory period. Thus intensity of stimulation is translated into frequency in the CNS. Further, since different afferent cells have different limens, a stronger stimulation excites more cells, which again means an increased frequency of firing. Thus the all-or-none principle applies to a single impulse in a single fiber, but not to the repetitive firing of the fiber nor to a bundle of fibers.

At this point in such discussions it is customary to introduce a simple but untrue diagram like Fig. 36, *A*, to explain the nerve impulse, so let us introduce it by all means. In the resting state the cell has positive ions on the outside, negative ions inside, separated by a membrane which is semipermeable (i.e., it allows some ions to pass through, not others). This is an unstable equilibrium; a very slight disturbance in the neighborhood of the membrane can upset the balance and allow the positive ions on the outside to pass through the membrane. When this happens the outer surface of that part of the neuron becomes negative, an electrical effect referred to as the "action potential." The polarization (i.e., the separation of positive and negative ions by the membrane) has disappeared; the depolarization then spreads by disturbing the equilibrium of the region next to it, so that it travels along the axon. No sooner is the equilibrium upset, however, than the cell begins to restore it by moving the positive ions outward, a process that takes altogether about 1 ms; the nerve impulse, that is, lasts about 1 ms at any one point in the cell (0.5 ms in large fibers, 2.0 in small).

The whole process is known to be more complex than this; the positive ions moving inward are sodium ions, but positive potassium ions are moving outward while this is going on (just to confuse the picture), and no one knows how the sodium ions are moved out, in the process of recovery. Something must do it, and this is known as the

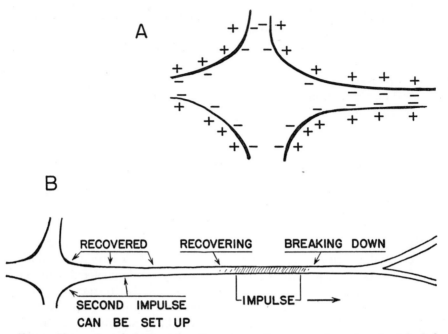

Figure 36.   *A,* polarization of resting neuron. *B,* passage of one impulse (shaded region) along the axon: showing that two or more impulses can occur at the same time in the neuron, since a second one can be started in the "recovered" region as soon as the first has moved along the fiber and the cell-body has recharged itself. The process is known to be far more complex than diagram *A* would suggest.

sodium pump, an entity that has some relation to unicorn or phoenix, or the celestial spheres that move the stars in their courses. Psychologists frequently have to give names to things they have not seen and do not understand; it is reassuring to observe that others must too.

The all-or-none action of the axon makes possible a rapid conduction to distant points. A further contribution to this end is made by the myelin sheath, a fatty covering surrounding many nerve fibers (this is what makes the white matter white). At intervals of a millimeter or so there are gaps in the sheath (at the "nodes"); it seems probable that electrical potential at one gap produces an excitation in the next, starting what is really a second nerve impulse at that point. The myelin sheath over the intervening part of the fiber appears also to prevent the impulse from occurring in the internodal region. Thus the impulse, it is believed, does not travel continuously along the fiber, but jumps from node to node at a faster rate than continuous travel would permit (and also demands less energy expenditure).

Fatigue in the neuron is, first, the refractory period. The absolute refractory period lasts for the length of the impulse, about 1 ms. Following this the cell may be excited again, but recovery from a single firing takes from 80 ms (in large fibers) to a second or so (in small ones). Secondly, a cell that is fired at a rapid rate begins to have a kind of supply problem: the sodium ions are not excreted completely for some time after each firing and so accumulate when there is prolonged activity. Full recovery may take an hour or more.

Inhibition is a hyperpolarizing (instead of the depolarizing that occurs

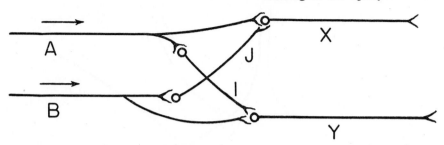

Figure 37. The mechanism of inhibition. Neuron *A* excites *X* in the usual manner; a collateral also excites *I*, which is specialized for inhibition. *I* then acts to hyperpolarize *Y* and prevent it from firing at the same time as *X*. Similarly, *B* excites *Y*, but (via *J*) inhibits *X*. (This is known as reciprocal innervation.)

when the cell fires), which prevents firing. It is probably produced by the chemical action of separate neurons specialized for this function. *Facilitation* is the opposite of inhibition: in one case, the impulse reaching the synapse tends to prevent firing, in the other it tends to produce firing. ("Facilitation" has exactly the same meaning as "stimulation," except that it is customary to distinguish between (1) events which excite the neuron from outside the CNS—these are referred to as *stimuli;* and (2) the excitation of one neuron by another—facilitation.) Figure 37 then shows how, by means of an inhibitory link, a neural activity may facilitate one path while inhibiting another.

Timing at the synapse

Physiologists have found that there are circumstances in which a single impulse cannot cross the synapse, whereas two or more can, by summation. There is also reason to believe that when two impulses arrive simultaneously, over two separate axons, they are more effective than two impulses arriving one after another in the same axon (Fig. 38). This does not mean that a single impulse cannot cross any synapse, but the probability that the second cell will fire must be greater when two impulses are delivered simultaneously. For example, the second cell may be fired by a single impulse when it is fully rested; but the summation of two or more impulses may be necessary when it is in the relatively refractory period. Since several impulses must arrive within a short time interval in order to sum, timing becomes an important factor in neural transmission.

With this in mind, we can better see the significance of certain structural features of the CNS. When fibers are laid down in parallel, as in the specific afferent systems, the excitation of a group of contiguous cells will be reliably transmitted at the next synaptic level because they all deliver their excitations to the same group of post-synaptic cells. This permits summation; when fibers conduct in divergent directions, there is no summation except when, by chance, two of them converge on a

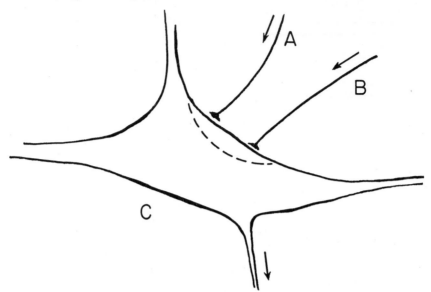

Figure 38.   Summation at the synapse. *A, B*, axons; *C*, cell-body. *A* alone may not be able to fire *C; A* and *B* together produce a greater area of breakdown and a higher probability that *C* will fire.

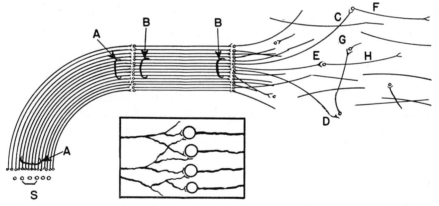

Figure 39.   Neural conduction: parallel on the left, divergent on the right. *S*, stimulation of part of a receptor surface, excites a group of neurons *A* which converge at the next synaptic level and provide summation in a post-synaptic group, *B*, which therefore fires reliably. At the next synapse there is divergence; *B* produces summation in *C, D, E,* and so fires them reliably, but there is no summation for *F, G, H* (some of these diverging paths may meet by chance, when a very large number is involved). *Inset:* the convergence in greater detail, showing the overlap of branching fibers that produces summation.

third cell. In Fig. 39, the stimulation *S* which fires a group of cells *A* will have a high probability of firing cell-group *B*, and also cells *C, D* and *E,* but there is a much lower probability that *E* (for example) will fire *H*.

At first glance it appears that the conduction in parallel is efficient, the divergent conduction inefficient, and it may be hard to see **why a** large part of the brain should be given over to the latter. The sensory excitation that is reliably conducted as far as neurons C, D and E is likely to peter out at the level of F, G, and H or (at the most) shortly thereafter. On the other hand, the conduction in parallel may be altogether too efficient for certain other functions for which delay in transmission is necessary; and conduction through the divergent paths of association cortex is possible in certain conditions which will be considered later in this chapter.

Synchrony and asynchrony: the EEG

It is implied by Fig. 39 that synchronized firing is characteristic of cells that conduct in parallel, but not elsewhere. Activity in the divergent-conduction regions of the brain is likely to show a lack of synchronization of the cells in any one small region. We may consider next the evidence on this and related points that is obtained from *electroencephalography*: a term to make anyone shudder, even electroencephalographers, who consequently are accustomed to speak of the *EEG* instead.

When the same electronic amplifying methods that are used to pick up disturbances in the atmosphere, otherwise undetectable, and to turn them into music or speech on the radio—when these methods are applied to the scalp of the living human subject, it is found that the brain too is broadcasting though not always in an equally entertaining way. Instead of turning the broadcast into sounds, it is made to operate a pen on a moving sheet of paper and thus produce a lasting record of the brain's activity. Such tracings, or "brain waves," are shown in Fig. 40.

One implication of the figure is clear. Since the record cannot be from a single cell, but must be from whole populations of cells beneath the points on the scalp to which the electrodes are attached, the size of the potential that is recorded (the height of the wave) will be greatest when all the cells in that small area are active at the same time. The activity may be dendritic, without actual firing. Large potentials then mean that there is a synchrony of activity; small waves mean asynchrony, and dispersion. The figure shows that the higher the level of excitation or arousal is, the smaller the potentials. Conscious processes therefore are primarily asynchronous, or diffuse, neural activity. Cells in any one small area tend not to be active at the same time. When the waking subject is relaxed, instructed to close his eyes and "let his mind wander," moderately large potentials appear at a rate of about 10 per second: the *alpha rhythm*. If at this point he opens his eyes, fixes his attention on some environmental event, or tries to solve some problem, a faster frequency with smaller waves (*beta rhythm*) immediately replaces the alpha rhythm.

Sleep, on the other hand, is accompanied by much larger potentials and slower waves (*delta rhythm*). These potentials are not caused by actual firing of neurons; they consist mainly of synchronized dendritic

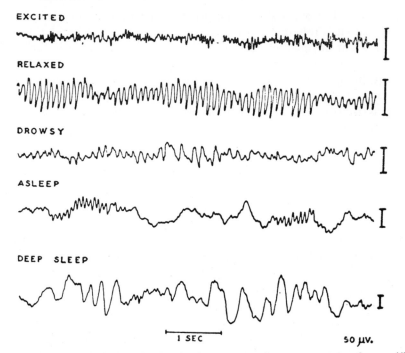

Figure 40.   The EEG at five levels of excitation. The tracing next to the top ("re-laxed") is the alpha rhythm. In the one next to the bottom ("asleep") the two places where a burst of short, faster waves occurs, on top of a slow wave, are "sleep spindles." The vertical line at the right of each tracing permits comparison of voltages (e.g., the bottom tracing would have much higher waves if on the same scale as the top trac-ing). (From Jasper, in Penfield and Erickson, *Epilepsy and Cerebral Localization,* Charles C Thomas, 1941.)

potentials which, as we have seen (p. 90), do not necessarily conduct as far as the cell-body and thus may occur often without producing impulses. When synchrony of actual firing occurs on a large scale, the result is an epileptic convulsion.

The evidence of the EEG indicates in short that thought is related to the occurrence of small fast potentials. The alpha rhythm, with larger and slower waves, means a momentary absence of attention or intellectual effort; delta waves indicate a still greater lack, and often a complete absence of consciousness. Two points are of interest here. Delta waves are also found in pathological conditions of the brain which are such as to impair thought. Secondly, it is of considerable significance that in the newborn infant these large, slow waves are continuously present, even in the waking state (together with some fast-wave activity). The fully adult pattern does not appear until the age of 14 or thereabouts. This suggests that the cortical processes of consciousness are not present in the young infant; such a conclusion is supported also by behavioral evidence, to be considered later, indicating that perception of the environment, in the adult sense, occurs only as the slow product of experience. Since thought processes develop presumably from perceptions, this implies also an absence of any real capacity for thought in the first months following birth.

Some writers, especially on psychoanalysis, have been puzzled at the lack of memory for the events of infancy. They seem to think that the infant is conscious in the same way as an adult, with the same kind of memory. It is even suggested that the fetus is conscious in the uterine environment, and later can be nostalgic for this idyllic state of existence. Such ideas, surely, are nonsense. We do not need to suppose that there is some special repression that explains the "forgetting" of uterine and early postnatal awarenesses; it is far more likely that such awarenesses, in any adult sense, do not exist. It seems likely, in other words, that the newborn infant is not conscious, and only gradually becomes so in the first five to ten months of life.

"Specific energies" and coding

Timing in nervous activity is related to another problem. How does the nervous system keep the different "messages" from the sense organs distinct, so that they are conducted to the proper destination? Chiefly, this is done by (1) having separate channels for separate groups of receptors, from the eye to the visual area of the cortex, from the ear to the auditory area, and so on; in this way, the effects of visual stimulation are kept distinct from those of auditory or tactual stimulation. There is also another mechanism (2), which allows two different messages to use the same channel, if they are "coded" differently.

This is an old question in psychology. Stimulation of the optic nerve always produces visual perception, sensation from the left foot never gets mixed up with sensation from the right hand. These facts are known as the *law of specific energies*. It does not matter how the optic nerve is stimulated: pressure, or passing an electric current through it, still makes the subject "see" light, so the optic nerve is "specific" for visual perception, once it is activated. And, clearly, the specificity is because the nerve leads toward the visual cortex. Stimulation of this region is enough, by itself, to produce the effect. A blow on the head that stimulates it mechanically makes one "see stars"; the surgeon, operating on the brain of a conscious patient, applies electrical stimulation to occipital cortex and the patient reports seeing a light—though his eyes may be closed and there is in fact no activity of the sense organ. So-called visual *awareness* thus consists of the activity of certain paths in or beyond visual cortex, auditory awareness an activity in the paths of the auditory cortex, and so on. The difference between these processes, their distinctiveness, is evidently related to the fact that each sense organ connects with a different region in the brain. Basically, the routes involved in tactual perception are separate from those in auditory or visual perception. A difference between two perceptions means the possibility of making distinctive responses; this is easy to understand if the sensory excitations reach different parts of the brain, and thus have clearly separate paths from receptor to effector.

The same separation of routes, of course, occurs within a single sensory system. We have already seen that each part of the retina is connected with its own part of the visual cortex: the existence of these different pathways within the visual system helps to account for the subject's ability to make different responses to stimuli in different parts of the visual field. The subject *knows* what direction a light is coming from, whether he responds to it or not. This means that with the proper summation from further stimuli (Chap. 2) he would point to it or direct his gaze toward it. Similarly, there are separate paths within the somesthetic system for different parts of the body. The subject knows when he is touched on the hand; if the stimulus is strong enough to produce a response, it is the hand that moves, rather than some other part of the body.

But now we can consider the second point. Specificity in sensation goes further than is accounted for by a complete separation of routes. Two sensory messages may use the same incoming lines, at least in part, and still be completely sorted out at higher levels in the CNS. This is achieved by a kind of coding, which consists of the frequency pattern of the impulses (one message, for example, may consist of regularly spaced impulses, another of intermittent bursts) plus the combination of afferent fibers.

As a first simple example of what this means we may consider the transformation of strength of stimulation (intensity) into (1) frequency of firing, and (2) frequency of the number of afferent neurons firing. In Fig. 41, a weak stimulus may fire cells A only, at a low rate. A strong stimulus produces a higher rate of firing in A, and also brings in B. The second-order neurons X and Y may thus be exposed to a low or a high rate of bombardment. Neurons differ not only in limen (the number of impulses at the synapse that are necessary to fire them) but also with respect to their frequency of firing. If pathway X therefore has a low limen, or is most readily fired at a low frequency, it is possible that a weak stimulus would activate pathway X and not Y. A strong stimulus might excite Y more than X, when both X and Y are exposed to a strong bombardment; and if, as suggested in the figure, activity in Y inhibits activity in X, the result would be that with a strong stimulus only Y would be active, with a weak stimulus only X would be active. Thus two "messages" use the same incoming lines, in part, but are sorted out in the CNS.

The details of how this occurs are not established experimentally. They are suggested here to show how the same afferent neurons, A, might contribute to two different sensory events, and to show what is meant by the term "coding." The sorting out into spatially discrete paths might not occur at this level, but in the cortex. What we do know is that discriminable sensory events do not always have entirely separate incoming paths; and we do know that, if they are discriminated, they eventually get on to separate paths in the CNS.

This last point, concerning the ultimate spatial separation, is a straightforward inference from behavioral evidence. If we have two sensory events A and B which can be discriminated by the subject, we can train him to raise his left forepaw or left hand to event A, and his right forepaw to event B. The excitation from A may use some of the same incoming paths as B; yet ultimately it is conducted *only* to the motor neurons that lead to the left forepaw. Even before this training has been done, therefore, we may say that though the excitations from A and from B utilize the same lines for part of their course, they ultimately get on to separate lines, or are capable of getting on to separate lines, at some point in the CNS. They may of course be brought back to the same lines, since we can also train the subject to make the same response to different stimuli; but the principle is clear that perceptual discriminability means a spatial separation in the CNS at some point.

A more interesting example of the problem of specific energies and coding occurs in taste. A weak acid on the tongue (which tastes sour) produces firing in three sets of afferent neurons, A, B and C. Salt solution fires set A plus set B; quinine, which is bitter, fires set A plus set C. Despite having a common activity in neurons A, these three afferent processes produce effects at higher levels that are quite distinct from

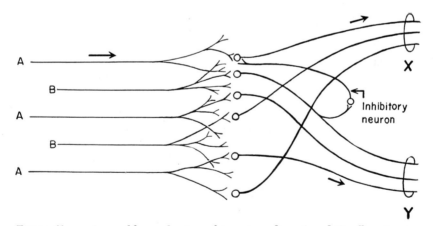

Figure 41. A possible mechanism of sensory coding. A and B, afferent neurons, A having a lower limen than B. A weak stimulus fires A only; a strong one fires A at a higher rate and also fires B. At the next synaptic level, internuncial neurons X may have a lower limen than Y, or respond more readily to a lower frequency of firing. With low-level activity in A alone, X will fire and Y tend to be inactive. When the level of bombardment goes up, however, Y begins to fire and inhibits X (for clarity, only one inhibitory neuron is diagrammed). Note that this is quite speculative; also, this sorting out into spatially discrete paths need not occur only at the first synaptic junction, but may occur farther on in the system as well.

each other. (Sour, salt and bitter, together with sweet—for which less physiological information is available—constitute the four primary taste qualities.)

Activity on line A, therefore, may contribute to any one of three different awarenesses (considered as neural activities in the cerebrum), depending on the total pattern of activity: A-B-C one central process, A-B another, A-C a third.

Another example is found in the perception of temperature. Steady warmth and steady cold have a considerable overlap in their use of afferent connections; but warmth produces a slow, irregular firing, cold a faster and regular firing. Ultimately these messages get completely sorted out, at some point in the CNS. They must, since they determine quite different responses.

It is not difficult to see how the sorting out might be achieved, although the synaptic mechanisms are not known specifically. In taste, A and B fibers may produce summation and fire cells that A and C do not (these cells in turn inhibiting any others that happen to be excited by A alone). As for warm and cold and differences of temporal pattern, we have seen that some cells may have a low limen for impulses at one frequency, other cells a low limen for another frequency, and this may be a factor in sorting out the "warm" message from the "cold" message.

To sum up: the specificity of sensory input is primarily in the existence of separate routes from different parts of the sensory surfaces. Secondarily, this is extended by the patterning and timing of impulses. Two different inputs may use, at least in part, the same afferent lines. But if so, they must be sorted out at some higher level. If the organism can respond differentially to two sensory events, either by giving them different names (i.e., making distinctive verbal responses) or by acting in one case to maintain the stimulation and in the other to discontinue it, then at some point in the nervous system there is a spatial separation of the two processes.

Diffuse conduction: the basis of higher behavior

Earlier in the present chapter it was noted that there are two quite different kinds of conduction systems in the CNS: parallel and diffuse. Where cells are laid down in parallel, their fibers beginning and ending close together, there is a high probability that an excitation in the path will be transmitted from one synaptic level to the next. In other regions, conduction is diffuse; cells may start out together but travel in different directions, so that the impulses cannot sum their effects at the next synapse. Such transmission seems inefficient and must often fail to carry through the network to reach the effectors, thus not influencing behavior. However, it is not desirable that every stimulation should be responded to—inattention to the trivial is necessary for concentrating on what is important—and the cortical organization that is inefficient in this sense is very efficient indeed in others. Let us see now how the diffuse conduction of the cortex allows us to understand, in principle, the selectivity of higher behavior (i.e., responding to some stimuli, not to others); the holding process, or the delay of transmission that permits a stimulus to have its effect at the proper moment; and, in general terms, the lack of a complete sensory dominance of the behavior of the higher animal.

Chapter 3 made the distinction between sense-dominated and voluntary behavior. If all conduction in the CNS were in parallel, all behavior would be in the first of these two classes. As we have seen, sensory afferents are laid down in parallel, and even when an animal is asleep or under anesthesia a sensory excitation reliably reaches the cortical projection area. This means that environmental stimulation can control the activity of sensory cortex completely. Each change of pressure on the skin, for example, must be reflected in the pattern of firing in the somesthetic cortex. If a neural cell is not stimulated from without it tends eventually to fire by itself, spontaneously, because it is a living thing and must be active; but this would not be expected to happen unless the neuron was left a rather long time without stimulation. Thus when the sense organ is exposed to the varying stimulation of the environment, as it normally is, the whole afferent pathway must remain under environmental control.

Now if conduction from the sensory cortex onward were also in parallel, the same conclusions would apply elsewhere in the CNS. The whole nervous system would be under direct control of sensory events and the organism would become an automaton, all of its actions being determined by the stimuli of the moment. Each sudden stimulation would produce a convulsive jerk of the muscles with which the sense organ was connected; the high efficiency of parallel conduction would guarantee that the excitation would reach the muscle and have its effects immediately. No delay of response until a more appropriate moment would be possible. There could be no thought process, and no voluntary behavior. Thought and "volition," as we have seen (Chap. 3), are the occurrence of processes which, themselves independent of the immediate sensory input, collaborate with that input to determine which of the various possible responses will be made, and when. Such collaboration could hardly occur if all conduction, throughout the CNS, were in parallel.

Instead, the rules of transmission change as the excitation leaves the sensory projection cortex, and whether it goes further or not, and where it goes, is determined now by what other events are going on in the system. In Fig. 39, whether neuron C fires F or not depends on whether some other neuron (not shown in the figure) delivers an impulse to F at the same time, with summation. Neurons of bundle A will reliably fire neurons of bundle B even when these latter are in the relatively refractory period, because they converge on B in volleys; but if F is in the

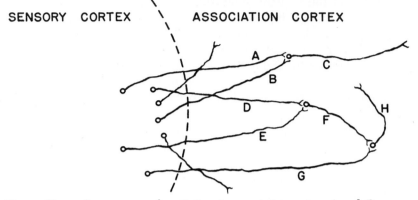

Figure 42.   Convergence of excitation in association cortex. A and B converge on C; D and E on F; F and G on H. These are assumed to be chance convergences, the diagram representing those, among the thousands of cells in the region, which have such relations.

refractory state it is most unlikely that C will fire it even with summation from another single cell.

We can now see the significance of the nonspecific projection system and arousal, in relation to cortical function. Its activity provides a diffuse bombardment of widespread cortical regions, increasing the likelihood of summation at the synapse, and thus makes cortical transmission more feasible. If C in Fig. 39 cannot fire F by itself, the probability of its doing so is greatly enhanced by the general bombardment. An impulse from the arousal system (though the axons from this system are not shown in the figure) arriving at F at the same time as one from C would sum with it; and the higher the level of arousal the greater the probability that such summation would occur.

Summation must occur also between cortical cells. Two cells that lie side by side in sensory cortex, and send their axons out into the neighboring association cortex, are not likely to send them to the same point; but the axons of cells that are not close together may converge (as D and E do in Fig. 42), and this must happen very frequently among the thousands or hundreds of thousands of cells involved. In Fig. 42, A may or may not be able to fire C with summation from the arousal system; but if B is active also the probability of firing C would be greatly increased. If sensory stimulation is such as to fire D and E at the same time, they are likely to fire F; and if the same sensory activity is firing G, so G sums with F, transmission would include H also. Whether H fires or not therefore depends on the timing of activity in D, E, F and G. If H had been fired immediately before by some other neurons not shown in the figure, or were now exposed to inhibition from other cells in the same region, it would not fire now, so that neural transmission of activity through this tangled network must be a function of all the other complex activity going on in the same tissue.

So much is a reasonably direct inference from the available anatomical and physiological evidence, and is also in general agreement with the behavioral evidence of set: the response made to a stimulus is a function of what is already going on in the nervous system.

But the behavioral evidence also indicates, as we have seen, that the brain is able to hold an excitation, without its dying out, so that it has its effect on behavior after an appreciable period of time. The only explanation that seems to account for the facts is the presence of the closed pathways, or loop circuits, which are found throughout the nervous system. Theoretically, excitation might continue for some time in such pathways (p. 55f.). We have no direct physiological evidence concerning their actual functioning in behavior and learning. Such ideas are therefore in the realm of theory, but they have considerably clarified our problems, and in the laboratory have led to new and significant research. Consequently this line of analysis may be taken with some degree of seriousness even though we must expect that the physiological details, as they can be suggested at present, are not always correct.

What we are discussing here is a physiological hypothesis about the mediating processes defined in Chapter 3. In brief, the hypothesis is that a mediating process consists of activity in a group of neurons, arranged as a set of closed pathways (cf. Fig. 43) which will be referred to as a *cell-assembly*, or of a series of such activities, which will be referred to as a *phase sequence*. Here and in the following chapters, the terms "cell-assembly" (or just "assembly") and "phase sequence" will be used when it is intended to refer to the specific physiological hypothesis that is about to be presented, "mediating process" when no such reference is intended. The student should note that it is often desirable in psychology to use ideas that may have derived originally from physiological considerations, but in a more general way and without specific physiological implications. Current physiological knowledge is of course incomplete, and some flexibility is needed when we apply it to psychological problems (cf. Chap. 13).

The loop circuits which are supposed to be the basis of the cell-assembly exist anatomically, laid down from the first by the growth processes that determine the whole structure of the CNS. We might suppose that they are ready to function from the first as holding mechanisms (or mediating processes) as already described. As we shall see, however (in Chap. 6), the evidence of behavior suggests that a prolonged learning process is involved also. Let us see how this might occur.

The fundamental physiological assumption of learning is that whenever an impulse crosses a synapse it becomes easier for later impulses to do so. More precisely: when a neuron A fires, or takes part in firing, another neuron B, some change occurs in A or B or both which increases A's capacity to fire B in the future. The change might be an enlargement of a synaptic knob (Figs. 35, 38); or it might be some chemical change. The student should note that this is a purely theoretical assumption, but one which is apparently necessary if we are to understand learning as a physiological process.

Now let us suppose that cells A, B and C in Fig. 43 are being fired repeatedly as a

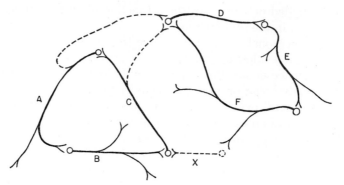

Figure 43.   To illustrate the way in which learning might modify the functioning of cortical circuits and establish a cell-assembly. It is assumed that *A-B-C* and *D-E-F,* in association cortex, are excited by the same sensory event (axons from the sensory cortex are not shown, but it is assumed that they excite these cells separately). If *A* then delivers impulses to *B* at the moment when *B* is being fired by axons from sensory cortex, the synapse *A-B* will be "strengthened," and similarly with the other synapses. As a result of this strengthening the excitation of one cell may become able to set up reverberation in the circuit. Broken lines show possible connections between the two circuits, which would permit them to function as one system.

result of a particular sensory stimulation. *A* delivers impulses to *B* at the moment when other cells (not shown) are doing so; thus *A* contributes to the firing, and the synaptic connection *A-B* is strengthened. Similarly with synapses *B-C* and *C-A.* Each of these neurons thus becomes more efficient at firing the next in the series; and eventually (with the background bombardment from the arousal system) excitation of one of them alone may be enough to set off a reverberation *A-B-C-A-B-C* and so on. At this point the system has become capable of an "autonomous" activity: the activity corresponds to a particular sensory event, but can continue after the stimulation has ceased, or if some other event in the cortex should trigger firing in one of the three cells, the whole system will respond just as if the external stimulation were occurring.

It is not likely, however, that one such circuit would function in isolation. Any one sensory event would excite a number of similar circuits, which theoretically would tend to establish interconnections with each other and thus merge in one larger system. The way in which this might occur is suggested in Fig. 43. *D-E-F* is another circuit in which the individual cells are fired by the same stimulus event that fired *A, B* and *C,* and in which the same kind of internal synaptic changes would occur and make reverberation possible. When two such closed pathways lie close to one another there is a rather high probability of chance connections between them, as represented by broken lines in the figure. If then the two circuits are active at the same time, excited by the same sensory event, *A* and *C* will deliver impulses to *D* when *D* is being fired. According to our assumption about learning, the synaptic connections *A-D* and *C-D* will be strengthened. If a cell such as *X* is also being fired by the sensory event, or if for any reason the synaptic connection *F-X* is well established beforehand so that *X* is fired whenever *F* is fired, *F* will similarly become capable of firing *C. A-B-C* and *D-E-F* will then be fused in one system, together with other circuits in the region which are fired by the same sensory event. This is the cell-assembly.

The formation of such an assembly is assumed to depend on the original chance interconnection among its parts (the connections then being reinforced by the learning process). The neurons involved in an assembly would be those, and only those, that happened to have the kind of interconnection described above. This would mean, perhaps, a tenth of one per cent of the neurons in the region. Two assemblies therefore may lie closely intertwined with each other, and yet function as separate systems, unless they are repeatedly active at the same time; in this case, they would establish effective synaptic connection in the same way as *A-B-C* and *D-E-F.*

All this is highly speculative, and such detail is given here only to show the student one direction in which psychological theory can establish meaningful direct relations with physiological and anatomical conceptions. But there are different forms such theory can take, and we do not have enough information, either physiological or psychological, to decide which of the various possible forms is right. Instead of getting completely lost in the details of one theory, or in the details of the firing of the hundreds of millions of individual neurons that must be involved in almost any action by a higher animal, we can make some general assumptions that will help us to keep things in perspective. These can be treated as dealing with the more specifically physiological conception of the "cell-assembly," or the less physiological "mediating process."

ASSUMPTION *1:*   A cell-assembly (or mediating process) is established in the first place as a slow development resulting from the repetition of a particular kind of sensory event, usually in infancy. (Anatomically, this may be set up in the cortex alone, but it is more likely that some of the loop circuits involved would be subcortical as well.)

ASSUMPTION *2:*   If two assemblies A and B are repeatedly active at the same time they will tend to become "associated," so that A excites B and vice versa. If they are always active at the same time they will tend to merge in a single system—that is, form a single assembly—but if they are also active at different times they will remain separate (but associated) systems. (This means that exciting part of A, for example, has a very high probability of exciting all of A, but a definitely lower probability of exciting a separate assembly, B; A may be able to excite B only when some other assembly, C, also facilitates activity in B).

ASSUMPTION *3:*   An assembly that is active at the same time as an efferent pathway from the same region will tend to establish connections with it, just as with another assembly. Most of the sensory events that form assemblies are accompanied by motor activities, so this amounts to assuming that most assemblies will have motor components: that is, they tend to produce overt behavior, visual assemblies producing eye movements, somesthetic assemblies movements of hand or foot, and so forth.

ASSUMPTION *4:*   Each assembly corresponds to a relatively simple sensory input, such as a particular vowel sound or syllable instead of a whole word, an increase of brightness, a simple odor, pressure on a particular skin area, a line of a particular slope in the visual field, and so on. Thus the perception of an actual object will involve not one but a number of assemblies. Activity of assemblies *ABCDE* is the perception of one object, of *ABCDX* a different object.

In the following chapters we shall see how these assumptions bear on a number of behavioral problems. The present chapter may be concluded by outlining the sort of picture that is provided concerning the direction of the thought process, and attention.

It is implied, for example, that transmission of excitations through the

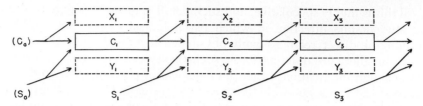

Figure 44. To illustrate the selective process in thinking. *C*, central processes (simultaneously active assemblies) at three successive moments in time; *S*, corresponding sensory inputs; *X* and *Y*, subliminally excited assemblies. *X* receives excitation from one source (central) only, *Y* from one source (sensory) only, so these have lower probabilities of being active. *C* consists of the assemblies which receive excitations from both sources and which consequently are active. Thus C_1 selectively determines which of the assemblies will be active, from among those that S_1 tends to excite; and contrariwise. This selective central influence is *attention*, represented by the horizontal arrows of the diagram.

cortex occurs by means of a series of assembly activities, or phase sequence. How would this work? An excitation cannot be reliably transmitted by a series of single assemblies, *A-B-C-D*, since each one has a limited probability of exciting the next (Assumption 2), and if the transmission succeeds at one point in the series it is likely to fail at another. But there are many assemblies active in the brain at the same time. If some of these others are also connected with *B*, *C* and *D*, so that each is excited by more than one assembly, transmission is much more probable. In other words, a stimulus has a good probability of affecting behavior if it fits into the processes already going on in the brain.

This sort of relation is diagrammed in Fig. 44. The actual activities that occur (C_1, C_2, C_3) are those that are aroused both sensorily and centrally. The sight of a stimulus object might arouse many different trains of thought; which one it does arouse is determined by the already-existing central processes, which (so to speak) select among these possibilities. This selective influence is what is referred to by the term *attention*.

Attention and set are closely related terms, both referring to the same sort of selective action by central processes. Set is commonly used to refer to selectivity among motor outputs (which of two possible responses will be made to a given stimulus?), attention to refer to selectivity between sensory inputs (which aspects of the stimulus object will be responded to?), but both imply the same kind of central mechanism.

Figure 44 shows how the course of thought can have some continuity and directedness, since at each moment the processes now going on tend to pick out, from among the many perceptions of the environment that are possible, those that are relevant to the activities that have gone before. Response to environmental stimulation will not be made at random.

However, this does not mean that the train of thought cannot be interrupted. If some sensory event occurs which has strongly established central processes, if it arouses its own group of cell-assemblies which facilitate one another's activities strongly, it is quite capable of setting up a new phase sequence which has no relevance to preceding phase sequences. In Fig. 44, S_3 may have central connections which do not overlap with those of C_3, but there may be sufficient overlap in the connections of the assemblies it *does* arouse to make possible a new phase sequence, and this in turn may perhaps inhibit other activities. An unexpected event, that is, may interrupt the present train of thought and begin a new one, with the consequent effects on overt behavior. This would be the case in which we speak of an environmental event as "catching one's attention."

Summary

Chapter 4 described the gross parts of the CNS and its main pathways; the present chapter focusses on the interaction between individual neurons. The nerve impulse is a tiny electrochemical storm that sweeps across cell-body and axon; it obeys the all-or-none principle. Excitation of a dendrite may facilitate the occurrence of an impulse starting at the cell-body, but is not itself an impulse since it does not obey the all-or-none principle and can occur without firing the cell-body and axon. The all-or-none principle means that intensity in the stimulus must be transformed into frequency of impulses—not bigger impulses.

The probability of transmission at the synapse is increased by summation of two or more impulses delivered by separate neurons at the same time; a single impulse has a low probability of transmission. This makes the timing of impulses very important. Also, neurons fire at different rates. These facts make it possible for two different "messages" to use the same lines: a difference in timing means that they are sorted out at the synapse, taking different routes from there on. The distinctive effects of sensory inputs ("specific energies") is partly determined in this way, partly by separate routes all the way from the sensory surface to the cortex.

The EEG shows that timing of neural firing in consciousness is primarily asynchronous; any great synchrony of firing is likely to cause a convulsion. In unconsciousness there is some firing, but the large EEG potentials are mostly dendritic in origin.

The need of summation at the synapse for reliable transmission means that parallel and divergent conduction systems are very different. Parallel conduction from sense-organ to brain guarantees that an excitation will get to the sensory cortex; but conduction from there onward is divergent, and whether it will occur depends on what other activities are going on, and whether these activities provide summation at the synapses in the association area. This, apparently, is why the arousal system must be active if the animal is to be conscious: the bombardment of the whole cortex increases the probability of summation at any synapse.

Another implication of these facts is that the divergent-conduction regions of the brain are necessary if the higher animal is not to be an automaton under complete environmental control. If all transmission were in parallel, each sensory stimulation would have an immediate effect on the musculature, no delay of response being possible; any strong, widespread stimulation would tend to produce a convulsion. The divergent conduction makes possible a screening of sensory inputs, and a selective response to those stimuli that are related to the animal's present behavior.

A physiological mechanism of formation of cell-assemblies (mediating processes) is proposed but these ideas, being very speculative, are not elaborated in great detail; instead, the kinds of properties they might have, suggested by present anatomical, physiological and psychological evidence, are summarized in four generally-stated working assumptions. The assumptions are then applied to the problems of thinking and of set and attention.

Notes

A number of chapters in Stevens (*General References,* Chap. 1, p. 19) deal with the various topics of the present chapter: see especially Brink, Chaps. 2 and 3; Lindsley, Chap. 14; Morgan, Chap. 20; Pfaffman, Chap. 29; and Jenkins, Chap. 30. These chapters may be supplemented by the more up-to-date but also more difficult writings of J. C. Eccles, *The Neurophysiological Basis of Mind,* Oxford University Press, 1953, and R. Granit, *Receptors and Sensory Perception,* Yale University Press, 1955.

The theory of cell-assemblies is developed in Hebb, *Organization of Behavior,* John Wiley & Sons, 1949 (a more adequate form of the theory is proposed by P. M. Milner, *Psychol. Rev.,* 1957, 64, 242–252).

Chapter 6

Heredity, maturation, early learning

THE preceding chapters have at several points touched briefly on the development of behavior. It is time now to consider the question in more detail. What is the course of development, and what factors determine it?

This involves us at once in the age-old question of the relation of heredity to environment: the question of intelligence or instinct, in this behavior or that; of the innate and the acquired; of maturation and learning.

As this question is usually asked, in one form or another, it sets up an opposition between two variables. Is intelligence inherited, *or* is it acquired? Is a particular perception learned, *or* is it independent of learning? But this is usually a false opposition; most such questions cannot be satisfactorily answered because they are wrongly asked. Much confusion derives, first, from thinking of two variables only, in growth and development; and secondly, from thinking of them as alternative to each other instead of collaborative. The present chapter tries to show how these pitfalls can be avoided.

A central issue in all aspects of psychological analysis is the nature of learning, and the part it plays in the development of adult characteristics. But equally central—the same problem in reverse, the other side of the coin—is the role of maturation and growth in determining the structures in which the learning must occur. In our thinking, theoretically, we can distinguish between these different kinds of influence, but in practice they are inseparable: there is no behavior that is independent of the animal's heredity, or of the supporting environment; and no higher behavior that is uninfluenced by learning. It is only recently that these conceptions have been clarified logically, and the student in his other reading will sometimes find them still used in an unsatisfactory way.

Instinctive behavior and maturation

"Instinct" is a term of doubtful scientific value, for reasons that we will come to later, but "instinctive" is more useful as a rough term for designating certain kinds of behavior. *Instinctive behavior* may be defined as complex species-predictable behavior: at a higher level than reflex behavior, not requiring special conditions of learning for its appearance, but predictable simply from knowing that we are dealing with a particular species in its ordinary habitat.

The distinction from reflex behavior (which of course is also species-predictable) is clear in principle, though the two classes shade into one another and a sharp dichotomy is probably impossible. A reflex response occurs in a specific group of effectors, and is evoked by stimulation of a specific sensory surface. Light falling on the retina results in pupillary contraction; acid in the mouth results in salivary secretion; stimulation of the palm of the newborn infant's hand produces clasping by that hand, and of the lips produces sucking movements. The pupillary reflex is not possible without the retina, the clasp reflex is not possible without the receptors of the palm, and so on. Instinctive behavior, on the other hand, is usually not dependent upon any specific receptors, and it characteristically involves a large proportion of the effectors of the whole body, rather than being limited to one gland or muscle group.

All instinctive behavior involves reflex elements,[1] so part of the pattern can be eliminated by loss of a sense organ or muscle group, but the over-all pattern may still remain fully identifiable. The instinctive maternal behavior of the female rat is only slightly affected by the loss of any one of the senses of vision, smell, or the tactual sensitivity in the

---

[1] As any complex behavior does. In the first place, any response must affect the animal's posture, which is reflexively controlled though higher centers can impose changes on these reflexes and thus produce what we classify as a nonreflexive action. If a leg is amputated, in a male animal, therefore, there will be a recognizable change in his approach to the female, but the over-all picture of male sex behavior will also be recognizable. In the second place, instinctive behavior in general includes two phases, *preparatory* and *consummatory*, and the consummatory phase is essentially reflexive. In food-getting behavior, the search for food and seizing it are preparatory, whereas mastication, salivation and swallowing are consummatory. Damage to throat muscles would prevent completion of the consummatory activity, but the instinctive pattern would still be identifiable.

snout. Loss of two of these senses does affect the behavior significantly, showing that they are all involved in the behavior; but no one is essential.

Instinctive sexual behavior by the male rat shows the same picture. Even if the genitalia are removed the pattern of mating behavior can be obtained, complete up to the point of intromission and ejaculation; thus an essential reflex element of the total pattern is missing, but the pattern is recognizable and complete as far as it is mechanically possible. Reflex behavior is primarily a local process; instinctive behavior primarily involves the whole animal (Fig. 45).

The special problem of instinctive behavior is that it does not have to be taught, or be acquired by practice. A female rat may be brought up in

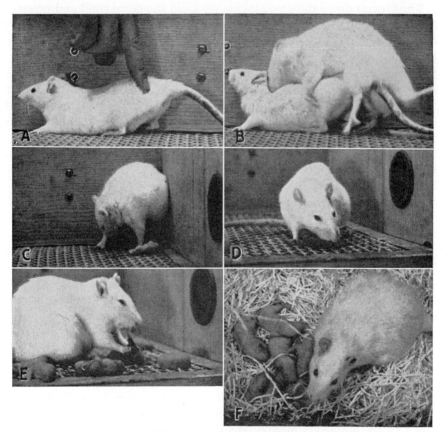

Figure 45.   Instinctive behavior in the female rat. A, tactual stimulation elicits the receptive posture. B, mounting by the male. C, delivery of the young. D, cleaning a pup and removing the amniotic membrane. E, eating the placenta (the mother seldom pays attention to the young until the placenta has been eaten). F, the litter has been gathered together in the nest; in a cold environment the nesting material would be pulled up over mother and young so that they could hardly be seen. (Photographs taken in the Laboratory of The Wistar Institute by Dr. Edmond J. Farris and William Sykes. From Farris, E. J., and Griffith, J. Q., in *The Rat in Laboratory Investigation*, J. B. Lippincott Company, 1942.)

isolation and never have an opportunity to observe another female caring for her young. At maturity the female is mated, and put in a cage in which strips of paper are available. A day or so before giving birth she begins gathering paper together to form a primitive kind of nest. When the young are born she promptly cleans them and collects them into the nest, and crouches over them in a way that makes suckling possible. With no opportunity for practice, in short, she performs a complex task quite adequately. Many such examples could be given: the web-building of spiders, each making a web characteristic of the particular species; the complex courting and mating behavior of birds; or the migration of some fish for great distances to spawn in a particular stream, and the nest-building and fighting patterns of others.

The farther down the animal scale we look, the more rigid and unvarying the predictable pattern of behavior is, but it is quite evident that there is much that is "species-predictable" about the behavior of the higher mammals, including man. Is this instinctive too? For man at least, the usual answer is No, because some learning is involved and instinct is supposed to be incompatible with learning. We shall see however that the question is more complex than this. An act may be unlearned, in the sense that one does not have to practice it or be shown or told how to do it, and yet be fully dependent on the prior occurrence of other learning. "Instinctive behavior" is regarded here as being only a rough designation because, in its long history, it has picked up connotations that prevent its being used precisely. It is not possible to give a clear Yes or No to the question as to whether man has instincts, because of these connotations. Instinct is thought of as a substitute for learning, or for intelligence; man shows some very marked forms of species-predictable behavior at a complex level, which (according to the definition above) means that it is instinctive, yet it is evident also that learning and intelligence are involved in the behavior, which (according to the connotations referred to) means that it is not instinctive. Such contradictions require that we use other terms in discussing human behavior, as well as when we wish to be precise in any context.

Two kinds of behavior, learned and inherited?

Much of our difficulty with these questions comes from thinking of behavior as being of two different kinds, learned and unlearned, with the idea that the learned is more or less independent of heredity and the unlearned determined by heredity alone. But now consider this case. Neither a human nor a chimpanzee baby needs to learn how to have a temper tantrum. The behavior is complex but quite characteristic in form, so that no experienced observer has any difficulty in identifying it. The baby does not have to practice it (nor to see how others do it) in order to produce, on the first try, a first-class sample. It is therefore "unlearned."

But it is not independent of learning, for the baby must have learned to want something outside his reach which is being withheld from him. That is, the tantrum itself is not learned, but *is* dependent on the existence of other learning.

Another example is the fear of strangers, which occurs only when the child has first learned to recognize familiar persons, but does not require that he have any previous exposure to strangers, or any unpleasant event associated with strangers. Another example is Pavlov's experimental neurosis (p. 12): the dog's breakdown in behavior was not learned, but could not have occurred until after the conditioning process had established the discriminative behavior with oval and circle.

There are other situations in which similar relations hold. Shall we then conclude that there are three kinds of behavior: (1) learned, (2) unlearned but dependent on other learning, and (3) unlearned, determined by heredity alone? Instead, we might ask whether this kind of classification is justified at all. Let us now consider two other sets of relevant facts, one concerning maturation, the second the effects of early experience; we will then be in a position to make a different approach to the whole heredity-environment question.

Maturation

It is obvious that some of the changes of behavior following birth are due to physical growth, especially the increase of the infant's muscular strength. It is not so obvious that growth is also going on in the nervous system, and that learning is not the whole explanation of other changes that are observed. The human brain at birth has all the neurons it will ever have, but many connecting fibers are still incomplete. Learning processes cannot strengthen synaptic connections between two neurons until axon and dendrite, or axon and cell-body, are in close proximity. Learning, that is, cannot occur until physical maturation has reached the proper stage.

Thus we think of the infant as learning to walk, once his muscles are strong enough to hold him. But in this period, apparently one of practice, what is going on is at least partly the completion of a certain level of growth in the nervous system. When this stage has been reached, a comparatively short practice period is enough to achieve walking.

Another example is the feeding behavior of young chicks. Shortly after hatching, as the chick begins to peck at things about it, it will succeed in hitting kernels of grain, holding them in the beak and swallowing them. But errors (failing to hit the kernel, but more often failing to hold it until it can be swallowed) are frequent. The accuracy improves rapidly in the first five to ten days, as the chick practices, and this looks like learning. Figure 46 gives the results of an experiment which shows instead that much of the change is due to maturation. Some chicks began their peck-

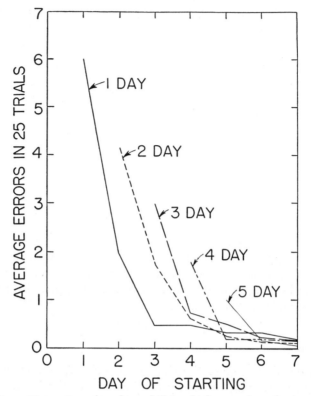

Figure 46.   Maturation of pecking skill in chicks: number of misses ("errors") made by chicks allowed to begin practice at different intervals after hatching. (After W. W. Cruze, *J. Comp. Psychol.,* 1935.)

ing one day after hatching; others were kept in darkness and fed by hand for one to five days before they began to practice pecking. The figure shows two things: the older the chick, the more accurate it is without any practice (e.g., the curve for the 3-day group begins at a lower level of errors than that for the 2-day group); but the practice has its effect also, for the 3-day group does not begin at the level which the 1-day or 2-day group has reached by the third day.

This example is particularly instructive. For one thing, it shows clearly how physical growth and learning processes can collaborate in the development of behavior. They are not opposed but work together, and only by ingenious experimentation can they be distinguished, for theoretical purposes. Another important point is that the learning must occur at the right time; if the chick is kept in darkness very long, grossly abnormal feeding behavior is likely to be the eventual result. We must note also that learning is not essential for all aspects of the behavior: the tendency to peck at small objects is present in the newly hatched chick, and it has been reported that no prior experience is needed to make the chick peck at rounded objects rather than sharp-cornered ones.

This innately established pecking may perhaps be classed as reflexive. Reflex paths are in general laid down by heredity and growth processes. Some of them are functional at birth, like the chick's pecking tendency or the sucking reflex of the newborn mammal, but others apparently have to wait until the neural fibers involved have made connection with each other. When the sole of the foot is scratched in the newborn infant the toes curl upward and outward ("Babinski reflex"), but in the older child or adult they curl downward (a Babinski reflex in the adult means that motor paths in the spinal cord have been injured).

Another classic demonstration of reflex maturation is one in which larval salamanders are placed in an anesthetic solution before any swimming movements have begun. The anesthesia prevents any movement during the period in which others from the same hatch seem to be learn-

Figure 47.   Jed, a nursery-reared chimpanzee infant at four months, the age at which fear of strangers appears. The leg posture is the normal one for the sitting animal; an abnormal posture appears in Fig. 48. (Courtesy of H. W. Nissen and R. K. Helmle, the Yerkes Laboratories of Primate Biology.)

ing to swim. Then they are taken out and placed in ordinary water, and as soon as the anesthesia has worn off they show swimming movements identical with those of their normally reared fellows. The development of swimming in the normal animals therefore is a product of physical maturation, with no important effect from practice.

Maturation is an important phenomenon in primate behavior. An obvious example is sexual development, which depends on the growth of the gonads. Another example is the baby's fear of strangers, which characteristically does not appear until the age of four months or so in the chimpanzee (Fig. 47), six months in man. Still another is the fear of imaginary creatures or events associated with darkness, which in the human child is rare before the age of three years, common thereafter. In these examples we are not dealing with maturation in the narrower sense of physical growth alone (a distinction is made later between physical and psychological maturation), but it seems highly probable that the physical development of the nervous system is an essential factor determining the delayed appearance of such phenomena.

The effects of early experience

In the phenomena of maturation the probability that learning is going on strikes the eye, and the experimental problem is to find a way of showing that the development of behavior is not due to learning alone. Now we turn to another complication: to examples in which the problem, on the contrary, is to show that any learning is occurring. The very young infant seems to be doing nothing much but eating, defecating and growing; vegetating in the intervals between feedings, with some random movement of the limbs and eyes, and some random noise-making, but not learning anything relevant to his later behavior. Only recently has it been discovered how pervasive and all-important for mental development is the learning that is going on in this period: the product of *early experience*.

In a technical sense, experience may be defined as the pattern of sense-organ stimulation: the combinations and sequences of stimuli affecting the organism, apart from the question of possible conscious processes arising therefrom. Thus we may speak of the early experience of the goldfish, or of the newborn baby, without implying that either organism has neural processes that are sufficiently elaborate to be dignified by the term "consciousness" or "awareness."

Even before birth, the mammal is exposed to complex tactual stimulation, in the various pressures exerted by the uterine wall and by contacts of one part of the fetal body with another. From birth onward, the complexity is enormously increased. The human baby lying in his crib is exposed to a continuously changing pattern of stimulation; even if he is in a quiet room in which nothing else is happening, his own movement of eyes and limbs varies the visual and tactual input, and there is auditory stimulation from his own breathing and any vocalization he happens to make. The baby appears to be unaffected by most of this; it seems that what is going on is almost entirely bodily growth, that the nervous system has to be further developed before much learning can begin. It has been shown that the young mammal in his first weeks or months of life is capable of a primitive kind of conditioning, but it used to be thought that on the whole this was a period of maturation, with learning coming in later when neural growth was more complete.

We know now that this is an erroneous picture. There is a great deal of learning going on whose effects do not appear until much later. This fact is revealed by the difference, at a later age, between the behavior of subjects brought up with and without exposure to some part of the varied stimulation of the normal environment.

First, *vision*. There are clinical records of a number of children born with cataracts (clouded lenses) which were removed when the child was half-grown or at maturity. Such persons learn to recognize colors readily, but they have only the most rudimentary perception of visual pattern, needing months to learn to see a square or triangle as normal persons do, and never acquiring the level of visual perception of those who have had vision from infancy. One girl who went through high school with a good record while still blind, thus giving evidence of above-average intelligence and ability to learn, nevertheless could not learn to recognize more than three persons visually, out of all her acquaintances; in a month of daily experimentation with two psychologists she did not learn to tell them apart by sight. The effect of early experience on the visual perception of normal persons is discovered only when we see how different vision is in the congenitally blind who are given their sight later.

Experimentally, animals have been reared in darkness from birth onward, with similar results. The normal chimpanzee by the age of 16 months makes excellent use of vision, and learns readily to make selective responses to new visual stimuli. He gets a mild electric shock once or twice from a new object, and thereafter will not let it come near him. He recognizes those who care for him daily, welcoming their approach and showing rather extreme fear and avoidance at the approach of a stranger. But the chimpanzee reared in darkness to the same age can be shocked repeatedly, day after day, before beginning to avoid the object that accompanied shock. It takes weeks of living in a normally lighted environment before he begins to show signs of discriminating visually between friend and stranger. When the animal first comes out of the dark room, in fact, he appears totally unconscious of his visual environment.

That is to say, the visual reflexes are present and well developed, but the activity of higher centers in the CNS appears unaffected by optical events. The general behavior of the animal is exactly as if he were still in complete darkness; there is no sign either of curiosity or of fear, and none of the (perhaps fumbling) investigation that one would expect of an animal as sensitive, intelligent and curious as the chimpanzee when suddenly offered a new sensory universe.

Another fact is very important for the interpretation of these phenomena. It is not the absence of sensory stimulation alone that produces them, but the absence of varied *patterns* of stimulation. When the chimpanzee is brought up with sensory stimulation in the form of an unbroken field of light, produced by enclosing his head in a translucent dome of plastic which permits a normal intensity of stimulation without the contours of the usual visual environment, he is just as "blind" as the one brought up in darkness. It was thought at first that the visual incapacity of the animal reared in darkness was some failure of physical maturation of the eye or the optic nerve, due to the absence of stimulation; there are defects of this kind in the eye of the animal reared in darkness, but the presence of well developed reflexes shows that the retina can still function well, and the equally great incapacity of the animal reared in unpatterned light shows that sensory defects due to rearing in darkness are not the whole explanation.

The development of the normal capacity merely to see the distinctive objects of the visual world, their similarities and dissimilarities (apart entirely from their meaning, or learning to respond distinctively to them), requires a prolonged period of simple exposure to patterned visual stimulation. During early infancy when the normal infant appears to be learning nothing, when his eyes are moving apparently aimlessly about, there is actually a great deal of learning going on in addition to the physical maturation which of course is also going on.

A similar conclusion has been established for *somesthetic perception*. Here it is not possible experimentally to establish the complete control of sensory input that is possible with vision, for reasons that should be obvious. The degree of control that was achieved, with one chimpanzee infant, showed however that tactual perception also develops as a result of early experience. The chimpanzee was reared normally in all respects except that cardboard tubes covered the hands and feet, fastened to arm or leg near the elbow or knee in such a way that fairly free movement of the joints was possible but exploration of the environment, or self-stimulation of the body, was ruled out for the hands and feet (Fig. 48). At two and a half years of age (which corresponds roughly to an age of three and a half or four years for the human infant), somesthetic perception was tested in comparison with that of normal animals. A situation was set up in which the chimpanzee could not see his hands, and in which the food reward was presented sometimes from the left, sometimes from the right. The left hand was touched when the food could be obtained on the left side and similarly on the right. A normal chimpanzee of the same age served as control animal (i.e., for comparison: see Chap. 11). He required 200 trials for learning to turn always to the correct side. The experimental animal had not fully mastered the problem after 2000 trials.

When the normally reared animal was pinched at some point on his body (vision being prevented), he would reach directly and accurately to the spot, to stop the pinching. The experimental animal made inaccurate movements, with apparent need of exploration, before reaching the right spot. A most interesting further observation was this. To make sure that the animal was doing his best to find the spot as quickly as possible, pinprick was used. The normal animal objected vociferously, and wasted no movement in removing the painful object. The experimental animal, on the other hand, showed no sign that the pinprick was disturbing, and even acted as if it were pleasant rather than unpleasant. There is a great deal yet to find out about these phenomena, but there is no doubt that even the limited control of early somesthetic experience that was possible in this experiment produced grossly atypical later behavior.

These results have the same implication as the visual-deprivation studies. It seems clear that normal adult perception is a function of early experience, and the learning processes determined by it. This has a further implication: any higher behavior which depends on perception is also dependent on the learning processes of infancy. Actually, we have evidence for vision and somesthesis only, so this statement is a generalization that may have to be qualified later; but there is little higher be-

Figure 48.   Rob at 30 months of age, as reared in conditions of somesthetic restriction. The cylinders permitted fairly free joint movement but radically limited his tactual experience. Note the abnormal sitting posture (cf. Fig. 47). (Courtesy of H. W. Nissen, from Nissen, Chow and Semmes, *Amer. J. Psychol.,* vol. 64, 1951.)

havior that does not depend on either visual or somesthetic perception for its guidance, so we do not actually go far beyond the evidence in concluding that all higher behavior (above the level of the reflex or simple stimulus-response relations) is a function of learning.

But it is perfectly obvious that all higher behavior is *also* a function of heredity and the growth processes that give us eyes and ears and skin receptors and a nervous system in which learning can occur. Instead of asking whether a given action is hereditary or learned—opposing these two influences to one another—we usually need to ask how the two have collaborated in producing it.

The student should note that heredity, by itself, can produce no behavior whatever; the fertilized ovum must have a nutritive, supporting environment for its growth, before behavior is possible. Similarly, learning can produce no behavior by itself, without the heredity and the prenatal environment that produce the structures in which learning can occur. The two collaborate. Further, it seems highly probable that heredity makes some kinds of learning easy or inevitable, others hard, and thus guides learning. Some things that are considered to be unlearned, for example in the insects, may in fact be the result of a very rapid learning which the sensory and neural structure of the insect makes inevitable.

In the higher animal too some learning is inevitable, in ordinary circumstances, but now there is a larger mass of neural tissue involved, and if we assume, as in the preceding chapter, that cell-assemblies must be developed before effective transmission at higher levels can occur, this implies that the first course of learning will be very slow. This is in fact what is indicated by the course of learning in the visual- and somesthetic-deprivation studies. Theoretically, therefore, we may consider that the function of early experience in the mammal is to build up the mediating processes which, once they are established, make possible the very rapid learning of which the mature animal is capable.

Codifying the factors in development

In all matters touching on the heredity-environment or maturation-learning question, long experience shows that it is extremely difficult to think or speak with logical consistency, or without omitting some obviously important factor from discussion. A codification of the factors in development is presented in Table 1, which may oversimplify the question, but which will help to avoid the worse oversimplifications that abound in the literature: not only the literature of psychology, but also that of medicine, zoology, genetics—in short, the whole field of biological investigation, as far as it touches on the determinants of physical or behavioral growth.

The purpose of Table 1 is to provide a working classification only, one that will keep us reminded at least that there are more than two kinds of factors in development, and allow us to talk about them less ambiguously. The scheme is really a sort of mnemonic device, not an exhaustive analysis; if carried too far shortcomings will appear. Factor I is classed as genetic, for example, as if the ovum consisted of genetic structures alone. Many ova consist of genetic structures *plus* nutritive matter (as birds' eggs clearly do), which means that Factor I as defined overlaps Factor II, the nutritive environment of the developing embryo. This probably applies in some degree to mammalian ova as well. Factor II should include also temperature, which is physical, and so on.

But if we regard the table as a working approximation, it will help us to avoid certain common fallacies. Much of the discussion of instinct is based implicitly on this kind of argument: such-and-such behavior needs no special experience—that is, it does not require practice, or observation of others' performance—hence it must depend on heredity alone. Table 1 permits us to restate this: Factor V is not involved, therefore Factor I alone is the cause. But this omits Factors II, III and IV (assuming that VI is not involved). In other words, the roles of the nutritive and constant-sensory environments, as causal factors in behavior, have been overlooked—and there is plenty of evidence to show that they must not be overlooked.

The schematizing of Table 1 will help one to remember that no behavior whatever can be caused by one of these factors alone. No "learned behavior" is possible without Factors I to III, which together make possible the existence of the sense organs, nervous system and so forth. No "innate behavior" can be produced by Factor I alone; the nutritive environment must act on the fertilized ovum to produce something that can manifest behavior at all.

Factor I, evidently, is the hereditary variable in behavior. Factors II to VI are the environmental variables. Factors II and III are the same in principle, but in practice II is apt to be forgotten; also, II is harder to control experimentally, III easier, so it is worth while (especially for mnemonic purposes) to separate them. Similarly, Factors IV and V are

Table 1.   Classes of factors in behavioral development

No.	Class	Source, mode of action, etc.
I	genetic	physiological properties of the fertilized ovum
II	chemical, prenatal	nutritive or toxic influence in the uterine environment
III	chemical, postnatal	nutritive or toxic influence: food, water, oxygen, drugs, etc.
IV	sensory, constant	pre- and postnatal experience normally inevitable for all members of the species
V	sensory, variable	experience that varies from one member of the species to another
VI	traumatic	physical events tending to destroy cells: an "abnormal" class of events to which an animal might conceivably never be exposed, unlike Factors I to V

the same in principle—though IV is predominantly a cause of early learning, V of later learning, which in higher species have rather different
properties—but Factor IV is again hard to control experimentally and is
very often overlooked, so these two may also be kept separate in our
codification.

Factors I to III, and Factor VI, together comprise the *constitutional*
variables in behavior, Factors IV and V the *experiential* variables. The
student will find in his other reading, especially if he ventures into the
clinical literature, references to something that is called "organic" and
something else called "functional." One symptom is called organic, for
example, while another is functional. In modern psychology these terms
have no good justification: what they are really getting at is the distinction between an effect of some constitutional variable, and that of some
experiential variable. If a mental illness is considered to derive from the
abnormal growth process of a tumor inside the head, or from a head
injury with destruction of cells, it is said to be organic—that is, it has its
origin in Factors I to III, singly or in combination, or in Factor VI. If
instead it is considered to derive from some conflict of learned behaviors
in the patient, it is said to be functional—that is, experiential. There is no
harm in using the older terminology, provided its real meaning is kept
in mind, but it tends persistently to make people think in terms of a
different meaning, including a mind which is somehow not a function
of the organism.

Next, in speaking of maturation, we may mean either of two things:
the influence of Factors I to III, which we may refer to as *physical
maturation;* or the influence of Factors I to IV, referred to as *psychological maturation.* The student will find that these two things are confused
in the literature. For example, in the case of children learning to walk,
let us say between the twelfth and the fifteenth month, we arrange it so
that none of the children in one group are allowed to practice—that is,
to get into a vertical position with feet on the floor—until they are
12 months old. We see how long it then takes for walking to occur. Ten
per cent, let us say, are walking after three days' practice; in another
group, not allowed to practice until the age of fifteen months, we find that
perhaps 75 per cent can walk after three days' practice. We say then
that the difference between the two groups must be due to the "maturation" that occurs between the twelfth and the fifteenth month. But is this
physical maturation, the operation of Factors I to III alone? During this
time we have not controlled all the aspects of somesthetic experience
that come under the heading of Factor IV, and their effects cannot be
excluded. We have seen that some sort of somesthetic learning, or development of perception of tactual locus and of the position of the limbs
with respect to the body, is going on in this period. We cannot doubt that
physical maturation is also going on, but such experiments as this do not
show that physical maturation alone produces the increased walking

readiness of the child at fifteen months as compared with twelve. On the other hand, the change is not due to practice in the specific acts of walking, and we can speak of it as psychological maturation: the operation of Factors I to IV, apart from the ad hoc learning of Factor V.

Further on Factor IV and instinct

The conclusion has been drawn that perceptual development depends essentially on exposure to the patterned stimulation of the early environment. It has been seen that our experimental evidence on this point actually is for vision and somesthesis only, but we must assume that the same principles must apply in audition, the other sense mode in which the pattern of stimulation has a predominant role.

Certain common knowledge further strengthens the assumption. A foreign language is rarely, if ever, learned at maturity in the same way as in infancy. It is rare that an adult learns a language so well that he can pass in every respect as a native: the intonations, the subtle shifts in precision in less formal situations (the "perfect" speech of the foreigner is too perfect), and the free use of colloquial forms, are not mastered at maturity to the same degree. And further, the foreigner cannot detect other foreigners as a native can. One's "ear" for the rhythms and nuances of speech must be acquired early.

The patterns and combinations of stimuli falling under the heading of Factor IV are so ubiquitous and so inevitable that they are frequently overlooked entirely in the analysis of behavior. Except in the case of foster-care in captivity, *every* mammal makes its first social contact with an adult female of the same species (unless an obstetrician catches it first, delaying this contact for a short time); and generally for an extended period the young mammal receives no other social stimulation than from one or two adults, the parents, and from young of the same species, the siblings. The fact can hardly help influencing the course of subsequent social behavior. The act of vocalization is *always* accompanied by corresponding auditory stimulation (except of course for the deaf child). Proprioceptive stimulation from flexing fingers is practically always the prelude to further tactual stimulation as the fingers meet the palm or close on an object held in the hand. The most frequently encountered object in the young animal's early movements is its own body. The effects of gravity on weight-bearing surfaces are constant and inevitable. And so on, almost endlessly.

All this is obvious, though the operation of Factor IV is hard to control experimentally. But when it can be controlled, and significantly modified, the result frequently is a significant modification of later behavior.

This includes instinctive behavior. Male cichlid fishes reared in isolation attempt to mate indiscriminately with males and females, unlike those normally reared. If two species of ants, which normally attack and kill each other, are placed together less than 12 hours after hatching, no fighting occurs; and this amicability is permanent, though any other intruders are promptly killed. The "gregarious instinct" of wild and tame species of sheep is considerably modified if the young animal is captured and brought up by human beings; being offered now the opportunity to consort with its own species it may follow the human caretaker instead, and if put into the same field with other sheep tends to graze by itself.

Birds "instinctively" choose their own kind for mating. Is this independent of learning? In many species a phenomenon of *imprinting* can be observed (it is probably general, but most marked in certain birds), which shows at least that the behavior can be affected by experience, and strongly suggests that experience is an important factor in all cases—that the bird chooses its own kind rather than others partly because it was exposed to them in an early formative period. If the eggs of the graylag goose are removed from the mother and hatched in an incubator, the young geese attach themselves socially to the species to which they are first exposed on leaving the incubator. At maturity their courting behavior, the preliminaries to mating behavior, is directed toward the foster species. The foster species, also, need not always be another kind of bird, but might be a dog or a man. Jackdaws reared by human beings directed their sexual display at maturity toward human beings, rather than other jackdaws.

In its most marked form, imprinting is a kind of irreversible learning that occurs in early infancy ("forgetting" occurs in less extreme cases). Under ordinary circumstances, the imprinting is to the animal's own species, strengthening and making part of the instinctive social pattern of response.

Instinctive behavior, then, is frequently unlearned but dependent on other (perceptual) learning. It is unlearned in the sense that it does not require practice, or the special learning conditions that are comprised by Factor V of Table 1. But in higher animals at least it is a function of the perception of environmental objects and events, and normal perceptual development depends on Factor IV, exposure to the normally present stimulus patterns of the early environment.

All our evidence thus indicates that it is wrong to think of instinctive behavior as a separate class, wholly distinct from another class of learned behavior. Instead, the two shade into one another, with no clear line of demarcation. As for the term "instinct," it must be by definition that process within the nervous system that produces instinctive behavior, and we can see now why it is a misleading term. It implies that instinctive behavior is produced by a *special* activity or part of the brain, separate from the brain processes that control learned behavior, and separate from those that make up what we call intelligence. But this is not so.

In addition to the facts already discussed, there is another kind of evidence to show that instinct is not separate from learning or intelligence.

Learning ability in the male rat, as measured by maze performance, is correlated with the level of sexual activity. The better learner copulates more efficiently and frequently. Sex behavior in the female at this phyletic level is largely reflexive, and does not correlate with learning ability; but maternal behavior does. The female that is best at maze learning is the best mother. Similarly, cortical removals which affect intelligence and learning ability in the rat produce a lowered rate of copulation in the male, and deterioration of maternal behavior in the female.

There is no ground, therefore, for thinking of instinctive behavior as having a special kind of neural control, immune to the effects of learning, and distinct from the operations of intelligence. Instinct by definition is that which determines instinctive behavior—that is to say, it is the presence in the individual animal of certain neural paths which are characteristic of the species. How are these paths determined? Also by definition, instinctive behavior does not depend on practice (or imitation), and thus is not learned in the usual sense of the term; yet, as we have seen, the learning induced by Factor IV may play a significant part in it. What we conclude is that instinct is the neural organization, over and above reflex paths, which is common to a whole species: determined by a common heredity *and* the common features of the environment. The learning that is part of it is learning that inevitably occurs in the whole species (except when an individual animal's environment differs significantly, and produces aberrant behavior). Growth processes and early experience between them determine the presence of neural paths which mean, when the animal is faced for the first time with a particular class of situation, that he will tend to respond in a particular way. These processes are incredibly complex, and we have hardly begun to unravel them, but in principle there is nothing any more mysterious about instinct than about other aspects of behavior.

The student should be clear for example that instinctive behavior does not imply advance knowledge of its end effects, inherited from his ancestors. It is done for its own sake, not for what it will achieve in the future. The pregnant rat builds a nest before her first litter is born because she feels like building a nest, not because she knows why her belly is swollen and that the pups will need shelter. The primary reason for human sex behavior is not to produce another generation of troublemakers in this troubled world but because human beings like sex behavior.

It has already been said that it makes for confusion to apply the term instinctive to man's behavior, because of the word's persistent connotations. It is almost an article of faith for many psychologists that man has no instinctive behavior, no matter how the term might be defined. The student however should recognize how species-predictable human behavior is, in many of its aspects.

If instinct is a poor theoretical conception we must abandon it for technical purposes, but we must not forget the problems of behavior to which in the past it has been applied. Man everywhere has a fondness for the sound of his own voice, singing and listening to songs, telling elaborate tales for their own sake (some of them being true), or talking when there is no need of communication. Man everywhere uses tools, organizes social groups, avoids darkness in strange places. All cultures are said to have developed string games, related to the childhood game of cat's cradle. The taboos of incest or of food use, the belief in spirits good or evil, the tendency to ornament the body in particular ways and to impose strong sanctions against ornamenting it in other ways—all these are things which, in detail, are subject to the influence of special learning but which in one form or another spring up in every society of which we have knowledge. In detail, therefore, they are not species-predictable; but in a larger sense they are very much so. The fact that the specific way in which the hair may be worn varies from culture to culture, or from one time to another in the same culture, does not change the fact that all cultures at all times have such rules, and that they play an important part in the behavior of man in the presence of his fellows. We cannot predict the content of folk tales in a culture encountered for the first time; but we can safely predict that there will be folk tales, learned and passed on from generation to generation. A false opposition of the "instinctive" to the "learned" has tended in the past to prevent us from seeing these common features of human behavior and from recognizing that they must result, much as the instinctive behavior of rodent and carnivore does, from (a) the way we are made, and (b) the universal features of the human environment.

The development of intelligence

The classical view in psychology held that intelligence is determined essentially by heredity. This view seemed to be supported by such experiments as the following.

Learning ability was tested in a large number of laboratory rats. The brightest males and females, those with the fewest errors, were then bred with each other, and the dullest likewise. The second generation was tested and the brightest offspring of the bright group were bred, and the dullest offspring of the dull group. This was continued, until by the seventh generation it was found that there was little or no overlap in the scores of the bright and dull groups; practically all of the bright made better scores in maze learning than any of the dull.

This seems to show that intelligence is not dependent on environment, but on heredity alone. However, there are other experiments that contradict this. One experimenter equated heredity in two groups of infant rats by the *split-litter* method: taking several litters of pups, he put half of each litter into one group, half into the other. One group was reared in a restricted environment, each animal in a small cage which he could not see out of, containing no objects and presenting no opportunity for problem-solving. The other group was reared in a "free environment," a very large cage which was a sort of amusement park for rats, containing a variety of objects, and barriers which gave experience with varied paths (direct and indirect) from one point in the cage to another. The two groups were tested at maturity for problem-solving ability, and the ones reared in the free environment had a lasting superiority to those reared in the restricted environment. Similarly, dogs reared in rather extreme isolation in small cages show marked deficiencies in learning and problem-solving; physically, they are healthy and vigorous (Fig. 49), so the deficiencies are not attributable to a failure of bodily development. These experiments show that intelligence is a matter of environment, not heredity.

But do they? Let us look again at the two kinds of experiments. In the

Figure 49. Littermate Scotties, one reared normally, one reared in restriction. Visitors to the laboratory were sometimes invited to tell which was which, and usually made the wrong choice. The normal dog is at the left, rather bored with the photographic process; the restricted dog did not have enough brains to be bored but kept on being interested in the most trivial events.

breeding experiment, all the animals are brought up in identical small cages, effectively equating environmental factors and keeping them from influencing the results. In the second kind, the rearing experiments, hereditary variables are equated, which removes their influence. The two results therefore are not contradictory at all. Both these influences are important; if one is held constant, it does not affect the outcome of the experiment—and thus is easily forgotten; but it must not be forgotten.

With this point in mind, we can examine the result of a related investigation of human intelligence. Identical twins are ones which, according to genetics, originate from a single fertilized ovum and thus have the same hereditary characteristics. If they are brought up in different environments, we should be able to see what kind of effect variations of environment have upon intelligence. Psychologists have therefore been very interested in identical-twin orphans adopted in different families. It has been found that the IQ's (Chap. 12) are very similar, and this fact has sometimes been used as argument that man's adult intelligence is determined by heredity and not by environment.

But if we examine the evidence, we find that most of these pairs of children have been brought up in very similar environments. When a pair of twins is orphaned, one of two things happens. They may be adopted by the neighbors, which implies similar environments—the same community, plus the fact that all the families in one neighborhood are apt to have about the same economic and social status. Or the twins may be taken charge of by a social agency, to oversee adoption, and this again means that they will get into environments that have much in common, social workers having strong ideas about who is fit to bring up children. In this kind of "experiment" differential effects of environment are minimized, and it is hardly surprising to find similar IQ's in identical twins with similar environments. The fact that identical twins have IQ's which are more alike than those of fraternal twins is a valid argument that heredity is important, just as the rat-breeding experiment was a valid demonstration of the same point; but it does not show that heredity is the *only* variable. To show this we need to have one of each pair of twins brought up in the worst possible environment, the other in the best possible one: if then there was no significant difference in IQ, we could conclude that intelligence is unaffected by the sensory environment. This experiment however is not likely to be done, and in the meantime there is a great deal of evidence to indicate that such a result is in the highest degree improbable.

Sometimes it is recognized that heredity and environment both affect intelligence, but the writer then goes on to say *how* important each is. The student may find it said for example that 80 per cent of intelligence is determined by heredity, 20 per cent by environment. This statement is, on the face of it, nonsense. It means that a man would have 80 per cent of the problem-solving ability he would otherwise have had, if he were never given the opportunity to learn a language, never learned how people behave, and so forth. Conversely, it means that 20 per cent of a man's problem-solving capacity will result from a good environment, no matter *what* heredity is involved, which we know of course is not true. What we must say is that both these variables are of 100 per cent importance: their relation is not additive but multiplicative. To ask how much heredity contributes to intelligence is like asking how much the width of a field contributes to its area.

It is reasonable to ask how much the *variations* in intelligence are determined by variations of heredity, or of environment, but this is a very different question, and the answer cannot be generalized. In a very homogeneous community, culturally, practically all the variability of intelligence might be determined by heredity, but this would only occur when environmental variation in the group studied is at a minimum. It has been found repeatedly that cultural differences can affect intelligence-test scores to a very marked degree. For example, children growing up on canal boats in England, thus removed from many of the normal experiences of other children, showed a sharp decline in intelligence: IQ 90 at age 6, 77 at age 7½, 60 at age 12. An IQ below 70 is ordinarily considered to mean mental deficiency (p. 226), whereas 90 is within the range of normal ability. Again, a very similar picture (IQ 84 at 7, IQ 60 at 15) has been found for growing children in isolated mountain communities in the United States. The higher IQ's for the younger children show that the low scores, at later ages, do not mean deficient heredities—otherwise all the IQ's would be low. Instead, it appears that the social and cultural environment is sufficiently stimulating for a normal development of intelligence in the first four or five years of life, but progressively inadequate from then on.

None of this means, of course, that the child's heredity is unimportant. Intelligence is the joint product of heredity and of the physical and social environments. Emphasizing the importance of one of these factors does not reduce the importance of the others.

Summary

The development of behavior depends on a number of influences, classified here as Factors I to VI. An animal's heredity (Factor I) by itself cannot produce any behavior whatsoever; nor can learning by itself, without the heredity and the nutritive environment that produce a nervous system in which learning can occur. Experience (Factors IV and V) is not involved in the unconditioned reflexes; but all other behavior, including instinctive behavior in mammals and much instinctive behavior in other animals, involves the generalized early experience of Factor IV.

The term maturation is used in two senses: physical maturation (determined by Factors I to III) and psychological maturation (Factors I to IV—that is, including the effects of early nonspecific experience).

The term instinct is unsatisfactory, implying a special agent in behavior distinct from (or substituting for) learning and intelligence. The term instinctive behavior is less misleading, provided it is not defined so as to deny all effects of learning; it is the behavior that can be predicted from knowledge of the species, independent of special experiences, but not independent of the early experience that is common to the whole species. Instinctive behavior in birds and mammals is not identical with reflex behavior, which is a stereotyped local response to specific stimulation, whereas instinctive behavior may be independent of any particular sense organ and is a function of the whole animal (and also involves early experience).

Level of intelligence must not be regarded as due *either* to heredity *or* to environment; or partly to one, partly to the other. Each is *fully* necessary. Heredity can produce intelligence only with the collaboration of the nutritive environment, pre- and postnatal. There is also clear evidence to show that generalized experience, the effect of the stimulating sensory environment, is necessary to normal intellectual development.

Notes

Much of the background of this chapter can be found in Stevens (*General References*, Chap. 1, p. 19): Chap. 7 (Sperry) on neural development, and particularly on the independence of reflex responses from experience; Chap. 8 (Carmichael) on postnatal development; Chap. 9 (Hall) on genetic factors in behavior; and Chap. 12 (Beach) on instinctive behavior.

On congenital blindness, and the later course of development after an operation has made vision possible, the main reference is M. von Senden, *Raum- und Gestaltauffassung bei operierten Blindgeborenen. . . .*, Barth, 1932, which brings together all the case reports in the literature, from 1066 onward. (Two modern references in English are: J. B. Miner, *Psychol. Rev. Monog.*, 1905, 6, 103–118; and Latta, *Brit. J. Psychol.*, 1904, 1, 135–150. Three related papers, comparing space perception in the congenitally blind and in those who have had vision, are G. Révész, *Amer. J. Psychol.*, 1937, 50, 429–444; R. H. Sylvester, *Psychol. Bull.*, 1913, 10, 210–211; and H. Carr, *J. Exp. Psychol.*, 1921, 4, 399–418.) The experiment on rearing chimpanzees without pattern vision is by A. H. Riesen (*Chicago Med. Sch. Quart.*, 1951, 13, 17–24), that on rearing with limitation of somesthetic experience by H. W. Nissen, K. L. Chow and J. Semmes (*Amer. J. Psychol.*, 1951, 64, 485–507). An extensive review of this whole field (the role of early experience) can be found in F. A. Beach and J. Jaynes, *Psychol. Bull.*, 1954, 51, 239–263.

The distinction of reflex from instinct is Lashley's (*Psychol. Rev.*, 1938, 45, 445–471), but the general point of view of the present chapter is based on a paper by Beach (*Psychol. Rev.*, 1955, 62, 401–410).

The studies of human intelligence in restricted environments are reviewed by W. S. Neff, *Psychol. Bull.*, 1938, 35, 727–757.

Chapter 7

Problems of learning and memory

Up to this point our emphasis has been on the methods and the general conceptions one uses for the analysis of behavior. Now the emphasis changes somewhat. Instead of focussing on the behavior that fits into our theoretical conceptions we can take a wider view. The student should never forget how far we are still from understanding behavior: not only man's, but that of lower animals as well. We must now consider the whole picture of behavior, and see how far our conceptual tools are capable of dealing with it.

We begin with the problems of learning and memory: the way in which behavior is modified by experience, and retention of the modifications. Essentially, the question is in what circumstances these changes of behavior appear and disappear.

"Learning" comprises events that occur, apparently, in very different conditions. The housewife may learn to operate a new can-opener from reading instructions on the box, or by trying to operate it. One way involves practice on the task, the other does not: what have they in common? Or what has either in common with learning to sleep in a noisy room—that is, learning *not* to respond to stimuli? There is also the "learning to see" (discussed in Chapter 6) by patients born with cataracts that were removed at some later time. The fundamental process may be the

131

same in all these cases, as we assume; but if it is, there are complicating factors which produce very different end-products.

It seems therefore that "learning" is another one of our global terms which can be used very effectively in a general sense, but which needs qualification when we wish to be more precise. Instead of discussing learning in general, we may need to say whether it is conditioning or maze learning that is in question; or may need to distinguish perceptual learning from motor learning, and rote learning (blind memorization) from intelligent or insightful learning.

As for "memory," it too is a global term without precision. Broadly, it refers sometimes to the capacity to form lasting connections (or to retain the effects of past experience), sometimes to the presence of such connections formed in the past. This is clearer with an example: the cases of brain damage in which there is what is called "loss of immediate memory." This is a condition in which new connections are hard to establish, but old ones are not lost. It might be said of such a patient that his "memory" is impaired, but his "memories" are not; evidently, the term can be used in different senses.

As we shall see later (Chap. 12), there are different methods of measuring the retention of past learning, and these also imply different conceptions of what memory is. In one method, the subject repeats what he has learned—if he cannot repeat any of it, his memory score is zero. But either savings or recognition method would give a higher score. That is, sometimes we use "memory" to refer to what can actually be recalled in effective form; at other times we use it to refer to any lasting effect of earlier learning, no matter whether the subject can reproduce or use what he learned.

Memory is clearly an integral part of the question of learning; what learning would there be, in any meaningful sense, if a man forgot something in the very instant of learning it? If there were no retention at all, how could we determine that there had been any acquisition, and what meaning would it have? The conception of learning itself implies the conception of a short-term memory, at least; the two terms do not refer to different things, but to different aspects of the same phenomenon.

Phenomena of conditioning

Some workers in the past have considered that the conditioned reflex, or CR, is the simple and elementary form of learning, all others being complications thereof. This seems to oversimplify matters, but the CR certainly is a relatively simple form, especially in comparison with serial learning and the acquisition of motor skills. In it various factors that affect learning can be well controlled, and study of it has taught us a great deal about the whole process.

Pavlov, who developed the method, concentrated almost entirely upon a single response, secretion of the salivary glands; but any simple stimulus can be conditioned to almost any simple response. The method has already been described for salivary secretion to food (p. 30) and for avoidance of electric shock (p. 50). In general terms, an unconditioned stimulus (UCS) is used to evoke an unconditioned response. The neutral stimulus, which is to become the conditioned stimulus, must precede the UCS. With Pavlov's method, about 40 trials are needed to produce a reliable CR in the dog. The number of trials varies from species to species, and also with the kind of stimulus and kind of response. With the normal adult chimpanzee, for example, an avoidance response may be obtained after one trial in which the animal is pricked with a hypodermic needle; the animal will not allow it to be brought near his skin again. On the other hand, hundreds or thousands of trials may sometimes be needed for conditioning, for example with a barely liminal stimulus and a weakly evoked autonomic response.

Conditioned inhibition can also be established. In Pavlov's procedure, a metronome beating at 120/sec. is first made a positive CS for salivation, by feeding after each presentation. A beat of 60/sec. is now presented, but not followed by food. At first this also elicits salivary secretion—the phenomenon of generalization referred to earlier (p. 23f.). After some repetitions, however, the unrewarded metronome-60 elicits no secretion. There has been a learning not to respond, but this is not merely a negative process, an absence of response. There is also an active inhibition. This is shown by the following facts. Immediately after metronome-60, metronome-120 is presented, but no secretion is obtained. Whatever process prevented secretion to the first stimulus (M-60) continues for some seconds, and prevents secretion to the other (M-120). However, the inhibitory process itself may be disturbed; if some unusual sound is presented, immediately following metronome-60, the dog will now secrete saliva to metronome-120. The sound has a "disinhibiting" action, disrupting the inhibitory process and allowing the CR to appear.

Another phenomenon of some importance is the *higher-order CR*. Assume that a CR has been established to a light, which has always been followed by presentation of food. Now the light is presented together with a specific tone, but *not* with food. After five such combinations of light with tone, the tone presented by itself elicits a small secretion of saliva. Since the tone had never accompanied food, this is a second-order CR. Third-order conditioning has also been achieved occasionally.

A good deal has been made of this phenomenon theoretically, to account for certain kinds of learning which are not directly established CR's. Thus chimpanzees can be trained to work for poker chips instead of food, when there is a slot-machine in the cage which will give up grapes in return for the poker chips (Fig. 50). In these circumstances, the chimpanzee does not always take each poker chip and go direct to the slot machine for his reward, but may first accumulate a number of the

Figure 50.   Subject Kambi is shown about to drop a token into the slot of a chimpomat to "purchase" food. (Courtesy of Yerkes Laboratories of Primate Biology and H. W. Nissen.)

tokens. This corresponds fairly well to the human accumulation of money for its own sake: the idea is that a man's responses which result in the acquisition of money are secondary CR's. One difficulty with this kind of explanation is that the secondary CR in the laboratory is weak and unstable; whereas human money-getting tendencies, even in those who already have more than enough to satisfy all bodily comforts, are very strong and persistent. Also, they are not as subject to the process of *extinction* as one might expect from the laboratory data.

Extinction is a form of forgetting, but it has certain peculiarities which show that this is not a simple loss of the connections that were made during learning. After establishing a salivary CR to skin stimulation of the back (for example), we now give a series of CS's in close succession, without presentation of food. The salivary secretion decreases on each trial, until the eighth trial let us say, when the secretion is zero. Has the animal forgotten? Not at all, for when he is brought back and tested next day the CR is present again at its earlier level, or nearly so. We may call this temporary extinction, obtained by *massed trials* (i.e., presented at short intervals).

If instead *spaced trials* are used, separated in time, a permanent extinction can be obtained. The CR will not reappear spontaneously. But here again the extinction is not a case of simple loss of connections, just because time has passed without the animal's experiencing CS and UCS together; for if we merely keep him out of the experimental room, and not expose him to the CS at all, the CR will last for months or years. Extinction is a form of forgetting in which an active learning process is involved—that is, the animal in a sense learns *not* to respond in the same way as before. Logically, this makes it an example of retroactive inhibition (p. 147ff.), the addition of new learning that interferes with older learning.

THEORETICAL IMPLICATIONS.   Our primary theoretical approach to the CR is to treat it as a set of connections from receptors to effectors, like the UCR but established by experience (p. 50). This interpretation is quite feasible for some CR's, but as we have seen there are difficulties with others, such as delayed CR's (p. 51), in which it appears from our present knowledge that a mediating process must operate rather than the simpler through-route connections.

Another major difficulty is this. In its simplest form, the theory implies that whenever a stimulus is followed by an unconditioned response, connections will be set up from the excited receptors to the effectors that are active immediately afterward (Figs. 13, 14 and 26 represent this in a crude way). This implies that the same response is made to CS and UCS: a new stimulus is connected to the old response. But taken as a whole, the CR is frequently not identical with the UCR; some of the components may be the same, but others are changed or absent. Pavlov's analysis dealt only with the secretion of saliva, which may be the same both as CR and as UCR; but the total pattern of response in these experiments is quite different, since the CS does not make the dog reach into the food dish and begin chewing and swallowing. These parts of the UCR are almost wholly absent from the CR; they appear only when the food is presented. If conditioning were just the substitution of a new stimulus, retaining the earlier response unchanged, the CS should elicit all these activities.

When a rat is conditioned to jump off a grid to avoid electric shock, the UCR (the response to shock made before learning has modified it) involves squealing, biting the bars through which shock is delivered, and other ineffective actions (including occasional "freezing") as well as the final escape. When the avoidance CR is finally established, the motor pattern is considerably changed; at the presentation of the CS the animal promptly jumps off the grid. The pattern of movement is not the same from animal to animal (some animals which freeze at the first shock may actually continue to do so), but each will develop a stereotyped response which (1) can reasonably be described as a CR but which (2) is not merely a reinstatement of the UCR. Instead, it usually differs greatly in total pattern.

The change in pattern may be regarded as simply due to the dropping out of some components of the original unconditioned behavior. Why should they drop out? In this question lies the crux of the theoretical problem of learning.

Contiguity, repetition and reinforcement

The view that we have been considering implied that what is needed to set up a CR is simply to have the CS followed repeatedly by the UCS-UCR combination. This statement gives us the two important learning principles of *temporal contiguity* and *frequency*. Contiguity refers to the fact that two events to be associated (such as an auditory sensation and a secretion of saliva) must occur closely together in time. Frequency refers to the obvious fact that learning involves repetition of the stimulating conditions (one-trial learning is a limiting case; even here, it is likely that the "single" trial involves a number of stimulations, or else we are dealing with *transfer* from earlier learning: see below).

Now, however, we turn to a third principle, *reinforcement:* contiguity and frequency are not sufficient to account for the occurrence of learning for, as we have just seen, the response that is repeated often in contiguity with the conditioned stimulus may drop out instead of being strengthened. What is the factor that reinforces or fails to reinforce?

The problem becomes very clear in the case of serial learning, as for example in the maze. As the rat goes from starting box to goal, in the maze shown in Fig. 51, he passes three choice points. At each he is exposed to a complex of stimuli—visual, tactual and olfactory. These can become *cues* (stimuli which direct behavior) to turn right, or turn left. At A, for example, the rat turns right and goes to the end of the blind alley, having then to retrace his path before he can proceed to point B. The same thing happens, let us say, for the first four trials. What learning do we expect to result from this repetition? In practice we know that the rat will stop entering the blind alley. But theoretically, if we think of learning as being established by contiguity and repetition, this should not happen. The sights and sounds and smells experienced by the rat at point A are followed, closely in time and repeatedly, by a right turn: should this not establish a CR to turn right, when the animal is exposed once more to the stimuli of point A?

Contiguity and frequency are, therefore, not the only determinants of learning. In many circumstances, repetition of a response strengthens the probability that it will be made next time, but in others the probability is decreased. The term reinforcement refers to an effect of what happens immediately after a response, to strengthen or weaken the tendency to make that response again when exposed to the same stimulation.

The nature of the effect is not clear, though this is a crucial point in the theory of learning. Concentrated research for some decades has shown that the problem has more complexity than one might have thought, and a clear solution has not yet been reached. At present, consequently, there are differing ideas of how reinforcement occurs.

These ideas take three main forms: (1) reinforcement may occur only because the response takes the animal away from the stimulus—the S-R connection is "reinforced" (i.e., continues to exist) because no other connections can be formed with the same stimulus, to compete with or weaken the connection; (2) reinforcement may be a special effect of satisfying a need, or of stimulation associated with such satisfaction; and (3) reinforcement may depend on some kind of interaction between sensory input and mediating process.

1. To illustrate the first of these explanatory ideas: the rat in the maze of Fig. 51 reaches point A and turns right. This strengthens an S-R connection which will produce a right turn when next he reaches point A. However, the right turn also puts him in a blind alley, which forces him eventually to return to point A. Now he cannot turn right, so whatever he does a new S-R connection is formed, tending to produce a different response to the cues of point A. The new S-R connection may perhaps abolish the preceding one entirely, or it may just weaken it: in either case, turning right at A

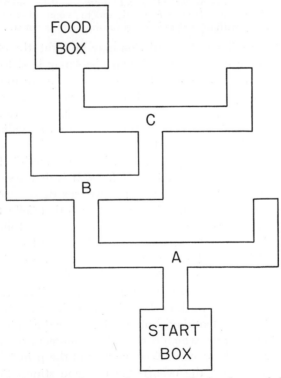

Figure 51. Plan of simple maze for the rat. The bend in each blind alley prevents the animal from seeing that it is a blind alley before he has actually entered it. A, B, C, choice points.

results, in the end, in a weakening of the tendency to do so again. But if the animal turns left at point A, he continues on to B and does not see A again on that run; so no new responses to A get established, and the left-turning tendency remains undisturbed.

2. The second type of explanation relates to the *law of effect*, proposed originally by Thorndike, a pioneer in the study of animal learning (a more modern form of the theory will be discussed below). The law proposed that when a response to stimulation is followed by a satisfying state of affairs the S-R connection is strengthened; when followed by an annoying state of affairs, it is weakened. When the rat in the maze turns right at A annoyance results (as he encounters the block at the end of the blind alley) so the strength of the tendency to turn right on subsequent trials is reduced. A left-turning tendency at A is of course not weakened; and when the rat reaches food this satisfying state of affairs strengthens the tendency to repeat whatever responses preceded it. The student should note that this is a strictly mechanical process: if the animal turns right at C, enters the blind, then turns round and reaches food, this series of actions is reinforced; but since he reaches food sooner if he turns left at C, a left turn here will be reinforced more than a right turn.

3. Finally, when a hungry rat has been put in the maze several times and has wandered at random until reaching food, certain expectancies will be established. The various stimulus combinations arouse mediating processes, one after another, and these mediating processes will become associated, or connected, so that one arouses the next. The animal has repeatedly experienced A, B and C, followed by food, in that order. If the corresponding mediating processes have become connected, experiencing A will produce an expectancy of B (mediating processes A excite mediating processes B, before B is actually experienced). If the animal turns left at A, B is actually seen and smelt, which strengthens further the connection between the two sets of mediating processes (confirms the expectancy); and also strengthens the connection between the motor process of turning left and the concurrent mediating process. If the animal turns right at A the expectancy of seeing B is not confirmed, and the connection of the mediating processes of expectancy with motor processes of turning right is not strengthened.

One of these three lines of speculation may be right, the others wrong; or, more likely, some combination of such ideas may lead to the answer. A combination of the law of effect (in one of its more modern forms) with a theory of mediating processes is rather generally accepted, though there is little agreement on details and some investigators give more weight to law-of-effect conceptions, others more to mediating-process conceptions, in working out their theories.

Now the law of effect in more detail. It has been modified in different ways, but a main line of thought is as follows. It is first assumed that all behavior is energized by *drives:* hunger drive, sex drive, drive to escape pain, and so on (see Chap. 8). It is then assumed that "effect" in the law of effect becomes *drive reduction:* the response that is followed by reduced drive is the one that tends to be repeated. The hungry dog learns to "beg" for food because he gets food after sitting up on his hindquarters: food reduces the hunger drive, and the reduction strengthens the tendency to repeat the response immediately preceding. When punishment is used instead of reward, in this scheme of things, it is not the pain as such that reinforces learning, but relief from pain; reinforcement is again a reduction of drive, which occurs at the moment of escape.

This is *primary reinforcement.* Now we extend the principle to include *secondary reinforcement:* the occurrence of some stimulation that was previously associated with primary reinforcement (cf. secondary conditioning, p. 133). The rat that was fed after entering a white goal-box is more likely now to enter that box than a dark one in which he was not fed. In the same way, the anomalous behavior of human beings, who often act in a way that increases discomfort instead of decreasing it, may be due to the operation of secondary reinforcement such as praise, or receiving money. Though we shall see in Chapter 8 that this is probably not the whole explanation of such behavior, it seems clear that it is an important part.

Now let us return to the rat in the maze of Fig. 51. He is hungry on his first run, and wanders through the maze until he encounters food. Eating produces a drive reduction; the drive reduction is also associated with goal-box stimuli and stimuli from nearby points, which thus acquire (especially with repeated trials) properties of secondary reinforcement. On one trial the rat reaching C turns left and drive reduction occurs quickly, since this leads direct to food. On the next trial, perhaps, he turns right, enters the blind alley, and must retrace before reaching food: drive reduction is delayed. Hence a left turn at C is reinforced more than a right turn. With repeated trials, *habit strength* is built up enough to overcome chance fluctuations of behavior due to possible distracting events, and so the rat always makes a left turn at C.

Next, we may extend this by including an action of mediating processes. The stimulus traces excited by point C can be expected to be still active when the rat reaches food: therefore, they will be associated with drive reduction, and C itself will (like the goal-box) acquire secondary reinforcing properties. Thus the rat may proceed to learn to make a right turn at B in the same way as he learned to make a left turn at C,[1] and conceivably this effect could be extended to include A.

However, we know that this is not the whole story. If the rat is put into a maze with no food in the food-box, he still learns much about it; for if later he is put back in the starting-box, with food in the food-box, he learns the correct path more quickly than rats without such prior experience. A suggested explanation of this result is that the rat experiences discomfort when he enters a blind alley and has to turn round in a narrow space. This implies that more than one kind of reinforcement is involved in maze learning by the hungry rat—not reduction of food drive alone.

Another possible explanation is a "short-circuiting" of a mediating-process series: the rat turns left at B, experiences the blind alley, and returns to B before going on to C. This happens repeatedly, setting up a mediating series (B)-(end of blind alley)-(B)-(-open alley). On a new run the animal now reaches B and starts to turn left into the blind alley; but the mediating series runs off in advance of his actual locomotion. As

[1] This may be clearer for the student if put another way. Secondary reinforcement has the same kind of effect as primary reinforcement, but weaker; so now, when C has become associated with food, it acts as if the animal got a tiny bite of food here. The effect can then extend to B, and so on.

he turns left, the mediating process corresponding to perception of the blind end occurs, and associated with it a turning movement; what an observer sees is the rat starting to enter the blind, turning around and proceeding to *C* instead. On still later trials the short-circuiting proceeds further, and the animal does not even start to turn left at point *B*.

These are some of the main lines of inquiry that are being worked with by psychologists at present. Since the problem is not solved, we do not know whether the answer will be found along one or other of these lines or whether the development of some further theoretical conceptions will first be necessary.

Drive reduction: a possible hypothesis

It seems evident from ordinary observation, as well as from laboratory experiment, that satisfaction of a bodily need and the consequent drive reduction are frequently decisive factors in determining what is learned or unlearned. In some situations, at least, they are crucial. But if we ask why this should be so, physiologically, the answer is far from plain. Here we may consider briefly the only explanation that has been suggested: a hypothesis which, if it should be verified, has some interesting implications with respect to behavior.

Let us assume that drive is *arousal* (this hypothesis will be considered further in Chapter 8). If so, a relation of drive to learning would at once be evident. We have seen that there is little transmission through cortical synapses without arousal; and if there is no synaptic transmission, there can be no learning. Learning thus would depend on drive; but when we consider the details of this idea more closely, the hypothesis implies that it is not necessarily drive reduction that is important. With low drive levels, on the contrary, it may be an increase that results in reinforcement; and changes of drive level may not be significant at all within some intermediate range.

With a high level—according to the hypothesis we are now considering, a high level of bombardment of cortical synapses from the arousal system such as might be produced by giving an experimental animal a strong electric shock—there is a tendency to activate all cortical pathways, including ones that inhibit each other, and ones that produce conflicting behavior (moving forward and backward at the same time, or holding the breath and vocalizing). The effect of the shock thus is a tendency to break up the phase sequence and to produce ineffectual behavior. Also, any sensory event that accompanies this activity will tend to establish connections with all the randomly firing cortical paths; it will be conditioned, that is, to a pattern of disruptive and incoordinated activity. In these circumstances either of two things may happen.

1. As a result of the cortical disruption, no phase sequence occurs

whose motor effects remove the animal from the grid that is shocking him. The only effect of learning is to strengthen the pattern of incoordination, and the animal "freezes" where he is instead of escaping. This would account for the behavior of rats which, shocked in one compartment of a two-compartment apparatus, fail to learn to escape the shock. It would also help to explain why dogs reared in isolation in small cages are much poorer than normal dogs in learning a similar habit: the rearing tends to prevent normal establishment of the phase sequences that produce movement from one place to another, so the probability of freezing would be higher in these animals.

2. Second possibility: the cortical disruption is not complete, and a "locomotor phase sequence" occurs. This takes the animal off the grid, there is an immediate decrease of the cortical bombardment, and therefore a decrease of the disruptive cortical activity. Such a phase sequence, that is, creates sensory conditions that make its own continuation more likely. The sensory cues that preceded and accompanied shock will be conditioned both to the incoordinated activity, and to the movements of escape. The latter are the only organized behavior which these stimuli evoke, and when the behavior occurs before shock is actually delivered we say the animal has learned to avoid pain; but there is, of course, a learned emotional reaction also, evinced by the incoordinated activity and the heightened level of excitation (Chap. 8).

These are conditions in which we can understand how drive reduction strengthens one form of behavior and abolishes others. But the explanation applies only when drive level is high enough to produce some degree of cortical disorganization.

Suppose that the experimental subject has a low drive level instead, and has two courses of action before him, A and B. Course A is such that it produces no increase of arousal; B raises it. When a phase sequence occurs that produces behavior A, it must exist at a time when cortical transmission is uncertain, not strongly established (since bombardment from the arousal system is below the effective level), and behavior A does not change the situation in this respect. The probability that the phase sequence will continue is low. But when the phase sequence occurs that produces B, it promptly results in an increased bombardment of the cortex, increasing the probability of synaptic transmission necessary for the existence of the phase sequence, and the probability that learning will strengthen the phase sequence. This phase sequence, consequently, is likely to recur when next the animal is put into the same situation.

In summary, the hypothesis implies that behavior which causes an *increase* of drive, from a low to a moderate level, will be learned; one that *decreases* drive, from a high to a moderate level, will also be learned; but within the middle ranges of drive level, high enough so that efficient cortical transmission is possible but not high enough to produce incoordination, changes of drive level will not be crucial to learning. In the well-fed, normal waking subject, that is, there need be no change of drive level in order that learning should occur. In the following chapter we shall see that these speculative conceptions have some clarifying value concerning motivation, helping one to understand the higher animal's tendency to both seek and avoid certain kinds of stimulation.

The student should realize, however, that psychological knowledge is in a period of very rapid development and that our present theoretical ideas, none too satisfactory anyway, may be subject to drastic revision at any time. Two recent developments that have not yet been effectively incorporated into the general theory of learning should be mentioned.

One of these concerns "habituation," or "negative adaptation": the disappearance of responsiveness to accustomed stimulation, so that the subject pays no attention to the stimulating event if he is awake or, if asleep, does not wake up. At least in part, the learning not to respond occurs in the arousal system itself. How or where this happens is not known in detail; and the answer when it is obtained may affect our ideas about other learned responses. It is conceivable, for example, that "positive" learning (establishing a new response pattern) depends as much

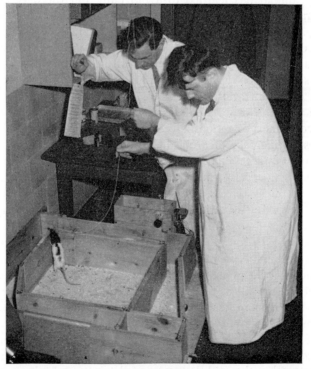

Figure 52.   Rat with implanted electrodes, connected with a light flexible wire so he can move about freely. If the experimenters give a brain stimulation in this corner of the maze, the rat will persist in coming back to it, just as if he were hungry and found food there.

on eliminating wrong movements as on establishing a new connection in the CNS. Learning to type is to a large extent learning not to hit the wrong keys; in the later stages of learning this is very nearly the whole problem. Eliminating wrong responses may not be related to habituation, but there is a parallel here that is possibly very significant.

The second development concerns the existence of possible "pleasure areas" in the brain, whose activity produces reinforcement of learning. In the rat one of these areas is the "septum," just ahead of the hypothalamus. An electrode is inserted into the septum, under anesthesia, and connected with a small block of plastic attached to the skull. When the animal comes out of anesthesia he has, no doubt, a mild headache but actually shows no sign of discomfort and pays no attention to the plastic where it protrudes through the scalp. But now, some days later when the scalp has healed round the block, thin flexible wires can be attached to the ends of the electrodes, and the brain can be stimulated directly while the animal is free to move around (Fig. 52).

When this is done, the animal acts as if it gives him what a human subject would call pleasure. If he is stimulated when he holds his head to the right, he keeps his head on that side; if stimulated whenever he goes to a particular place in a maze, he stays there or returns if he is moved to another place. If he is put in a "Skinner Box" which contains a lever connected with a switch, such that each pressure on the lever gives him electrical stimulation, he keeps on pressing the lever at a high rate (sometimes as high as 2000 or 3000 per hour). It is too soon to say whether the effect is "pleasure" or not (some human actions that are compulsively repeated are not described as having pleasant effects); but it is certainly "reinforcement," by definition, since the animal repeats any action that is followed by the stimulation.

There are other areas in the brain in which stimulation has an opposite effect. Here the animal avoids the action that is followed by stimulation, or will perform any action that stops stimulation by the experimenter. In this case, possibly, pain pathways are being excited. However, neither effect is fully understood as yet, and it may be expected that such experiments will lead to considerable changes in learning theory.

Relation to prior experience: transfer

Learning in the mature animal is based on prior learning, and particularly the learning that occurs during the early growth period. It extends the earlier learning, modifies it, or inhibits it; learning in a new situation at maturity is largely a matter of combining old learnings in a new pattern. What can be learned at maturity, then, depends to a great extent on the learning that has gone before.

Transfer of training refers to this carry-over from previous experience: *positive transfer* when it aids new learning, *negative transfer* when it hinders. There is a large technical literature, into which we shall not go, concerning the conditions in which positive or negative transfer will occur from one task, learned at maturity, to another. Theoretically, we would expect positive transfer when stimulus and response are both similar to those of the original learning; negative, when a new response must be made to an old stimulus, since the earlier S-R connections obviously should conflict with the ones now being set up. In practice, however, it is often hard to say what is a new stimulus or a new response (in view of all the learning done by the subject in other situations), and thus predictions often miss the mark.

Transfer of training from early experience is of great interest. We have seen that ordinary visual learning, as we know it in normal persons, is not possible for the congenitally blind when they are first given sight; only after prolonged exposure to the visual world is there anything like the normal capacity to see something and remember it. Somesthetic learning in the chimpanzee is impaired by lack of some of the usual tactual stimulations of infancy. Maze learning in the rat or dog is impaired if the growing animal lacked experience in finding his way about a complex environment. The learning that normally occurs during infancy, therefore, is prerequisite to the learning capacity with which we are familiar in the adult; that is, adult learning essentially consists, to a large extent, of transfer from the learning of infancy.

If this is so, adult learning is not the acquisition of wholly new connections in the brain (whether from sensory to motor system or in the development of new assemblies) but largely a recombination of connections established earlier.

There is also evidence in the structure of language to show that man characteristically learns to think about new phenomena, or ones that are more difficult to understand, in terms of old phenomena and simpler ones. This evidence is the figures of speech that show how much we think in terms of analogy. The "spring" and "fall" of the year, the "rotation" of the seasons, the person who is "peppery," the "soft heart," or the "iron determination": there is no end of these in everyday language; and scientific language includes them too, as in the "wave" of sound (very different from the visible waves on a beach), or the "cycle" (literally, circle) of weather changes over a period of years; the "island" of Reil and the "aqueduct" of Sylvius in the brain, or the "optic thalamus" (literally, the "inner room" of the third ventricle to which the eye seems connected by the optic nerve); the electrical "resistance" of a wire, the chemical "affinity" (liking) of one substance for another, the electron that "jumps" from one atomic "ring" or "shell" to another; and so on.

There is reason to believe that it is often easier to learn a new use for an old term, in this way, than to learn the meaning of a new term; the figure of speech is an aid to memory. This can only mean that the learning process itself freely utilizes earlier learning, and therefore—once more—that the rate of new learning at maturity depends on transfer from earlier learning.

There is of course no reason to suppose that such transfer is only from infant learning, though this may be where it is most extensive. At maturity, the monkey can acquire a *learning set* (or learning how to learn) when given a number of problems of the same kind. Something (it is not very clear what) happens with the earlier problems in the series which transfers to the later ones, producing much faster learning.

Data from such an experiment are represented in Fig. 53. Two new stimulus objects were presented to the monkey in each problem, and a choice of one was rewarded with food. No cue was given on the first trial as to which was the correct one, so the choice was not counted as either success or failure. But this trial tells which is the right stimulus object, and no error need be made on the second trial. The second trial therefore is the crucial one. In the first series of problems the subjects did little better than chance but after having 80 to 100 such problems they were making over 80 per cent correct choices on second trials, some monkeys solving 20 to 30 problems consecutively with no errors after the first blind trial on each one.

Development of learning sets must be one of the most important features of the educational process. Much of the specific content of what we learn in school disappears completely in a few years as far as any direct use of the material is concerned; but the student still remembers how to attack such material, even when it is not identical with what he has been exposed to before. What he chiefly retains is the learning set.

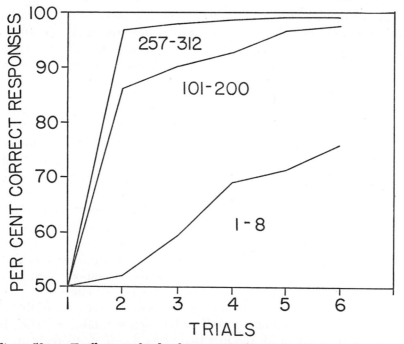

Figure 53.   To illustrate the development of a learning set. Curves of acquisition are shown for the first 8 trials, the second 100 trials, and the last 55. The data are for the first six trials on each problem. Since the monkey has no cue to the correct response on the first trial, this one is at a chance (50 per cent) level; the significant point is the change of performance on the second trial. (After Harlow, 1951.)

We have no very good explanation available as to how learning sets work, in any detail, beyond the possibility that they focus attention on the relevant stimuli; that is, that responses to other stimuli are extinguished as training goes on.

There is one other way in which previous experience with a particular kind of material can promote further learning. This occurs in situations in which the stimuli are not very familiar but become so with further exposure, so that more accurate responses and better learning become possible.

We have already seen that one most important feature of early learning is simply to enable the subject to perceive the objects of his environment. This process is not restricted to the period of infancy. Teaching adult rats to respond selectively to certain aspects of stimulus objects in one situation makes them able to learn better with these stimuli in other situations, even though a new response is to be made. Exposing human subjects to meaningless scribbles, and requiring attention to them, produces a greater distinctiveness in their perceptions of scribbles. In the determination of sensory limens (Chap. 12), the subject tends to get better and better as testing goes on: he develops finer discriminations, even when he is not "rewarded" for the correct response by being told that it is right.

Some of this effect can be understood by supposing that there is a development of cell-assemblies, with a more selective and accurate sorting out of afferent messages to the cortex. Though not all of the effect seems accounted for by this hypothesis, the phenomenon is an important one in the study of learning.

Forgetting and distortions of memory

There are three forms of "forgetting": (1) a simple loss of learning, with *disuse;* (2) temporary *extinction,* considered earlier in this chapter; and (3) what is known as *retroactive inhibition.* Let us look at each of these.

1. The first, disuse, is the ordinary view of forgetting. It seems obvious to common sense that the effects of experience can just disappear if the experience is not repeated. We shall see in a moment that something else can happen: forgetting is often due to some kind of suppression or distortion by later experience—that is, by retroactive inhibition. Most of our experimental evidence, in fact, is concerned with this effect.

But there is also evidence to support the common-sense view that disuse can produce forgetting, as well as retroactive inhibition. The child who has normal vision for the first two years of life or thereabouts and then becomes blind loses all the effects of visual learning; at maturity he is indistinguishable from the congenitally blind. (We have seen, in Chap. 2, that the perception of space and tactual form of the congenitally blind differs from that of persons who have become blind later in life.) These clinical observations have been confirmed experimentally: a chimpanzee was reared normally to the age of 7 months, then in the dark room until 24 months. At 7 months (corresponding to an age of 10 or 11 months in the human baby) he had been making an effective and extensive use of vision; after coming out of the dark room, 17 months later, he had lost all signs of visual learning and made no more response to visual cues than animals reared in the dark room from birth onward.

This loss cannot be wholly attributed to retroactive inhibition. Retroactive inhibition may occur because new responses have replaced old responses to the same stimuli, or because new responses to other stimuli conflict with or suppress the earlier stimulus-response connections. This perhaps would account for some forgetting of responses to visual stimuli, whenever new responses to auditory and tactual stimuli (learned in the dark room) actually prevented one of the earlier-learned visual responses from being made; but it does not account for the disappearance of other responses and the fact that, except for reflexes, the chimpanzee was not responsive at all to his visual environment.

Early visual learning, therefore, is reversible; forgetting can occur by disuse. Clinically, however, it is known that if the human subject has had vision long enough its effects do not disappear. If the child does not become blind until the age of four or five, the learning becomes more "ingrained" and disuse has little or no effect; in these circumstances, the subject never becomes like the congenitally blind.

As to an explanation of these facts, which otherwise might seem very puzzling: the synaptic changes that are the basis of learning may consist of a fluid ("ameboid") outgrowth of the cell wall, making closer connection with another cell. The growing neuron certainly acts in this way, sending out "pseudopods" as an ameba does; if learning also depends on such protrusions, it is possible that with disuse the cell wall slowly retracts, to produce forgetting; and it is possible also that if the connection is maintained for very long periods some further change (like the calcification that makes a child's bones more rigid) may occur to prevent retraction. The learning then would be permanent. But this of course is speculative.

2. The second form of forgetting—which is not forgetting at all, in one sense—is the extinction that occurs with massed trials. Pavlov's evidence indicates that giving the CS repeatedly in a short time without the UCS rapidly builds up inhibition, in some manner that we do not understand, but does not weaken the connections of the CR otherwise. Thus when the animal is brought back into the experimental room next day, when the inhibition has dissipated, the CS elicits the CR again.

Extinction with spaced trials is a different matter. Here there is no spontaneous recovery of the CR. Either the connections are weakened and finally abolished altogether, or—much more probable—we are dealing with the third form of forgetting, to which we turn next.

3. The third form, retroactive inhibition, is an effect of subsequent

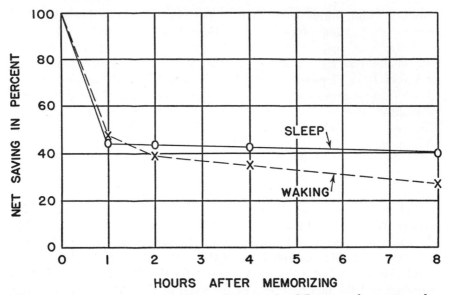

Figure 54.   Retroactive inhibition: shown in the differences of retention when the interval between learning and a later test is spent in sleep, or in waking. (Adapted from Woodworth and Schlosberg, after van Ormer.)

experience upon the retention of what has already been learned. The greatest effects are found when the subsequent experience involves exposure to the same kind of material as that involved in learning. The least effects are obtained when the subject is "experiencing" as little as possible, during sleep. Figure 54 shows retention curves for nonsense syllables, using the method of savings (Chap. 12), for subjects who were tested 1, 2, 4 and 8 hours after the original learning. In one condition, the subjects spent the intervening time in their usual activities; in the other, they slept. The differences are consistently in the direction of higher retention in the sleep condition, and the difference for the 8-hour period is statistically significant (Chap. 11).

This kind of result has been obtained repeatedly, in subjects ranging from the cockroach to man, and there is no doubt that much forgetting is of this nature. Theoretically, it is intelligible that adding further neural connections to those already made can alter the connections between cell-assemblies in such a way as to change the whole nature of the response, even though the original synaptic connections are still there.

The first learning, for example, connects assembly *A* with assembly *B*, which is already connected with assembly *C*. When a stimulus is presented that fires *A*, therefore, the result includes the firing of *B* and *C*, in that order. Now suppose that further experience, without decreasing the strength of any of these connections, *adds* a strong connection between *A* and *C*. Now when the stimulus is presented, firing *A*, the effect is to fire *B* and *C* at the same time, or even to fire *C* before *B*. The response is changed with the changed timing of motor excitation from *B* and *C*.

Many responses that we think of as quite different involve the same

components, but in different combinations or timing. For example: "less" and "sell" would be regarded as quite different responses in a word-learning experiment, but these are made up of the same components in a different order. When we are dealing with more complex responses, the addition of another component or the rearrangement of those already involved would mean that a quite "new" response appears—by the addition or strengthening of synaptic connections, and without any weakening or inhibitory process. Assuming, however, that some of what is "added" is also inhibitory, producing further change without necessarily involving any weakening of the earlier-formed connections, it is evident that retroactive inhibition could produce a forgetting that would be quite different from the weakened connections of disuse.

These ideas have two interesting corollaries. One concerns certain phenomena of memory in old age, the other the distortions of memory that are common in the adult but particularly characteristic of the young child.

1. On memory in old age: suppose that certain combinations of mediating processes are well established in childhood and early manhood, but later overlaid by the addition of further learning, by the retroactive-inhibition mechanism just discussed. The rearrangement would mean a "forgetting" of the earlier learning, the experiences and thoughts of childhood. Perhaps they might be evoked again, with the right stimuli, but most of the time they would simply not recur at all. Now suppose, secondly, that many of the early, long-established, synaptic connections have complete permanence, but that those established in middle age have not. With advancing years (as the degeneration of brain-cells proceeds) the learning that was added in middle age, the learning that produced retroactive inhibition, would regress more than early learning; and the old man would then find himself "thinking of things I haven't thought of for years."

2. The second corollary concerns certain distortions of memory. The theoretical proposals above, concerning retroactive inhibition, imply that the addition or subtraction of elements in a learned pattern can change the nature of that pattern, and might change it out of all recognition.

It is evident that memory for complex events is especially dependent for its accuracy on getting things in the right order. An elementary example: if Susie hits Willie with a stone, and Willie then hits Susie, the later social consequences for Willie will be very different if it should be reported to the parents that Willie threw the first stone. But memory mechanisms are such as to make it quite possible for such a change of order to occur. The sequence of ideas A-B-C can become A-C-B simply by strengthening the A-C connections, with no loss of any element and yet a complete distortion of the whole.

Furthermore, it should be emphasized that memory is not the reinstatement of sensory events, but of the thought processes that the events gave rise to. If a significant feature was not perceived, obviously it cannot be recalled. If what the subject recalls does not make sense to him, he is likely to fill in something that gives it coherence—whether the right coherence or not—and makes what seems to him a sensible picture of the whole incident. It must also be emphasized that this can be done unwittingly; the subject may have no awareness that his later account has been changed by his own rehearsals of the incident. When survivors are questioned in the first few hours after a disaster, the account they give of their own activities, and others', differs greatly from what will be obtained from them a day or two later. Human behavior in such situations is apt to be very peculiar, does not "make sense," and the subject thinking over what happened tries to find sense in it—and thereby changes it. Memory of complex events is to a considerable extent a reconstruction, which may or may not be accurate, but is very unlikely to be accurate when the situation was both emotion-provoking and unfamiliar to the subject. What he remembers eventually is a mixture of his original perceptions and the thoughts he had about those perceptions later.

The practical problems of learning

Laboratory research on learning has in general followed two directions. One is an attempt to find simple cases of learning in order to get at the essentials of the process. What *is* learning? What *is* reinforcement? This line of work, discussed in the preceding pages, is more and more being followed with animal subjects, and as we have seen it has not yet achieved definitive answers.

The other direction is empirical: the study of human learning at a more complex level, with the educational process in mind. It too has presented difficulty in reaching satisfactory generalizations.

There has been a good deal of work, for example, to determine whether children learn better with praise for doing well, or reproof for doing badly. No single answer can be given to this question; it depends on the nature of what is to be learned, the age of the child, his attitude to the teacher, and the situation in which the teaching occurs. Reward (i.e., praise) could be expected to work better than punishment in teaching a complex skill to a fifteen-year-old, but not in teaching a five-year-old to stop breaking windows. The punishment (i.e., reproof) in one social situation may only irritate an adolescent, even making the behavior worse; in another, the same words might cut deep and produce an abrupt cessation of the behavior.

Another problem concerns the use of the "whole method" in learning, as distinct from the "part method." When the student has a poem to memorize, he seems quite naturally to tackle it one verse at a time. It was a valuable discovery to find that learning often goes much better if the student instead tries to learn the whole thing at once. But this does not mean that the whole method is always superior, irrespective of the length of the passage to be learned and the maturity of the learner. The result of much later work, comparing part and whole methods, is that sometimes one is better, sometimes the other.

We should really ask, How big should the units be in learning? and the answer varies with the subject and with the kind of material. In teaching a four-year-old to repeat a poem of three stanzas, each four lines long, it is quite possible that even one stanza is too big a unit to work with; whereas for a fifteen-year-old, it is very likely that the best learning—quickest and most lasting—would be achieved by taking the whole 12 lines as a unit. But if now the fifteen-year-old were to take on *The Ancient Mariner,* he might well find himself making better progress by taking advantage of the author's own subdivision of the poem into seven parts—the whole is too long for effective study.

The "whole method" would be better thought of as the "large-unit" method. It is important for the student to realize that small units tend to be inefficient and that, with practice, he can increase the size of unit that he can work with effectively. One main difficulty with large units is that motivation suffers; at first one seems to be making no progress, and becomes discouraged, but if one persists this may change rather suddenly. Frequently one obtains the best results by use first of large units, then concentration on a smaller segment where one has difficulty, and finally a return to the larger one: that is, a combination of "whole" and "part" methods.

A final practical problem concerns the distribution of practice. The student naturally would like to know how to allocate his time so as to get the most results for the fewest hours of study (not to mention the least effort). This is the question of *massed* versus *spaced practice,* and here again the answer varies with the individual and the material to be learned. This statement, like the similar ones in the preceding paragraphs, may appear to be of no practical usefulness, just avoiding the issue; but the student should interpret it as telling him that he can experiment with his study methods so as to find out what works best with him for any given material. Being disinclined to study uninteresting material that others thrust on him, the student tends to let the work pile up until it can be avoided no longer, and then slave at it until it is done. Sometimes this works surprisingly well—it is the only way some of us ever get some jobs done—but on the whole it produces less results for more effort; and spaced learning, of ten minutes, half an hour or an hour at a time, generally produces much more with much less pain.

The big problem here is motivation. The student who has trouble studying should regard himself and his work habits as a behavioral problem that can be solved. In what circumstances, and with what methods of study, can I make myself *like* work? There need be no taint of nobility about this attitude: even if a man is lazy, wanting just to get through the course with as little pain as possible, ordinary intelligence will tell him he would be better off to fool himself into enjoying the work, and doing it the easiest way.

Many another man who is not lazy, who wants to do as well as he can, has failed because of not finding out how to study. In every class there is a group of students who have not found this out. Many of these students think that one studies a book on history, for example, by passively reading. Then, when they find their attention wandering, they frown harder (this is what they call "concentration") and read some more.

The lack of various devices to make reading *active* distinguishes these people from those who know how to study. Making a précis, reading through hastily to find first the main points before getting down to details; hunting through the chapter to find things one can disagree with, or could formulate better; looking for the evidence that bears on an idea of one's own: these approaches to a book—analyzing it, recasting it, criticizing it—are very different from simply reading with intent to remember. Because they keep attention focussed on the material, they lead to much better recollection of the whole thing.

This is not a text on study method, however; the student who is having trouble with study should consult his instructor for the name of a good book on the topic. Then, as suggested above, the student should treat himself as a problem in motivation; he will find that the problem is soluble.

Summary

Learning can be, and is, studied at different levels of complexity. The fundamental principles remain somewhat obscure; as a result, psychologists for the present are concentrating on theoretical issues rather than the practical problems of the student.

The present chapter presents some further aspects of conditioning (a topic introduced in Chap. 2): conditioned inhibition, the higher-order CR, and extinction. Also, the fact that the CR is not identical with the UCR raises the problem of reinforcement.

The first requirement, if a given stimulus is to evoke a learned response, is a repeated contiguity in time, S followed by R. But this is not sufficient, because the repetition in some cases results in a disappearance of the response, or some components of the response, instead of strengthening the connection. Reinforcement is an event following the response that determines whether it will continue to be made or not.

How reinforcement works is the crucial question, still unsolved. Various theoretical ideas are outlined, including the earlier "law of effect" and the more recent ideas of primary reinforcement by drive reduction as well as secondary reinforcement. A possible hypothesis concerning drive reduction, relating it to arousal, suggests that drive reduction is reinforcing only when drive is at a very high level.

It appears generally true that learning is a function of earlier learning, an influence referred to as transfer of training. Transfer may be positive (promoting the present learning) or negative (hindering it). Learning set is a form of positive transfer, a "learning how to learn" which must be an important part of what the student gets from the formal educational process.

Three forms of forgetting are discussed: disuse, transient extinction and retroactive inhibition. Either disuse or retroactive inhibition can produce forgetting, independently. The nature of transient extinction is not understood (it may be a conditioned inhibition, as Pavlov held), but permanent extinction seems to be a form of retroactive inhibition. A hypothesis of retroactive inhibition is discussed, which would account for some puzzling features of memory in old age and the distortions of memory that commonly occur when describing a complex event.

The practical problem in this field is to know how to study better, or how to teach in the classroom. Studying and teaching are complicated by many factors, so the general principles of learning, as we know them today, are subject to exceptions when applied in the particular case. Teaching remains an art: we do not yet have the kind of information that would enable us to take any intelligent student and make a good teacher of him. As to the art of study, some acquire it with little aid, others need advice; for these latter, there are no specific rules to be given that guarantee success and each one should regard himself as an experimental problem, and find out what particular procedures work in his case.

Notes

A general account of the present state of learning theory may be found in E. R. Hilgard, *Theories of Learning*, 2nd ed., D. Appleton-Century-Crofts Co., 1956, or in B. R. Bugelski, *The Psychology of Learning*, Henry Holt & Co., 1956. An earlier but still valuable book is E. R. Hilgard and D. G. Marquis, *Conditioning and Learning*, D. Appleton-Century, 1940. A first-hand account of learning set can be found in Harlow, Chap. 7 of Stone, *Comparative Psychology*, 3rd ed., Prentice-Hall, 1951.

Discussion of the effect of increased familiarity with the stimuli in a learning situation is based on the experiments of D. H. Lawrence (*J. Exp. Psychol.*, 1950, 40, 175–188) and J. J. Gibson and E. Gibson (*Psychol. Rev.*, 1955, 62, 32–41).

The loss of visual learning when a child becomes blind before the age of two years or so seems to be part of the common lore of ophthalmologists; however, there is some experimental evidence to back this up:

see the papers of Révész, Sylvester, and Carr cited in *Notes* for Chapter 6 (p. 130). Further, Riesen's paper (cited there also) establishes the point clearly for the young chimpanzee.

The reference to rat learning, when the animal is put in the maze with no food present and tested later with food in the food box, is based on a paper by K. MacCorquodale and P. E. Meehl (*J. Comp. Physiol. Psychol,* 1951, 44, 367–371), reporting a modification of Blodgett's earlier experiment. The work on habituation (negative adaptation) was done by S. K. Sharpless and H. Jasper (*Brain,* 1956, 79, 655–680); that on "pleasure areas" in the brain by J. Olds and P. M. Milner (*J. Comp. Physiol. Psychol.,* 1954, 47, 419–427). For brain stimulation producing avoidance, see N. E. Miller, *Amer. Psychologist,* 1958, 13, 100–108.

The "chimpomat" experiments (on token reward with chimpanzees: Wolfe, and Cowles) will be found in any of the *General References,* p. 19.

Chapter 8

Motivation: needs, drives and emotions

THE term *motivation* refers to two rather different problems: (1) What makes an animal active rather than inactive? and (2) What makes one form of activity dominant over others, so that the animal for example seeks food instead of water, or persists in nest-building instead of seeking food?

The terms *need* and *drive* are closely related. Need produces an unstable equilibrium in the relation of the organism to its environment: a condition in which the animal is impelled to persistent activity until equilibrium is restored. Drive is a theoretical conception; it is the mechanism of motivation which is thrown into activity when a need exists. The *biologically primitive* needs occur when there is some lack in the conditions which are necessary to survival of the individual or the species; these are the needs for oxygen, water, food, maintenance of normal body temperature, the need to copulate at certain times (depending on endocrine processes) and to foster the young, and the need to avoid damage to bodily tissues. These are biologically primitive since they occur early in phylogenesis—otherwise the more highly evolved species would not have developed and would not now continue to exist—but they are not all psychologically primitive, or simple in their manner of operation. The need of oxygen or water, for example, is about the same in all mammals; but the drive that is involved in sexual need has evolved in higher

155

mammals at the same time as other behavioral mechanisms, and is more complex in the higher mammals than in lower ones.

Emotion is difficult to define precisely, or to use as a technical term. It refers to such states as joy, love, pride, jealousy, anger, grief and fear. The nature of all these is hard to comprehend in a single general statement. Emotion can be both organizing (making adaptation to the environment more effective) and disorganizing, both energizing and debilitating, both sought after and avoided. All that the various forms of emotion have in common, to justify the use of a single term, seems to be that the subject's motivation is somehow in a special state. The subject is "e-moved," "moved out of himself," likely to act for the time in a more or less unusual way.

The deviation from normal, however, occurs in several directions. It may be (1) in the strength or persistence of the subject's response; (2) a hyper-responsiveness to stimulation, with a lowered limen for trivial stimuli (e.g., "nervousness" or "irritability"); or (3) a kind of overflow phenomenon, with the occurrence of irrelevant, inappropriate or conflicting responses in addition to, or in place of, the appropriate response: crying, blushing, trembling, excessive autonomic activity, "shouting for joy," or the peculiar disturbance of breathing and vocalization that we call laughter.

We may think of "emotion," therefore, as more a commonsense than a scientific term; what it appears to mean is, crudely, that something exceptional is going on inside the subject. It concerns the subject's motivation in general, but does not refer to any one specific motivational process.

Motivation and drive

We may assume that the original problem of motivation, for primitive man, was to understand how the organism could move itself, unlike the sticks and stones which are moved only by forces external to them. Movement must have a cause, and the cause was conceived of as a demon of some sort inside the organism (a demon is not necessarily evil) to move the limbs. But such animism was not a very satisfactory solution, since it only transferred the problem to a new locus: what moves the demon? As knowledge of anatomy and physiology accumulated, scientists began to think in terms of various analogies with machines. Now a machine has two properties that affect one's thinking in this matter.

First, power has to be supplied, either from outside or from a special power source built into the machine, separate from the gears and connections that determine what *kind* of action is performed. Secondly, the operation of the machine is controlled from outside. A button is pressed, light falls on a photoelectric cell, or the handle of a valve is turned, to start or stop it and to determine how much power the machine will develop. With these things in mind, and observing that animals are sometimes inactive, sometimes active in varying degree, it is inevitable that one should tend to think of the animal's nervous system as containing something like a power system (or systems) apart from its S-R and mediational connections—which are the steering mechanism—and of stimuli from the environment as pushing the buttons that turn on the power system.

Thus we arrive at the conception of drive: some process which provides the energy of movement but which, like the engine of an automobile, does not determine what the movement will be. Stimuli then have two different roles in behavior. One, which we shall call the *arousal function,* is to make the animal active, or tend to do so, apart from determining what form his activity will take. The other, the *cue function,* guides the response; it determines whether arousal is to be channeled into fighting or fleeing, whether a right turn is made instead of a left turn, and so on; it may even, like a driver throwing out the clutch, determine that the arousal is not to initiate movement at all, as when a hungry cat remains motionless until the robin is within reach.

The same stimulus may have both arousal and cue functions. The smell of food can excite hunger (a tendency to seek food) and also guide to where the food is; feeling a pinprick may both initiate movement of the hand and guide the direction of movement, away from the pin. Often, however, different stimuli serve these two functions: when hunger pains, from rhythmic contractions of the empty stomach, are the arousers of hunger, the eyes or nose must provide the guidance to food. A high air temperature may initiate a search for a cool place, but not guide the search.

Such conceptions work well over a wide range of behavior, so well that we cannot abandon them. Certain qualifications however are necessary, because the analogy between an animal and a machine is of course limited. The animal is not made up of inert parts but of living cells, each of which is as it were a separate engine—that is, it gets its energy direct from the blood stream, not from another cell specialized for the purpose. The energy of muscular response does not come from the CNS; nor does the energy of neural response come from one part of the CNS, or from the stimulus. A stimulus *triggers* neural firing, but all neurons are being provided continuously with energy from the extracellular fluids surrounding them, and if they are not triggered tend eventually to fire anyway. Spontaneous neural activity occurs in this sense.

It therefore becomes quite comprehensible that an animal might be active without any special prodding from the environment. When an animal moves from one place to another, the reason need not be a particular stimulation. The animal may in fact have moved because the level of stimulation was low. Essentially, animals are made to be active, and will be active. However, though all this is true, and though it seems to make the drive idea unnecessary, we actually cannot abandon the idea.

The spontaneous activity of neural units is uncoordinated, and can have little effect on behavior, unless there is activity in the nonspecific projection system (Chap. 4). This in turn depends on afferent input to the system; therefore, though no one *particular* stimulus is always needed to initiate an animal's movement, behavioral activity still requires a background of sensory stimulation. The CNS is made up of some 10 billion neurons, and the spontaneous firing of widely scattered individual neurons could have little observable effect. Even the neuron that is directly connected with a group of muscle cells would produce only a slight momentary twitch. Significant effects on behavior must result from coordinated activity in large numbers of cells. Normally, this is possible only when environmental stimulation is maintaining activity in the arousal system (abnormally, it also occurs on a small scale in tics, cramps, etc., and on a large scale in the epileptic convulsion).

Thus activity in the arousal system has the essential characteristics of a drive: it does not literally provide the energy of response, but it determines whether the energy will be available or not, without determining how it is to be directed. Also, by identifying drive with activity in the arousal system we become able to see how a stimulus can have both cue function and arousal function, since the afferent pathways branch in the brain stem to pass through both the specific projection systems (cues) and the nonspecific (arousal).

Is there more than one drive? The arousal system may be a single, generalized drive mechanism which can be excited by different conditions, including primitive needs as well as others; alternatively, there may be a pain drive, a hunger drive, a sex drive and so forth, involving different segments of the arousal system—presumably with parts of it in common, but also with other parts specialized for the separate drives.

SINGLE-DRIVE THEORY.   An older, unsuccessful attempt to simplify the problem proposed that all primitive motivations can be reduced to some form of pain from which the organism is trying to escape. Hunger was equated with pain from the empty stomach ("hunger pangs"), thirst with sensations from a dry mouth and throat, maternal motivation with discomfort from distended mammary glands which create a need to suckle the young, and so on. This is now known to be unsatisfactory. The patient whose stomach is removed surgically still is motivated to eat; thirst occurs before dryness is detectable in mouth or throat, and the desire to drink is not decreased when a large part of the region is anesthetized (in the patient, for example, who is suffering from throat cancer). Maternal motivation, and care of the young as far as it is possible, appear unimpaired when the mammary glands are removed surgically from experimental animals.

In addition, the motivation to explore and to manipulate the environment, or to escape from conditions of monotony, is very hard to explain on the basis of escaping from pain or conditions associated with pain. Pain motivation is extremely powerful and, through the process of secondary reinforcement (p. 138f.) and the acquired motivation to avoid stimuli previously associated with pain, can affect behavior in many situations in which no pain actually occurs; but it seems clear that there are aspects of motivation that cannot be reduced to this one drive.

The other single-mechanism theory of motivation which we may consider is that of the arousal system, the assumption that there is one drive state which differs only in the degree to which arousal occurs. This is the best unifying conception that is available to us at present, but it too is probably unsatisfactory as it now stands.

This theory implies that anger and fear, for example, have the same common core of undirected, and undirecting, emotional excitation (i.e., arousal), and that the differences which obviously exist between these two states lie in the cue functions, not in the kind of arousal. In anger, for example, the stimulus excites the arousal system, and also excites S-R connections and mediational processes that result in attacking behavior. In fear, the stimulus excites the *same* drive state, but different cue functions, which determine flight.

Some of the facts support this idea. In some circumstances fear readily turns to anger, suggesting that they are closely related. The victim of a practical joke who is first frightened, then becomes angry when he perceives the situation, is an example; a comparable case is that of a chimpanzee who, not hearing the experimenter approach, showed startle and fear on being touched, and then when she saw what had happened became angry. Here it does not seem that the arousal itself differs, and the distinction between anger and fear in these cases seems to lie in cue functions only. Testosterone in the blood stream facilitates both sexual behavior and pugnacity in the male, and it has been suggested on occasion that sexual arousal and jealousy in the female have some connection. It is very frequently observed that sexual excitement can overflow into aggression, even to the extent that the sexual behavior drops out and the male or female simply attacks the partner. Contrariwise, generalized excitement appears to contribute to sexual arousal in many circumstances. Finally, studies of emotional development in infancy have led some workers to the conclusion that there is first an undifferentiated emotional disturbance from which the more specific emotional states arise, to some degree at least as a product of learning (which means that the differentiation would lie in the cue function).

However, there are difficulties. It has already been suggested (p. 79) that the arousal system probably does not function in a unitary way, differing only in the amount of activity, since it is not a single mass of cells and fibers but consists of a number of discrete nuclei, highly organized separate structures, in which the *pattern* of activity could be highly variable. This would imply that drive states would vary qualitatively as well as quantitatively, and some of the behavioral evidence agrees with this.

For example, testosterone does not equally facilitate fear and rage in the male. It should do so if the arousal in the two cases is the same. Or we may take the example of fear and laughter. Both can produce strong muscular effects, which may be very disorganizing: a man may be "helpless with laughter," or "paralyzed with fear." The widespread disturbance in both cases may be regarded as due to overflow in the CNS, the excitation of arousal spreading to motor pathways which serve no adaptive purpose at the moment. But the pattern of overflow is clearly different in the two cases and, if it is directly due to the arousal, the latter must differ also. The time course of arousal in laughter and in fear differs as well, recovery from laughter being much quicker. We have no good experimental basis at present for a final conclusion, but it seems that we must recognize that there is at least some qualitative variation in the arousal function.

MULTI-DRIVE THEORY.   The difficulty encountered by a theory of multiple drives is that once we begin postulating separate drives to account for different classes of action, we find that we have to postulate too many. Among those that have been proposed are a pain drive, a hunger drive, a thirst drive and a sex drive. All are biologically primitive, of long standing in evolution and thus with equally good claims for entry in the list. To this it seems we must add a maternal drive (or parental drive, in view of the protective behavior of the male toward the young of many species) and, as we shall see below, an exploratory drive. Further, we must also provide for certain powerful causes of emotional disturbance such as loud noise, loss of support, the fear of snakes in primates, or the anger that results from certain social situations. No satisfactory simplifying assumptions have been found to reduce this list to reasonable length. The most plausible approach, perhaps, is to assume separate drives for the biologically primitive needs, each with its own pattern of activity in the brain-stem arousal system but still overlapping others, and to assume that other drive states originate in cortical processes and the "down-flow" action of cortex upon the brain stem.

Acquired motivations, real and apparent

The problem of the number of drives, one or many, is not solved. It is important to recognize, however, that we do not have to assume the existence of a special drive for each different form of behavior. Even though we have not succeeded so far in reducing all motivations to a single drive, we do know that many apparently special and distinctive motivations have actually arisen from a more primitive and general one, by a process of learning. These we may call acquired motivations.

A stimulus can acquire drive properties by being associated with a primitive need or its satisfaction. This has been shown by a number of experiments, and is illustrated here by two examples.

Rats were placed one at a time in an apparatus with two compartments, one black, one white. They showed no clear preference for either. Then each rat was placed in the white compartment and given an electric shock through a grid in the floor. Ten trials were given in this initial training period, the rat being permitted each time to escape to the black compartment. Then a door was closed between the two halves of the apparatus, which could be opened by moving a wheel placed near the door. Now the rat was put in the white compartment, but *without* shock. The drive-producing properties of the stimuli formerly associated with shock were clearly shown by the disturbed behavior of the animals and their attempts to escape—though they were not subject now to pain. Most of the animals made contact with the wheel in their attempts to pass the door, and moved it enough to make the door open. These animals learned promptly to move the wheel and escape. The situation which was originally neutral was no longer so, but aroused strong avoidance.

The second example is from an experiment referred to in Chapter 7, in which a neutral object acquired motivating properties which were positive instead of negative. Young chimpanzees were trained to exchange poker chips for food. When this was established, the animals would work for poker chips as their reward, even when they were not able to exchange the chip immediately but had to accumulate from 10 to 30 of them first.

These two experiments provide genuine examples of learned motivation, which in various forms must pervade the behavior of the higher animal. Now let us look further. It was an important feature of the above experiments that the object sought or avoided was more or less neutral in the first place, having in itself negligible motivating properties. When the test object is not neutral, however, false conclusions may be drawn from such experiments.

For example, it is possible to produce a strong avoidance response in a young child (about the age of 9 months) with a white rat as test object. The rat is offered to the child and as the child reaches for it a sudden loud noise is produced, which causes crying and withdrawal. This is repeated several times, until the child whimpers and avoids the rat whenever it is offered to him. Similarly, since sudden loss of support also produces emotional disturbance and crying in the young child, a fear of dogs may result when the unsteadily walking child is upset by a friendly dog. Both fears, of the rat experimentally associated with loud noise, and of dogs after being knocked down by one, seem to be learned. But this is only partly true. A child does not fear tricycles even after having fallen off one repeatedly; tumbling downstairs may make him a little more cautious, but not much. And experimentally, if one tries to condition fear of a block of wood or a piece of glass in the same way as described above for a rat, one does not succeed. Certain stimulus objects, among them insects and small mammals, have some property that makes such conditioning very easy in primates. Furthermore, fears of these very objects are found in the adult primate in circumstances in which no conditioning process can have occurred: namely, on the first exposure to the stimulus object. These "spontaneous" fears are not learned, though other learning is prerequisite; they increase in frequency and strength as the child grows. Such facts show clearly that a child's fear of animals is only in part a product of conditioning, which may serve to reinforce a response tendency in which psychological maturation is also involved.

Fear of snakes and certain strange objects

The fear of snakes is the extreme example of the way in which maturation can be involved in motivational development. Because it does not usually occur in small children it has been thought to be learned. Also, it may not develop at all in the child who has frequent opportunities to play with snakes during growth. But this, it seems, is evidence that such children have learned *not* to fear snakes, rather than that others have learned to do so.

We have two pieces of experimental evidence to guide us here. First, a study was made of the attitude toward snakes among a group of city children and adolescents (up to the age of 17 years). These subjects had not been exposed to a snake before. A somewhat sluggish snake was presented, the subject being shown that it was harmless. Avoidance was found to increase with age, both in frequency and in intensity. The experimenters gave rather convincing reasons for their conclusion that the responses could not be accounted for as due to a fear of being injured.

However, literature is full of very unfavorable references to snakes; perhaps verbal learning accounted for the behavior, in some way that is not very clear (in view of all the other things which are really dangerous but not feared in this culture—such as going on an automobile trip, or crossing a busy city street). The second piece of experimental evidence rules out this explanation.

All adult chimpanzees fear snakes; the strength and frequency of the avoidance response increase with maturation, just as in man; and it has been shown that the chimpanzee that never saw a snake before—and certainly did not learn to fear one through conversation or reading—shows just as strong a fear response as another chimpanzee or a man. The fear of snakes is therefore spontaneous in primates (as well as in some other animals). That is, the avoidance response does not have to be practiced, and is not based on association with some other, more primitive, source of fear, such as pain.

However, a further point must be recognized. Such fears are not learned, but they require that certain other learning has taken place. This learning is the perceptual development produced by exposure to the animal's ordinary environment, classified under the heading of Factor IV (p. 121). Though we have no detailed information as to how it works, there is some form of conflict between the effects of the present sensory input and the reaction patterns set up by past experience. The normal environment of the species establishes certain ways of reacting to common sensory events; after this has happened, and only then, the sight of a snake can have its disruptive effect.

Our most definite information about this kind of process comes from the reaction to strangers by the infant primate. It is not observed until the age of about four months in the chimpanzee, or six months in man. It does not usually occur if the infant has always been exposed to the sight of many different persons; but when he is used to seeing only a small number of persons (the regular caretakers or members of the family group) the close approach of a stranger produces something called "shyness," though it may actually be as violent as any fear based on pain.

In the normally reared infant the response is at full strength on the first exposure, showing that it is not learned. But if the chimpanzee has been reared in darkness, or if the human child has had congenital cataract until after six or eight months of age and has then been operated on, the response does not occur at all on first exposure. The infant must first become visually familiar with a small group of persons, which takes a month or so for the chimpanzee after coming out of the dark room; only after this does a stranger evoke the fear reaction.

The reaction is therefore not independent of learning. Also, it is not produced by a generalized susceptibility to any new stimulus. If it were, it should appear at the time of the first visual experience, when the chimpanzee is brought out of the dark room, or the cataract removed from the human eye. It seems instead that "fear of the strange" is a fear produced by events that combine the familiar and the unfamiliar—not by the totally unfamiliar event.

This implies that some kind of conflict is involved. The conclusion is strongly supported by the following observation. Dr. R. and Mr. T. are regular attendants in a chimpanzee nursery; the infants are attached to both, and eagerly welcome being picked up by either. Now, in full sight of the infants, Dr. R. puts on Mr. T.'s coat. At once he evokes fear reactions identical with those made to a stranger, and just as strong. An unfamiliar combination of familiar things, by itself, can therefore produce a violent emotional reaction.

As normal development proceeds, both chimpanzee and human child steadily widen their experience; objects that are strange and exciting to the infant are no longer so to the adult. But this does not necessarily mean that the adult has become less subject to emotional arousal. He is less sensitive to some stimulating situations, but more so to others. We have seen that this kind of arousal depends on previously learned processes. In some situations the previous learning that is necessary may take a long time, so the conflict can occur only in older subjects. One example is the so-called fear of the dark, which does not occur until the age of three years or so. What the subject really fears is the horrendous creatures conjured up by his imagination. Until the development of mediating processes has gone far enough to make such imaginings possible, darkness can hold no terrors.

Another important example is the emotional disturbance produced by dead or mutilated bodies. Like the fear of snakes, this may never appear in the subject to whom such objects are familiar from early infancy on; also, it can be minimized or abolished by prolonged exposure at maturity, in the soldier, the medical student or the undertaker's assistant; but, as a visit to the dissecting room by the inexperienced subject will show, the reaction is likely to be powerful on the first exposure, and there is good reason to conclude that this too is not a learned response but a form of conflict. It appears of course also in the operating room and in milder form with exposure to persons who have recovered from grossly mutilating injuries (especially to the face).

Once more there is evidence from experimental work with chimpanzees to show that the varied but strong reaction to such stimuli is not due to prior verbal learning alone. We have already seen (p. 36) that the adult chimpanzee is panic-stricken at the sight of a model of a chimpanzee (or human) head. Other parts of the body have similar but weaker effect. This is clearly related to the human behavior we are considering. The strength of response is least in the younger subject, and this is probably true also of the human child exposed to horror stories from Andersen or Grimm or scenes of violence on television. Whether these things are good or bad educationally, it should be recognized that their emotional impact for the child is likely to be much less than for the adult.

Primitive motivations and homeostasis

Let us turn now to the motivations that are directly related to biologically primitive needs. An important conception here is that of *homeostasis*, which may be defined as the process by which a constant internal state is maintained in the organism.

For example, breathing is part of the homeostatic mechanism that tends to maintain a constant level of oxygen and carbon dioxide in the blood stream. If the CO_2 level falls, or if the O_2 level rises, breathing slows down and reverses the trend. A rise of CO_2 and a fall of O_2 cause faster breathing. Certain receptors in the brain stem (for CO_2) and in the carotid artery and aorta (for O_2) act like the home thermostat that turns on the furnace when the temperature falls, and cuts it off when the temperature rises. The body of course has its temperature-regulating mechanism also. When body temperature rises above the normal limits, sweating and panting occur: these are heat-reducing. When it falls, shivering occurs: this is heat-producing.

The oxygen–carbon-dioxide mechanisms, and those regulating temperature, function reflexively. As long as a reflexive mechanism is adequate, so that the rest of the nervous system is not called into play, we do not consider the homeostatic process to be motivational (i.e., it does not produce arousal, nor affect the course of other behavior). But when the reflex process is inadequate, motivation is affected at once. If breathing for example is interfered with[1] there is a prompt and vigorous reaction from higher neural centers that dominates all other activity. Ordinarily, the need of oxygen remains at a reflexive level and does not often involve motivation. Temperature needs however differ. Because the temperatures to which man is exposed daily go well beyond the capacity of the sweating-shivering mechanism, maintenance of body temperature within normal limits involves the general course of behavior rather than being reflexive only. The motivation that is involved in the search for warmth or coolness is the activity of a homeostatic process.

Hunger and thirst are also homeostatic mechanisms, since they act to produce behavior whose direct effect, in turn, is to maintain the normal concentration of certain substances in the blood stream. The motivation to avoid pain is not as clear a case; it does not directly concern the constancy of the internal environment, but it does act in the long run to do so by preventing injury to the defensive barrier of the skin, for example, or the loss of blood. But the remaining primitive motivation with which we are concerned here—sexual motivation—is clearly not a homeostatic one. Copulation does not act to raise sex hormones in the blood stream to a normal level, or lower them from a higher level.

Behavior can be considered homeostatic only if its effect is to regulate the internal environment, correcting deviations from some zero point or norm, and sex behavior as far as we know does not do so. Motivation may therefore be biologically primitive, and very powerful, without being homeostatic.

HUNGER AND THIRST.   We shall define hunger as the central neural activity that causes eating. There are a number of hungers for different substances, one of which is water; technically, therefore, thirst may be treated as a "hunger" for water.

A short-term learning is involved to a different degree in different hungers. Experimentally, we take the laboratory rat that has always had food available, and remove the food from his cage for 24 hours. The food is then put back, and eating times are recorded. We find that in

---

[1] But not if there is merely too low a level of oxygen in the air that is breathed, since pilots have to be specially trained to put on their oxygen masks at the proper altitude. This lack of an automatic protective reaction is like the lack of a pain reaction to strong ultraviolet light: the warning signals come too late, after the damage (sunburn) is done.

the first 60 seconds the experimental animal eats no more than the control animal which has food present continuously; in one experiment with 10 rats, the range of times spent eating was from 0 to 55 seconds. In the next five minutes, however, the rate of eating increased. As the experiment was continued, making food available for a 30-minute period daily, the eating behavior in the first 60 seconds of each day changed, and by the tenth day or so every animal ate voraciously at the first presentation of food. (The same experiment with water deprivation gives a different result: a definite thirst appears quickly. Either learning is not involved in the same way, or it is more rapid.)

A sudden, acute lack of food does not produce a strong motivation in the subject that has not experienced it before. A rat does not run well in the maze, for a food reward, until he has been put on a 24-hour feeding schedule for some time; only with repeated experience of hunger, followed by eating, will the rat work energetically for food. In human subjects, similarly, an acute need of food in the previously well-fed subject is far from being as strong a source of motivation as chronic starvation; in the latter case the need may dominate behavior completely.

The homeostasis of hunger is selective for a number of substances—carbohydrate, protein, fats, vitamins and salts—as well as for water. The animal whose food lacks calcium salts, for example, will prefer to drink a solution of a calcium salt rather than plain tap water. If the diet lacks fat, or thiamine, a food choice is made that tends to correct the lack. But learning is again involved in some of these choices. The adjustment is not always automatic and immediate. Learning can also interfere with the adjustment, since prior food habits ("dislike" for a particular taste, for example) may make the animal avoid the protein that it needs. In man particularly, earlier-established food habits can seriously interfere with homeostatic regulation.

ARTIFICIAL HUNGER: ADDICTION.   The various addictions of this society, to caffeine, nicotine or alcohol as well as to less frequently used drugs such as morphine or cocaine, are commonly referred to as "habits." They are not merely bad habits, however, like eating with one's knife, or mispronouncing some word. "Habit" implies learning, and this is certainly involved in addiction as it is in hunger; but like hunger, the addiction has the further effect of maintaining the level of a specific substance in the blood stream. In short, an addiction is a homeostatic process, even though the presence of the drug in the blood stream was not originally necessary, or biologically desirable. Once the addiction is well established the drug becomes necessary to stable neural functioning, and lack of it can be very strongly motivating.

There are two stages in the establishment of morphine addiction and presumably of others also: an intermediate stage of physiological dependence, and addiction proper. When young chimpanzees were given injections of morphine daily, physiological dependence developed in five or six weeks. Now when the animal was not given his injection he showed the typical signs of disturbance physiologically, with restlessness, yawning, scratching and so forth; these are called withdrawal symptoms. The chimpanzee was clearly "unhappy" but at this intermediate stage had not yet learned that it was the injection that made him comfortable again. If it was omitted, he did nothing about it.

The experiment required one to three months of further injections before addiction proper occurred. Now the animal would try hard to get the injection, dragging the experimenter to where the drug and hypodermic needle were kept, taking out the needle from its case and handing it to the experimenter, and so on (Fig. 55). At this stage, the chimpanzee would do anything in its power to get the injection, and now the need of the drug had become powerfully motivating.

In human beings who know that they are taking a drug, and know that it is the drug that produces the feeling of well-being, the intermediate stage and true addiction may coincide. Essentially, however, the two stages represent different kinds of process, the first being some physiological modification of bodily tissues, so that they now require the presence of the drug for "normal" (i.e., reasonably stable) functioning. Without it, there is irritability, restlessness, and disturbance of work habits and social behavior. The second is a learning process.

There is a good deal of evidence to indicate that there are considerable constitutional differences, from one person to another, which determine susceptibility to addiction. It is often thought that alcoholism, for example, is simply an attempt to escape from personal troubles, or is due to some form of neurosis. This may be partly true, but there are some neurotics who fail to solve their problems this way, and despite using alcohol do not become alcoholics. Others with little emotional excuse become addicted at once. It seems clear that emotional difficulties are often the decisive factor that turns the susceptible person into an alcoholic; but it also seems that physiological susceptibility is not the same for all persons. For some, alcohol is a deadly poison because of its capacity for rapidly making, in these persons, a homeostatic modification which is

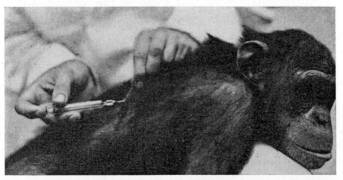

Figure 55.   Frank voluntarily taking an injection of morphine. (Courtesy of Yerkes Laboratories of Primate Biology.)

in effect irreversible and which thereafter is likely to dominate behavior, with personally and socially disastrous consequences.

PAIN.   Pain in normal persons appears to comprise two distinguishable processes: one a sensory event, the other a central reaction with a strong motivational component.

The most striking feature of pain as a sensory process is its tendency to take control of the animal's whole behavior. Unless light or sound becomes very intense it can be disregarded for fairly long periods (i.e., the animal may not respond at all to visual, or auditory, cues); but even a weak pain stimulus tends to be dominant over all others in determining the direction of behavior. How this comes about we do not know.

The afferent excitation is carried to the CNS principally by C-fibers, the smallest and most slowly-conducting ones in peripheral nerves. These produce an unconditioned flexion reflex in the limb, which of course tends to break contact with the noxious agent and prevent the occurrence of injury. The excitation is conducted from the spinal cord to the brain by special pathways separate from those concerned with touch and proprioception. So far this is consistent with treating pain simply as a sensory process. But the special pathways do not reach the cortex. This presumably is why any part of the cortex may be cut, burned or electrically stimulated by the neurosurgeon operating on a fully conscious patient, without causing pain. At the level of midbrain and thalamus the pathways become more complex, but their influence on cortical function appears to be solely via diffuse fibers, with no specialized area for pain.

At this level, therefore, pain may be more a motivational state, a generalized emotional reaction, than a sensation. Patients suffering from intractable pain are sometimes subjected to frontal lobotomy (p. 84) at a level which is anterior to sensory pathways. These patients give us a very curious report after operation: they say that the pain is the same as before the operation—but it no longer bothers them as it did. They are still able to identify the sensory event—that is, to recognize a pain stimulus—as well as before, but the pain has lost much of its dominating control of behavior.

Animal experiments suggest that some of the motivational aspects of pain are a product of normal experience during growth (Factor IV). The chimpanzee reared with cardboard tubes over hands and feet, preventing normal somesthetic experience and presumably with little or no experience of pain (p. 119), reacted very differently from normal animals to pinprick. Dogs reared in extreme isolation from the normal environment (p. 127), and with no experience of pain except what they may have inflicted on themselves, showed a most extraordinary unresponsiveness to noxious stimulation. They made little observable response to pinprick, or to having a tail stepped on. They would investigate a lighted paper match by putting a nose into the flame (thus extinguishing it); when another was lighted, it was investigated in the same way, and this was repeated on successive days of testing, with no evidence of emotional reaction. A normal control dog, if he had not encountered flame before, might put his nose into it once, but would not do so again. For the experimental animals, it was evident, pain stimuli had not acquired the same dominance as for the normal.

We cannot be certain as yet concerning the meaning of such data, but it appears that some of the problems concerning pain would be much less puzzling if this interpretation is sound: namely, that "pain" as the term is ordinarily used refers both to a discriminable sensory event, which in itself does not have strongly motivating properties, and to a motivational state to which the sensory event gives rise on the basis of past experience with pain. In short, it is suggested that "pain" in normal subjects is to a large extent an acquired motivation.

There is one peculiarity of the pain stimulus which might account for the strength of this motivation. The event which gives rise to pain, in ordinary circumstances, is one which injures tissues; once begun it continues, unlike the visual or auditory stimulus that can be discontinued promptly by closing the eyes or putting hands over the ears. (The violence of response to some tastes may be related similarly to the difficulty of getting rid of the substance that sticks to the taste surfaces, such as one of the oils.) Not only does the pain stimulation usually last for some time; it also frequently increases in strength before beginning to decline. The initial sensation would then be (a) in itself a mildly disturbing event, but also (b) a signal that disturbance will continue and perhaps increase in strength. These are circumstances that we could expect to establish a strong conditioned avoidance, to *any* pain stimulus.

SEXUAL MOTIVATION.   In lower animals, the most important single factor in sexual motivation is humoral: estrogens in the female, androgen in the male, both controlled to a considerable extent by the pituitary. As we shall see, however, sexual motivation is not completely dependent on this mechanism, especially in the male and in higher species.

The male of some mammalian species is sexually responsive only at one period of the year (the rutting season), but others, including the primates, are responsive continuously. The female on the other hand always shows cyclical motivation, ranging from a yearly cycle (in sheep, for example) to one of four days (in rats). This is directly related to the cycle of changes in the ovary. In lower species the period of estrus, or heat, is clearly distinct; copulatory behavior cannot be elicited except when the blood-estrogen level is high. In the chimpanzee, however, a few females show sexual responsiveness at all times during the ovarian cycle, though it is very weak at the stage at which other females are unresponsive. Motivation in the human female is still less controlled by the ovarian cycle; however, though there are great individual differences, the fluctuations of sexual responsiveness still show a relation to the cycle.

The nervous system of the normal animal, male or female, contains the patterns of organization for both male and female behavior. The presence of androgen in the blood stream of the male sensitizes the neural structures involved in the male behavior pattern, but also sensitizes those of the female pattern. The male pattern is dominant and is always displayed when a receptive female is available, but sexual arousal in the normal male makes it more probable, not less, that the female pattern can be elicited from the same animal if he is mounted by another excited male. Conversely in the female: one reliable sign of estrus is often the occurrence of mounting by the female. These facts are evidently of significance for the problem of homosexuality in man. It seems probable that constitutionally, by his nature, man is hetero- and homosexually motivatable, with heterosexuality dominant; and that the establishment of one of these modes of behavior as exclusive depends upon a learning process—that is, it is a function of the culture in which the subject lives, and of the accidents of his experience.

The relation of sexuality to cortical function and learning is of considerable interest. In the male rat, copulatory behavior is correlated with learning ability. It is also dependent on the cortex, and is impaired by cortical destruction in the same way as maze-learning scores. In the female of lower species, however, this relation does not hold. The behavior is much more at the reflexive level, and rather large cortical destructions do not lower the frequency of effective mating (what *is* impaired is the efficiency of maternal behavior). Also, there is little evidence that the female's copulatory behavior is affected by past experience. But at the anthropoid level, this changes. The experienced female chimpanzee copulates much more promptly than the inexperienced, though the difference is not nearly as great as with males. In the chimpanzee, and still more in the human species, ideational factors ("attitudes") determined by earlier learning are capable of greatly modifying sexual responsiveness, in both male and female; stimuli that have no directly sexual significance can heighten responsiveness or suppress it. In lower mammals copulation is a compulsive, stimulus-bound form of behavior, especially in the female but essentially in the male also. Strong as the sexual motivation of anthropoid or man may be, the behavior at this phyletic level has come under the control of mediating processes and is far removed from the reflexive characteristics to be seen in dog or cat.

Motivations primarily depending on cortical function

We have already seen that the nonspecific projection system of the brain stem, whose activity constitutes arousal, is excited by downstream paths from the cortex as well as by afferent paths. If we assume that arousal constitutes a general drive state (with or without qualitative variations as discussed in the earlier part of this chapter), we might expect to find cases in which arousal, and therefore drive, depend not on the presence of primitive need but on the complex cue functions of the cortex. Such cases in fact appear to make up an important part of the higher animal's motivations. Though they are not at all well understood it is essential not to overlook them.

When the mammal's primitive needs are reasonably well satisfied, when he is not under the control of stimuli directly associated with such needs, certain other motivations appear. In the primate these may be as compelling as noxious stimulation; they are less strong, but still clearly evident, in lower mammals. One example in the primate is the irrational fears of certain strange objects, which do not arise by association with prior injury but from a conflict of perceptions; another is the exploratory tendency which is so ubiquitous in vertebrates that it has frequently been treated as a special drive. Motivations of the kind that we are discussing now involve both approach and avoidance, and the great riddle that they present is in the fact that the *same* object or event can attract and repel. Which happens, apparently, depends on the strength of the disturbance produced, a weak disturbance attracting and a strong one repelling.

Placed in familiar surroundings, but with access provided to an unfamiliar region, the animal orients toward the latter. If he is in his home cage with the door open, he moves cautiously toward the dangerous outer world; he acts as though moving toward a point of balance between the strength of the exploratory motivation, on the one hand, and fear of the strange on the other, any sudden noise producing prompt retreat. Each exploration of course reduces strangeness, so the territory covered increases with time, and evidence of fear may vanish; but the significant point here is the earlier stage when the strange part of the environment excites both approach and avoidance.

Again, the chimpanzee that was exposed to the sight of a model head (p. 36) might be so disturbed that he ran screaming out of sight; but others, definitely frightened, retreated to a safe distance and then seemed unable to take their eyes off the object of fear. They were both repelled and attracted. Man in this society is definitely repelled emotionally by the dead body, flowing blood and gross bodily injury, and yet avidly reads or listens to accounts of traffic accidents or axe murders (a good axe murder is definitely more attractive than a poisoning, and a poisoning better than natural death).

A different example of this kind of ambivalence is the attraction of dangerous sports; here the human subject acts just like the rat venturing from home ground onto strange territory, very cautious at first but becoming increasingly venturesome as familiarity (and skill) increase. This sort of behavior has usually been explained by supposing that it is a search for prestige—in other words, it is in itself unpleasant, done only for extrinsic social rewards. This seems clearly untrue. The fact that people will pay money to get on a roller coaster, where no prestige is

Figure 56.   Two stages of a monkey's problem-solving for its own sake. All the experimenter has to do is to "set" the simple mechanical puzzles (which would offer a six-year-old child no problem at all), and the monkey will work at them. (Courtesy of H. F. Harlow.)

involved, makes it at least a doubtful explanation; and the further fact that animals behave in exactly the same way, in circumstances in which there is definitely no extrinsic reward, makes the explanation untenable. The "thrill" of danger in certain circumstances is sought for its own sake, as is the thrill of ghost stories and accounts of disasters.

A comparable ambivalence is found in the fact that man, who is undoubtedly opposed to work in many forms and especially when there is too much of it, promptly becomes unhappy when there is too little: here too, in other words, he seeks an optimum level. The statement includes mental as well as physical work, and may be misunderstood if the term "work" is interpreted in too narrow a way. Playing golf, physiologically, is work just as much as carrying another man's golf clubs. A game of chess is work, psychologically, and may be harder work than writing business letters. *Play*, in other words, may be defined for psychological purposes as work that is done for its own sake, without extrinsic reward. The frequency with which games have been invented that make intellectual demands as well as physical is a most important piece of evidence concerning the nature of human motivation. As with the dangerous sports, the explanation cannot be found in the search for social prestige; for there are forms of self-imposed problem-solving in which no prestige is gained (for example, playing solitaire, one form of which is widely known as Idiot's Delight), and here too the subhuman animals show the behavior when prestige does not enter into the question. For example:

Monkeys will work for hours at solving simple mechanical problems

(Fig. 56). Chimpanzees on occasion will work at learning tasks, if the tasks "interest" them, while leaving the food reward untouched. The rat that is offered a short direct route to food, and a longer route that involves passing through a simple maze problem, will frequently take the more difficult route (from 10 to 80 per cent of runs are indirect, depending on the difficulty of the problem and whether it is changed on every run: if it is unchanged it loses its excitation value and the rats revert to the direct route).

What these data tell us is that there are circumstances in which an animal will prefer to work rather than be idle, to do more work rather than less. The "principle of least effort" is extremely misleading as a general guide to understanding behavior in lower animals, and still more so in the primate. It may apply when behavior is motivated by a serious biological need, but not when such needs have been met: in the latter condition, it is clear, the principle is reversed and the organism's need is to expend energy. Moreover, the need is not merely for muscular activity, especially in the higher animal, for this could be achieved by monotonous physical exercises. There is, in effect, a need to exercise the brain as well.

This appears very clearly in the following experiment. College students were paid $20 a day to do nothing, lying 24 hours a day on a comfortable bed with eyes, ears and hands shielded to minimize perception of the environment (Fig. 57). These conditions were relaxed only to allow the

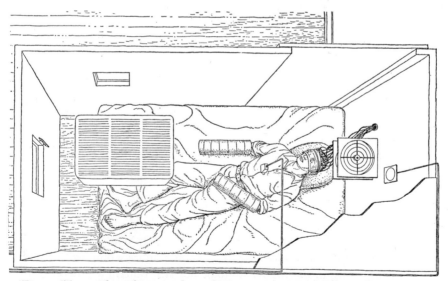

Figure 57.   The subject in the isolation experiment seen from above, with the ceiling cut away. Cuffs were worn to prevent somesthetic perception by the hands; the plastic shield over the eyes admitted light but prevented pattern vision. The subject had a foam-rubber U-shaped cushion covering his ears; here it has been removed so that EEG tracings can be taken. An air-conditioner is shown where it would be on the ceiling, upper left, and the microphone by which the subject could report his experiences is seen just above his chest. (From Heron: *Scientific American,* January, 1957.)

subject to eat or go to the toilet. Few could endure them for more than two or three days (the upper limit was six). Though the subjects were in need of money, they turned from this "job" to ones that paid much less but demanded much more of them in the way of physical and mental effort. They developed a need to be exposed to patterned stimulation of almost any kind, and this need to perceive and react to the environment eventually became overwhelming.

The experiment draws attention to what must be part of the explanation of the kind of motivation we are now discussing: the role of variety in maintaining arousal. With repetition, any one pattern of stimulation rapidly declines in arousal value. In the sleeping cat, for example, a series of unfamiliar sounds *A-B-C* produces arousal, waking the cat up. With a number of repetitions arousal decreases, and now the cat neither wakes nor shows the effect of arousal in the EEG (habituation, p. 142). Next, the pattern is changed to *C-B-A:* the cat again wakes up, and the EEG shows the full arousal picture. When an animal, therefore, looks at a fully familiar object or scene the arousal effects must be small, and if no need-associated stimuli are present the probability of response is low. But if a strange object is introduced, or if familiar objects act in an unfamiliar way, producing arousal at the moment when the animal perceives the new element in the situation, the probability of response is high.

We may suppose further that there is an optimal level of arousal, as implied by the earlier discussion of drive reduction and drive enhancement as factors in learning (p. 140f.). The subject will tend to repeat behavior that raises drive level from a low to a moderate level, and not to repeat behavior that raises it from a moderate to a high level. That is, he will seek conditions that produce a moderate level of arousal, and will tend to avoid monotony as well as pain.

It has already been said that this is a speculative line of theory. The statement can be reinforced by pointing out now a glaring defect: it makes no provision for sleep, a topic that psychologically and physiologically remains mostly mysterious. We know that there is a "waking center" which is part of the arousal system, and probably a "sleep center" as well; but how these achieve the 24-hour cycle is not known. External stimulation can postpone sleep, or lack of it can hasten it, but only to a certain degree. There appears to be in the brain stem a pacemaker, a physiological timing process, which is not very subject to sensory control. What it is we do not know; but in the meantime, the statements of the preceding paragraph need to be qualified by addition of the words, "during the waking state." An animal will seek a moderate level of arousal— until, as we say, he begins to "feel sleepy." Then he begins to seek conditions which minimize arousal.

The goals of the higher animal

This chapter may be concluded by asking, What are the mammal's goals, and especially, What are man's?

In the first place come the primitive biological needs involved in survival; when these are not met (particularly if the lack is chronic) the attempt to satisfy them generally becomes the dominant motive. Sexual needs, equally primitive biologically, become more complex and less directly compelling in the higher animal, but still remain a powerful motivating influence.

When such needs have been met, however, in the well-fed comfortable animal with adequate sexual opportunities, we find ourselves looking at a very different picture. Now we find the subject embarking on explorations even if these take him away from a safe and biologically adequate locus. We find him looking for or inventing problems to solve, and mild risks to be run, apparently for their own sake. In man, with his high in-tellectual capacity, these tendencies produce complex and expensive mechanical devices (e.g., racing dinghies, bathyspheres, roulette wheels) and endless verbal elaborations of soluble and insoluble problems (e.g., philosophy). The machinery of the nervous system, presumably enlarged under the influences of evolution as of value in seeking food and avoiding injury, has also developed certain intrinsic peculiarities which become very evident in an economically successful human society—a kind of Frankenstein's monster whose activities are not all undesirable.

Besides the seeking for excitement and the manipulation of the environ-ment, just referred to, there are also the irrational fears and dislikes discussed earlier (which as we have seen are more marked in the higher animal). Some of these tendencies are of incalculable value: problem-solving for its own sake, for example, is the essence of science. Others, such as the tendency to fear (and so be hostile to) the stranger, the one whose beliefs and habits differ from ours (Chap. 1), are potentially dis-astrous for the species. It is the problem of developmental and social psychology to learn how to handle these tendencies, to make the most of the valuable and minimize the dangerous ones. There is reason to believe that this can be done, but at present we know little of practical value about the problem. In view of man's present capacity to destroy himself as a species, this has become the most urgent of the problems of science.

Summary

Motivation refers broadly (i.e., it is not a precise term) to the state or process which makes possible activity of the whole animal, as distinct from a local reflex activity. Motivation does not supply the energy of response—this comes from the animal's oxygen and food supply—but de-termines whether the energy will be available for response, or for a particular class of response. Emotion is even less precise as a scientific term; it seems to mean that there is something special going on in the organism, motivationally, but the nature of this "something special" in the case of one emotion (e.g., joy) has apparently little in common with that of another (e.g., anger or despair).

The conception of motivation adds nothing, has no explanatory value, in the understanding of reflex activity. The behavior is produced by a system which is connected in parallel (Chap. 5) and which is always ready for action unless fatigued or inhibited by some other system. Some of an animal's biological needs are supplied reflexively, and as long as this happens such needs do not influence the animal's motivation: re-flexive breathing usually supplies oxygen and removes carbon dioxide, sweating or shivering controls temperature, and so on. But when a strong need is not satisfied reflexively, motivation becomes involved at once. The pattern of activity in higher centers changes, the behavior of the whole animal is directed toward meeting the need, and any competing behavior is suppressed.

Drive refers to a particular kind of hypothesis about motivation. It implies that there are separate processes in the CNS that determine the animal's level of behavioral activity, apart from the processes that guide this behavior. Roughly, this is like the distinction between the power system of an automobile and its steering system. We know that drive does not actually supply the power in behavior, the energy that cells use in being active; but it does seem needed to mobilize cellular energies in the CNS, to coordinate them so that they are available for behavior. There are differing ideas about drives and how they work; a hypothesis is discussed which relates drive to arousal, but no final answer to the problem is available at present.

Special motivations or drives may be acquired by learning (this is related to the conception of secondary reinforcement: Chap. 7). In some cases, however, as in the fear of strange animals, we are also dealing with maturation, and learning has a smaller role in causing the fears than it may seem to have. In some of these cases there is a species-predictable susceptibility, characteristic of the higher primates particularly. The nature of this susceptibility, however—the mechanism of response in these "irrational fears"—is not known. Factor IV learning is involved (see Chap. 6), and it is possible that the essence of the process is some conflict of present sensory input with pre-established mediating processes.

Homeostatic processes are ones that keep the "internal environment" constant. They include breathing, sweating or shivering, eating and drinking, and the "artificial hungers" of addiction. Hunger and addiction are partly learned processes, in combination with basic physiological changes. The avoidance of pain may also be considered homeostatic (though less directly); like normal hunger, pain is a complex process and not an elementary sensation, and is far from being fully understood at present.

Sexual behavior is biologically primitive also, but cannot be considered homeostatic since it is not a regulator of the internal environment. It is closely related to the level of sex hormones in the blood stream, but in the male mammal and the higher primates particularly it is also profoundly influenced by learning and mediating processes.

A special feature of motivation in higher animals, one dependent on a well-developed cerebrum, is an ambivalent attitude toward threatening situations and ones calling for mental as well as physical work. When there is a biologically-primitive need or serious threat of need, this tends to dominate behavior; but when need is absent or at a low level the higher animal (and particularly man) seems to seek out the threat-producing or puzzle-making situation. He avoids a too-easy or monotonous environment, and this motivation can be very powerful indeed.

Notes

For background material, see Lindsley on arousal and emotion, and Miller on learned drives, Chaps. 14 and 13 in Stevens; and the various chapters on emotion and motivation in Woodworth and Schlosberg (*General References*, Chap. 1, p. 19). Also, texts on learning are relevant, since the topics of reinforcement and motivation are difficult to distinguish: see Hilgard, and Bugelski (*Notes*, Chap. 7), and the treatment of learning in Osgood (*General References*).

An excellent discussion of chimpanzee motivation is found in W. Köhler, *The Mentality of Apes*, Kegan Paul, 1927: the concluding chapter is a readable and valuable account of social needs, irrational fears, hostility to the stranger, and so forth. R. M. Yerkes, *Chimpanzees: a Laboratory Colony*, Yale University Press, 1943, is also very readable, and reports more recent experimental work. A further discussion of some of these points is given in Hebb and Thompson, in the *Handbook of Social Psychology* (Chap. 1 *Notes*).

On the difference in ease of conditioning a child to fear an object such as an animal versus an object such as a block of wood, see C. W. Valentine, *J. Genet. Psychol.*, 1930, 37, 394–419; for the experiment on human fear of snakes, H. E. Jones and M. C. Jones, *Childhood Educ.*, 1928, 5, 136–143. The experiment on morphine addiction was by S. D. S. Spragg, *Comp. Psychol. Monog.*, 1940, 15, no. 7. The aberrant responses to pain stimulation in isolated dogs are reported by R. Melzack and T. H. Scott, *J. Comp. Physiol. Psychol.*, 1957, 50, 155–161.

The studies of problem-solving for its own sake by monkeys were made by Harlow and his students: see for example H. F. Harlow, *Psychol. Rev.*, 1953, 60, 23–32. For the rat, see J. Havelka, *Canad. J. Psychol.*, 1956, 10, 91–97; and Hebb and Mahut, *J. Psychol. Norm. Path.*, 1955, 52, 209–221.

A summary report of the perceptual isolation experiment, with human subjects, is given by W. H. Bexton, W. Heron, and T. H. Scott, *Canad. J. Psychol.*, 1954, 8, 70–76; and of a parallel experiment, with more rapidly appearing effects, by J. C. Lilly, *Psychiat. Res. Reports 5*, American Psychiatric Association, 1956.

Chapter 9

Perception, knowledge and response

Wᴀɪᴛᴇʀꜱ on perception have often considered it as only a question of input to the brain, hardly to be distinguished from sensation except perhaps by being more complex. It is true that perception may be inseparable from sensation in practice but it is important to distinguish between them theoretically, and it is very important to recognize the interaction of perception with response.

There are theories based on introspection that seem to explain perception fairly well—until we ask how it determines response, which of course it does. At this point the subjective theories break down. They solve only half the problem, and in thirty or forty years have shown no promise of dealing with the other half—the motor aspects—so we shall not consider them here. In the present chapter we shall approach the problem behavioristically, from the point of view of transmission through our automatic switchboard, the CNS, bringing together from earlier chapters the theoretical conceptions that bear on perception and seeing how far they are satisfactory or unsatisfactory.

What perception is

Where behavior is under immediate sensory control no problem of perception need arise theoretically. There is no reason, for example, to speak of an earthworm's perception of an obstacle it encounters in its path; sensory stimulation determines its responses directly. But in higher animals, where mediating responses share in the control of response, a complex set of events may intervene between first contact with an object and the adequate response (the one that we usually call "the" response); the animal looks, touches, sniffs, before finally carrying off the object, eating it, copulating with it, paying no further attention to it, or running away from it. The mediating processes that determine the final response must first be set up and adjusted, so to speak, and this preliminary adjustment is perception.

Sometimes the adjustment takes place very rapidly within the switchboard itself, and gives no motor signs of its occurrence; more commonly it depends on overt activity, which we speak of as investigatory. Mediating processes are set up and successively modified until a point is reached at which they determine the adequate response. The first stimulus, let us say, is the sight of something lying on the sidewalk as a child passes by; "the" response of the child is to put it in his pocket, but in between stimulus and response in this sense is a series of responses and feedback stimuli. The child first focusses his vision on the object, moves closer "to see what it is," and turns it over in his hand to feel its texture or to see it still better. The response series may take only two or three seconds if the object is not unusual in the child's experience, but the overt behavior is clearly necessary to the perception. Perception is essentially a preparation for the final response, and preliminary or investigatory responses essentially contribute to it in most cases. Discussion of perception as a kind of afferent input only is therefore unrealistic.

A *sensation* is defined here as an activity of receptors and the resulting activity of afferent paths up to the cortical sensory area. This is conduction in parallel, and the activity is completely subject to environmental control (p. 101). From a less physiological point of view, therefore, sensation might be defined as the sum total of processes resulting from stimulation of the sense organ and remaining directly under its control (beginning and ending at the same time). A *perception* is defined as the mediating processes to which sensation gives rise directly.

There is a long history of argument, based on introspection, over these terms. A sensation was once considered to be a simple element in awareness, perception a combination of such elements. Then it was shown that perception does not correspond to this description, and it was argued that there are no "true" sensations in consciousness at all; what was thought to be a sensation should be regarded, perhaps, as a simple perception. This view seems to have carried the day. "Sensation" has therefore lost all usefulness as a technical term for subjective description.

But now, in objective analysis, we encounter a new need of terms to distinguish between two theoretically-known processes, different in kind: one afferent and tied to sense-organ activity, the other central and, though initiated by the first, not completely determined by it. "Sensation" and "perception" meet this need perfectly, and it seems therefore that redefinition, as above, restores the distinction of terms to scientific usefulness.

The student will also find that the term perception is used in two senses. Usually this does not make any difficulty, but on occasion we need to distinguish between *perceiving* (the process of attaining a perception) and *percept* (the end product, the readjustment of mediating processes that produce the adequate response). The process of perceiving is not instantaneous except with very familiar objects; and even here, as we shall see, there is reason to believe that it consists of a rapid series of events in the brain, as shown by certain experimental data.

Visual perception (i.e., perceiving) in general depends on complex eye movements, tactual perception on movements of some part of the body (a hand, snout, or beak is characteristically brought into play). Auditory perception of strange sounds usually involves head movement (and ear movement in lower mammals); also, it often deals with series of stimuli, extended in time, a fact that is especially evident in the perception of a melody or of speech. Taste, or gustatory perception, utilizes movements of lips and tongue, smell utilizes changes of breathing (i.e., sniffing), unless the substance to be identified is very familiar. In short, perceiving takes time. Most past discussions of the problem have dealt with the apparently instantaneous identification of events in the environment—and usually optical events—but this is a very misleading emphasis. With very familiar objects or events no overt activity may be needed, and identification is apparently immediate. A single glance, one contact with the hand, is enough; no further investigatory movement is made. But even here, perception may consist of a temporal series of mediating processes instead of a single unitary event. Two experiments give us valuable information on this point.

The first experiment used the *tachistoscope,* a device that presents visual material very briefly: in this instance, for 1/100 second. The subject was instructed to fix his gaze on a point in the middle of a screen; he was told that letters would be projected on it, and that he was to report what they were. Various letters were presented, in groups of four, as shown in Fig. 58; sometimes left of fixation, sometimes right, sometimes with the fixation point in the center. The position varied randomly, and the subject was not told where the pattern would appear next. With all positions, the subjects showed great consistency in reporting the letters in this order: top left, top right, bottom left, bottom right—that is, in the order in which one reads printed matter in English. Further, the subjects *perceived* them in this order, even though they were presented instantaneously: the fewest errors were made in identifying the letter in the top left position (about 80 per cent correct), with errors increasing to a maximum at the bottom right (about 40 per cent correct), and the subjects reported that the top left letter was seen more vividly than the top right one, and so on.

There is no reason, in the objective conditions of the experiment, why the top left letter should regularly be seen first and most clearly; in fact, when the group is to the left of fixation, as in Fig. 58 *B,* the right-hand letters (*u* and *e* in the diagram) are nearest to central vision and should be seen best. The perceptual process itself imposes an order on the sensory input, in a way that is clearly related to the past experience of reading English (reverse results are obtained when this kind of experiment is done with skilled readers of Jewish material, which is read from right to left).

In another part of the same experiment, rows of letters were presented as in Fig. 59. When they were presented on one side only, either left or right, the average number of letters perceived correctly on the right side was higher. But when they were presented simultaneously on both sides, the average was higher for the left. Since the subject did not know in advance where the letters would appear, there was a sequence of events in his perception, despite the fact that it seemed instantaneous. First there was a discrimination, between (1) the situation in which there were letters on one side only, and (2) the one in which there were letters on both sides. In the first case, central processes then reinforced sensory input from the right more than from the left; in the second case, they reinforced sensory input from the left.[1] All this must have happened in a fraction of a second, but it shows that even when there is only a momentary stimulation the resulting perception may consist of a series of events.

The second experiment, with auditory perception, tells us more about the way in which serial processes can function in perception. The subject wore earphones which delivered two series of three digits simultaneously to the ears at half-second intervals (total time, 1½ seconds). The right ear received 3-7-5, for example, while the left ear received 8-2-9, 3 and 8 being delivered simultaneously, and so with the two following

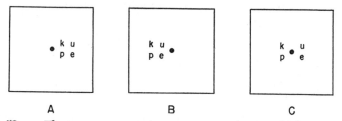

A   B   C

Figure 58.   The squares represent an exposure screen, on which groups of letters were presented tachistoscopically. The dot in the center is the fixation point. Different letters were used on different trials, not the same ones as shown above.

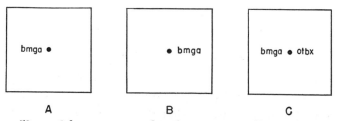

A   B   C

Figure 59.   Other patterns used in the experiment illustrated in Fig. 58.

[1] Theoretically, this is what is meant by saying that the subject attended to the right or left part of the field. The selective reinforcement of one sensory input over another is diagrammed in Fig. 44, p. 106.

pairs, 7 and 2, 5 and 9. The subjects were able to correctly report the digits they heard on 62 per cent of the trials, which in itself is an interesting result; but much more interesting, for our present problem, is the fact that in 157 out of 160 trials the subjects spontaneously (i.e., without being instructed to do so) reported the whole series for one ear, in the proper order, before reporting the series for the other ear.

Here again the perceptual process imposes a temporal order on material delivered to it sensorily. In this case, it changed the order of the sensory events from a series of three pairs of simultaneous events to two series of three single events (in the preceding experiment, the change was from simultaneity to a sequence). Subjects in this kind of experiment report that they hear the digits as constituting two separate groups, one in each ear, rather than as one series of six digits which have to be sorted out in thought before being reported.

In summary, perception is a setting up or modification of mediating processes, in preparation for an adequate response. Sometimes the adequate response to a situation is, in effect, no response, an inhibition of overt activity; so we do not conclude, from this definition, that perception is necessarily followed by observable motor effects. Perceiving, the process of arriving at a percept which determines what further reaction is to take place, normally extends over an appreciable period of time and involves motor activity together with the resulting feedback. With very familiar and simple events perception may appear to be instantaneous; but in some of these cases at least it can be shown experimentally that there is still a serial order of events within the mediating processes, even though of very short duration.

Perception without ensuing response: knowledge

Though perception is a preparation for response, it was remarked above that the "adequate response" in some situations is no response. There is one kind of situation in which this happens often, and which also helps us to see the significance of the terms *know* and *knowledge*.

In dealing with a familiar object, which has been encountered in different situations and by which different responses have been evoked in the past, the higher animal has learned not one but a number of ways of reacting to it. When he now encounters such an object, his perception of it is a preparation for more than one kind of response. In other words, there is not one adequate response but many. These may inhibit one another, so that no overt activity follows. At this point we may say that the subject has perceived something but does not respond to it further, or simply that he *knows* that the object is there. In either case, the meaning is that there has been a change of response potential; the fact that the perception has occurred will change the subject's reactions in any one of a number of situations that might occur later.

A simple example: Looking for glue in a friend's workshop I perceive a screwdriver lying under a pile of shavings. Having no use for the tool I do no more than let my eye rest on it for a moment, and go on with my search. But if my friend X should say, "Is the screwdriver on the bench?" I would at once say "Yes," instead of having to look first. If X should say, "The screwdriver must have been left outside," I answer, "No, it's here." If I should find the glue but cannot get the lid off, I reach directly for the screwdriver instead of looking for it first or getting out the pocket-knife I might otherwise have used. And so forth. Perceiving the screwdriver, or knowing that it is on the bench, has changed the response that I would make to each of a large class of potential stimulations; it would not be possible to list them all. Also, there is no single definitive way of reacting to a screwdriver (which may be used to drive screws or remove them, to pry cans open or to pierce them, to prop open windows, to close electrical circuits or to throw at cats). Consequently we cannot describe the original perception as an incompleted act, a partial activation of an S-R pathway (even an S-R pathway complicated by cell-assemblies). Essentially, it resets the switchboard, and it is this resetting that constitutes knowledge.

It follows from this that "know" and "knowledge" are useful terms when we are dealing with input to the switchboard which affects a large class of *potential* reactions, but not when dealing with through transmission in a specific S-R connection. When a rat hears a buzzer that has repeatedly been followed by shock, it adds nothing to say that he trembles because he knows that shock will follow: stimulus and response are closely and inevitably connected. Here the behavioral facts are adequately summarized by saying that the rat has a conditioned fear response.

Relation of perception to sensory control

To define perception as consisting of mediating processes implies some independence from sensation, but does not of course imply that the connection between them may not be close. The closeness of relation varies considerably, from cases in which a given stimulation seems always to produce the same perception to ones in which it is very difficult indeed to predict what perception will occur.

The relative independence of perception from sensory input can be observed in two ways. The same stimulus patterns may produce different perceptions, and different stimulus patterns may produce the same perception.

The classical demonstration of variability in perception, with a single stimulus pattern, is found in Fig. 60. This is an *ambiguous* (or *reversible*) *figure*. It may be seen as a bird-bath (or vase), or as two faces. If the student will keep his eyes fixed on the black dot between the two noses

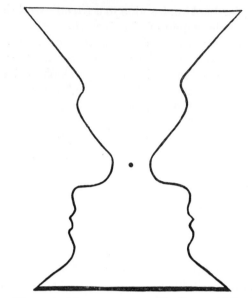

Figure 60.   Ambiguous or reversible figure. (After Rubin.)

(or in the center of the bird-bath), he will find that the reversal, the change from one perception to the other, does not require eye movement; though the movement definitely permits a clearer perception and affects the rate of reversal. The significance of this observation is to show that two very different perceptions can occur with the same sensory input.

Nothing in the sensory process, itself, accounts for this "flip-flop" action. Slow, steady changes might be intelligible, but not the discontinuous alternation of two distinctly different perceptions. It becomes quite intelligible by the mechanism diagrammed in Fig. 61, which assumes that the two perceptions consist of different assembly actions, or phase sequences, each of which prevents activity in the other.

Figure 60 is important also as illustrating the figure-ground phenomenon. The figure is the region in the total configuration that is perceived at the moment, the rest being ground (the alternation that occurs with Fig. 60 can thus be described as an alternating figure-ground relation). The student will find, when the vase is being perceived, that the space in the center of the figure appears closer and, in a vague way, more solid. When perception shifts to the two faces the central space recedes, and the two lateral spaces appear closer.

The figure-ground relation is fundamental in the perception of objects and regions of space. The unity of simple, clearly demarcated figures is present in first vision, as far as can be determined from the behavior of the congenitally blind who are given sight at maturity. With such objects, then, the figure-ground relation is independent of experience; but it also seems that other figures are much more a function of experience, and that the kind of variability of the figure-ground relation that is demonstrated in Fig. 60 increases as a result of perceptual learning.

Variability is a general property of perception, not found only with such special stimulus patterns as Fig. 60. The ambiguous figure is significant only because it provides an especially clear case. If the student will fix his eyes on some point of his environment, he will find himself perceiving sometimes this detail, sometimes that; sometimes the larger scene instead of details; and so on. If he looks even at as simple a diagram as Fig. 62 A, he will still find that his perception is sometimes of the crookedness of a line, sometimes the gap at the lower right; sometimes the whole triangle as such, or perhaps as a badly formed "4." With the dots of

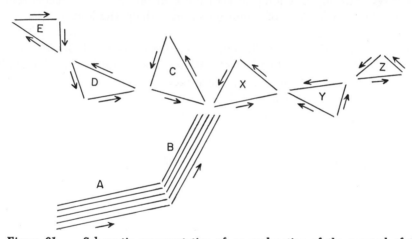

Figure 61.   Schematic representation of an explanation of the reversal of the ambiguous figure. *A*, *B*, afferent conduction (in parallel); *C*, *X*, alternating assembly actions. It is assumed that *C* inhibits *X* and vice versa. *C-D-E* constitutes one perception; *X-Y-Z* another (these assemblies must lie intertangled in the same regions of the brain, not spatially separate as above).

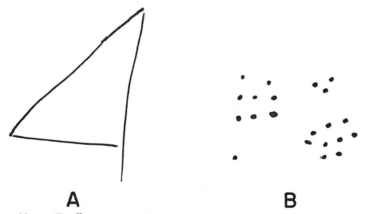

A   **B**

Figure 62.   To illustrate variability in the perception of simple configurations.

Fig. 62 *B*, he will see sometimes one group, sometimes three; sometimes individual dots, or the areas between them; and so on. The sensory input sets limits on what may be perceived; there is no chance that the perception of Fig. 62 *B* will be identical with that of Fig. 62 *A*; but within these limits variability is pronounced. The constancy of perception, with a given sensory stimulation, consists of a frequent recurrence of the process which is "the" perception, rather than maintenance of a single process.

Brightness and *size constancy* are two important examples of the case in which the stimulus varies while the perception remains the same. Brightness constancy refers to the obvious fact that a white object looks white whether in the light or in shadow. Now this is, in fact, rather surprising. "White" means that an object reflects much light, "black" that it reflects little light. A lump of coal lying in the sunlight reflects much more light than a piece of white paper in a deep shadow, yet the coal still looks black and the paper white. What is actually involved here is a phenomenon of *contrast:* though the coal reflects the light, it reflects much less than surrounding objects. When one arranges experimentally to focus intense light on a shiny piece of coal, and only on it (e.g., by fastening it with sealing wax to the end of a piece of wire, with no other surface near it to be equally illuminated), the coal becomes a brilliant silver in appearance. A piece of white paper in a dark shadow, seen through a reduction screen (which does not permit one to see the surroundings), becomes a dark gray. In ordinary circumstances, where contrast effects are not prevented, white paper moved in and out of a shadow does not appear to change its color but is perceived as white in both conditions: two different conditions of stimulation, but the same perception with respect to the color of the paper.

Size constancy is equally familiar, and equally surprising when one stops to consider what is happening. Visual size is basically dependent on retinal angle of projection; but it is also basically related to the perception of visual *depth* (i.e., distance from the eye), as shown by the fact that one's hand six inches from the eye, and twelve inches from the eye, does not appear to differ in size (or does so very slightly). Yet a hand at the six-inch distance has a retinal projection approximately twice as great as at the twelve-inch distance. A picture on the wall does not expand and contract as one moves closer or farther away; the face of a friend across the table does not appear three or four times as large as that of another friend at the far end of the room. This is size constancy. The constancy is not absolute, and at great distances apparent size is sharply decreased. Also, the constancy for some reason is much less marked with objects seen in the vertical dimension, up or down. A related phenomenon is the moon illusion, which makes the moon on the horizon seem larger than the same moon at the zenith. Experiments have shown that this is partly a question of the position of the body, and bending the eyes upward or downward, but why this should be so no one has explained.

Another phenomenon of visual perception is of some interest, partly from a historical point of view since it played a large part between 1912 and 1925 in convincing psychologists that the relation between two sensory events may be as important as the events themselves, in determining what one perceives. This is the *phi-phenomenon,* the perception of motion where no motion exists (as in moving pictures and illuminated signs). Nowadays the phenomenon is commonplace; but nonetheless it involves a really remarkable transformation, as between what happens on the sensory surface and what happens in perception.

In Fig. 63 two light sources are represented. *A* is lighted for 200 milliseconds; 60 ms after it has been extinguished, *B* is lighted for 200 ms. Instead of two lights, one after the other, the observer sees a single light that *moves all the way* from *A* to *B.* This is the phi-phenomenon. If the interval is too short, two lights are seen simultaneously; if too long, two lights are seen one after the other, without movement. The timing that produces the effect varies with the intensity of the lights and the angular distance between them. A number of suggestions have been offered to account for the phenomenon in physiological terms, but as yet there is no satisfactory explanation in detail. It cannot be accounted for by eye movement from *A* to *B* because, with two pairs of lights, apparent movement can be perceived simultaneously in opposite directions.

Now let us ask how all this is to be dealt with in objective terms. The subjective approach, which has continued to dominate the discussion of perception, treats the phi-phenomenon as if it meant that there is movement within the brain (or mind) which the mind can somehow apprehend directly by introspection. Whether this approach is right or wrong, it has great logical difficulties (how does the mind "look inward?") which are as serious in the study of perception as in that of learning or emotion; and—as noted at the beginning of this chapter—it has wholly failed to deal with the motor effects of perception. In modern psychology we are committed to a different approach, which must be applied in perception as much as elsewhere.

What does it mean when a subject reports that he sees a light move, in the experimental conditions of Fig. 63? It means, simply, that these conditions of stimulation produce, at some level in the brain, the same process that is produced by a light that does move from *A* to *B.* There

A   B

Figure 63.   A light *A* goes on, then off; a fraction of a second later *B* goes on and off. With proper timing, the subject sees, instead of two lights, a single one that moves from one locus to the other.

is no reason to conclude, necessarily, that there is any movement of an excitation in the visual cortex from one point to another; instead, it seems probable that there is not. The probability is that the sensory cortex reproduces the conditions of retinal excitation faithfully, and there is of course no excitation moving across the retina. We *can* conclude that the same assembly activities are aroused, either when the retina is stimulated by a light moving from A to B, or when the two corresponding points are stimulated with the proper timing. *Sensation* in the two cases differs, *perception* is the same. Both are theoretical constructs, events inferred from our knowledge of anatomy and physiology and from the responses made by the subject.

What does it mean when, with Fig. 62 *B*, a number of dots appear as a unified group, a single entity? We can interpret this as signifying that the processes aroused in some part of the brain are the same as would be aroused by a single object occupying the same space. The unity of such perceptions is not a mysterious thing. It implies that any response made to the group, or tendency to respond, is being determined by all of its members in the same way and at the same time.

Generalization

When an animal has been trained to respond to one stimulus object or event, the response can nearly always be elicited by presenting other objects or events of the same kind, though they are not identical and may not have been encountered before. When we train the young human subject to say "dog" when he sees a dog, about the age of two years, we find that he spontaneously transfers the response to other objects in the same general class, though they may vary in color, size or detailed configuration. Such spontaneous transfer is *generalization*. It is a fundamental feature of behavior.

For the purposes of analysis we must distinguish between (1) generalizations from one member of a simple series to neighboring members, and (2) generalizations involving pattern or form.

1. SERIES GENERALIZATION.   The first kind is a transfer from one intensity or frequency, for example, to other intensities or frequencies. If a salivary response is conditioned to a sound of given loudness, it will be elicited by other loudnesses; if the stimulus difference is great, the response will be weak or delayed; if the difference is smaller, the response will be more nearly identical with the original response. If the CS is a scratching of a particular point on the skin, the salivary CR can be elicited strongly by stimulating nearby points, weakly by stimulating distant ones.

The same relation is found to hold between auditory stimuli differing in pitch, and visual stimuli differing in brightness or size. In each of these cases the different stimuli vary along one dimension only; the differences are differences of degree. It is easy to define and to quantify them. The generalization is probably constitutionally determined (that is, independent of experience) though this has been shown for visual brightness and size only.

Also, the mechanism of this form of generalization is probably sensory, and does not primarily involve mediating processes. Because of overlap at each synaptic level in the specific afferent systems, there is an increasing spread of excitation as the cortex is approached. Two stimulations, S and S' (Fig. 64), quite distinct on the skin, must if they are not far apart produce overlapping areas of excitation in the cortex; the closer the two points, the more the cortical excitation would involve the same cells and excite paths leading to the same assemblies or the same motor outlets.

Where intensity is involved instead of locus, a similar explanation may be possible. When a response is conditioned to auditory loudness Y, a certain group of cells, y, is firing in the auditory cortex. If a weaker noise X is now presented, the cells that fire, x, will comprise many but not all of y; they will then tend to fire some of the same motor paths, but not all of them nor at the same rate of firing. The same response will be produced, but weaker. When a louder noise, Z, is presented, the cells Z that are fired

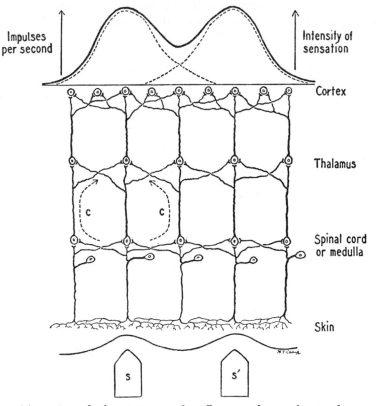

Figure 64.   Spread of excitation in the afferent pathway, showing how cortical overlap would occur with separate skin stimulations. The lower part of the diagram (from "skin" to "cortex") represents actual neurons; the curves at the top, instead, represent rates of firing in the cortex. The broken-line curves, c, show that though there is a spread, there is also a convergence toward the center, producing a peak in cortical firing that corresponds to the exact place of the stimulus. (After Ruch, in Fulton: *Textbook of Physiology.*)

will include the y cells, but also others which have not been conditioned to the specific response being measured. Some of the extra paths they excite may have inhibitory effects, or otherwise interfere with the action of the y cells, again tending to produce the same response, but more weakly. This second hypothesis, particularly, is speculative; the point however is that some explanation of this sort would fit in with the apparently unlearned nature of the simple-series generalization.

The kind of generalization we have been considering, from a single stimulus, is closely related to certain interesting phenomena to be observed when an animal is required to discriminate between two members of a series. Both higher and lower animals tend to discriminate on the basis of relative rather than absolute size, intensity or frequency. It is easy to train an animal to choose the smaller, or the brighter, of two objects; it is much more difficult to train him to choose always a particular size or brightness.

For example, in the apparatus of Fig. 4 (p. 25), we train a rat to go toward a lighted door of intensity 1, and avoid intensity 2 (i.e., twice as strong). When training is complete, we present intensities 2 and 4. The rat now chooses, if he chooses at all, intensity 2, which he was specifically trained to avoid. In other words, the original discrimination was on the basis of relative values. Or, if the animal has been trained to go to intensity 2 and avoid intensity 1 he will now, when offered 2 and 4, go to the new stimulus value, 4, instead of the one he was trained to go to.

However, the animal also shows clearly that he can discriminate between the new pair of stimuli and the old; there is an "equivalence of stimuli," but the equivalence is not complete. At the end of the training period, with the original pair of stimulus objects, the animal may have been taking five to ten seconds to make his response; now, with the new test stimuli, he takes perhaps one, two or three minutes. Not uncommonly, the animal stops choosing between the stimuli, and simply goes always right or always left (the student will recall that the positive, or correct, stimulus is presented with random alternation right and left; see p. 24). However, if such an animal is put back in the training situation for a few trials and receives punishment (electric shock) for a wrong choice, he usually begins to discriminate when returned to the test situation, and the discrimination will be on the basis of relative brightness. These facts show, therefore, that the animal tends in the first place to discriminate on the basis of relative value, but has the capacity to discriminate absolute values as well.

2. GENERALIZATION IN FORM PERCEPTION.   The second kind of generalization occurs with the perception of form or pattern. It is the same as series generalization in one respect, in causing a spontaneous transfer of response from one stimulus event to others of the same class; but it differs in other respects. It is not possible to deal with both problems in the same way.

For one thing, it is much more difficult to define the class of events within which the generalization occurs. Series generalization involves a single dimension of the stimulus: extent, energy, duration or frequency. It is easy to define the degree of similarity or distance between two sizes or brightnesses, with other variables held constant. When we deal with variations of pattern this is not so, because more than one dimension is involved at the same time. A measure of similarity is possible only by behavioral test: observing whether transfer occurs, how frequently, how strong the response is, or how much delay of response there is.

A further difference is found in the fact that series generalization is, on the whole, the same for the higher and the lower mammals, but generalization with visual patterns (the only sense for which any data are available) is not, as we saw in Chapter 2 (p. 30, and Fig. 10). Finally, pattern perception is much more dependent on experience (Factor IV: p. 123 and Table 1) than perception of brightness or size, and this also implies a difference in mechanism. Rats reared in darkness did not differ from those normally reared in rate of learning to discriminate brightness or size, but took six times as many trials to learn a simple pattern discrimination. The congenitally blind, given their vision at a later time, learn promptly to name colors (i.e., to make discriminative responses to them), but take months to learn to do so with patterns. Pattern generalization must, it seems, involve mediating processes built up by experience, but just how is not known. It is, in fact, a difficult process to account for. Most of our quantitative data concern series generalization, but the relations that have been found cannot easily be transposed to apply to pattern generalization.

The perception of space

The classical problem of space perception in psychology concerns *visual depth*. It seems easy to understand the visual perception of direction; the light reflected by objects in different directions from the eye strikes different parts of the retina, the light-sensitive receptor surface of the eye, which means that cues to direction are available. But the retina is a two-dimensional surface, like a photographic plate at the back of a camera: why therefore is the perceived visual world not flat, like a photograph? Why is depth so immediate and inescapable?

There is also auditory space perception, and here we have the problem of accounting for the perception of direction as well as distance. For both eye and ear we know in some detail what the cues are on which space perception depends, but the way in which they operate, physiologically, is much less clear.

The primary cues to visual depth are summarized as *accommodation, convergence* and *retinal disparity*. Of these, accommodation is the least effective; it is the degree of curvature of the crystalline lens of the eye which is necessary to produce a good retinal focus. The lens is elastic,

Figure 65.   Some of the varied secondary cues to visual depth are illustrated here: the smaller size of more distant objects, loss of detail, partial hiding by nearer objects, and so on. (Bahnsen, from Monkmeyer, in Gibson, J. J.: *The Perception of the Visual World,* Houghton Mifflin Co.)

and its curvature is reflexively controlled by the ciliary muscle. The amount of tension in the muscle that is necessary to focus the image, and the resulting proprioceptive sensation, is one cue to depth. Such effectiveness as this cue has is for near distances, up to about six feet from the eye.

A much more effective cue (but also mainly for near distances) is the convergence of the two eyes which is necessary if the image of an object is to be projected on the *fovea* in both eyes (the point of central vision in the retina, where acuity is highest). For far objects the axes of the eyeballs are parallel; for near objects, the axes cross, and the position of the eyes in their sockets becomes a cue to the distance of the object looked at. This is chiefly effective for distances up to, perhaps, 20 feet, though it may have some effect at greater distances.

Retinal disparity, or parallax, refers to the difference in the retinal images that are formed when an object is seen from different angles. Binocular disparity occurs when an object is observed with both eyes open, because the eyes, separated in space, necessarily see the object from different angles. The student can demonstrate this for himself by holding a pencil so that it points directly at his nose, at a distance of a foot or a foot and a half. By closing first one eye, then the other, he will find that the two eyes have distinctly different views of the pencil, one seeing the point and the right side, the other the point and the left side. Movement disparity is more obvious; either with one eye or two, one gets very different views of a three-dimensional object or scene as one moves the head from side to side, or up and down.

Both forms of disparity have a strong effect in the perception of the third dimension. The effect of binocular disparity is demonstrated best

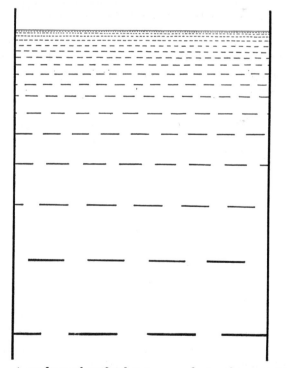

Figure 66.   A gradient of artificial texture, producing the perception of continuous distance. If this were a representation of a real surface, the grain and irregularities of the larger (nearer) component parts would be clear and large, and diminish proportionately for the smaller parts, producing a realistic texture and a more compelling impression of visual depth. (From Gibson, J. J.: *The Perception of the Visual World,* Houghton Mifflin Co., 1950.)

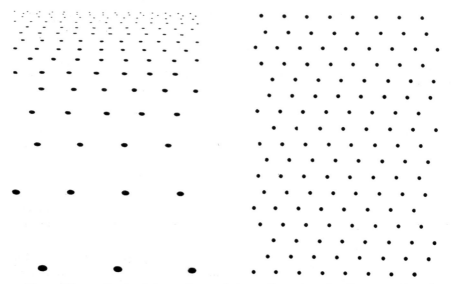

Figure 67.   On the left, gradients of size and spacing give the perception of a receding surface; on the right, the absence of gradients gives a "frontal" (non-receding) surface. (From Gibson, J. J.: *The Perception of the Visual World,* Houghton Mifflin Co., 1950.)

in the *stereoscope,* a device that allows one to see two slightly different photographs simultaneously, as if they were one. One photograph is seen by the right eye; the other, made by moving the camera to the left and taking a second photograph of the same scene, is seen by the left eye. The eyes then deliver to the same parts of the visual area in the brain slightly different patterns of excitation; but instead of two conflicting two-dimensional scenes, a single scene in depth is perceived. The brain, in some manner not at all understood, integrates the discordant patterns and adds a dimension in so doing.

There are a number of other cues to depth (Fig. 65): the smaller retinal angle of familiar objects farther away; the overlap of near objects over farther ones, partly hiding them; the loss of fine detail in farther objects, and their change of color (increasing blueness) at greater distances.

But all these are cues that apply to a single object (or two overlapping objects) without regard to the surrounding environment; and our discussion up to this point might suggest that in judging the distance of an object all one takes into account is the appearance of that object. In fact, except when one is dealing with objects flying or floating in the air, all one's judgments concern objects that are connected with (supported by) extended surfaces such as the ground, walls of buildings, ceilings, and so on; and these background surfaces have a most important influence on depth perception. As they extend away from us, they show gradients of *visual texture,* the units into which the surface is divided

(Figs. 66, 67) and the irregularities within the units (not shown in the figures). These provide cues to the direction of slope of the surface, with respect to the line of vision, and thus provide cues to the size and distance of objects close to or touching the surfaces (Fig. 68).

AUDITORY DIRECTION AND DEPTH.   To understand the problems posed by auditory space perception we must first consider the structure of the ear (Fig. 69). The outer passage ends at the eardrum, a membrane that picks up the vibrations of the air that constitute sound. The vibrations in turn are transmitted through the middle ear by three small bones, to the fluid of the inner ear. The inner ear contains the *basilar membrane* and the auditory receptors, coiled up within the *cochlea.* Hearing occurs when the basilar membrane is disturbed by the vibrations of the fluid in which it is bathed. (The bone cavity of the cochlea, as it happens, connects with that of the semicircular canals—see p. 58—and the same

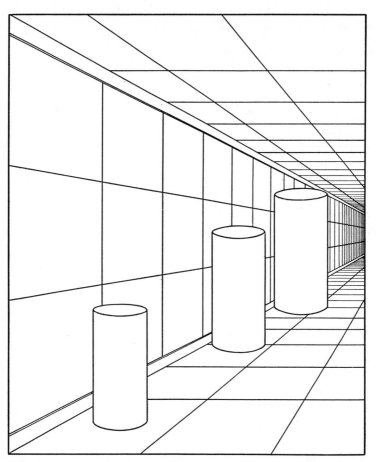

Figure 68.   Perception of size and distance of objects as related to receding surfaces. The three cylinders have the same retinal angles. (From Gibson, J. J.: *The Perception of the Visual World,* Houghton, Mifflin Co., 1950.)

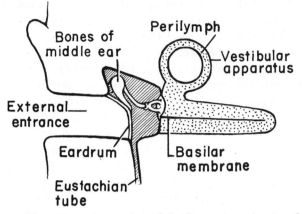

Figure 69.   Schematic representation of the human ear, showing the bones that connect the eardrum with the inner ear, the basilar membrane that carries the auditory receptors, and the cavity of bone filled with fluid (perilymph) which is continuous with the fluid of the semicircular canals, one of these being shown schematically. The Eustachian tube connects with the mouth, permitting air pressure in the middle ear to be equalized with external air pressure. The basilar membrane and the tube-like hollow of bone in which it lies are not straight as shown in the figure, but coiled like a snail-shell (after Békésy).

fluid is involved in producing both auditory sensation and the proprioceptive sensation of bodily motion.)

The design of this system, apparently, is such as to permit discrimination of frequency and intensity, but nothing else. In a sense this is true; but just as the visual system uses binocular disparity and other cues to produce depth discrimination though it seems at first not suited for such a function, so the auditory system uses the cues of frequency and intensity to produce discriminations of direction and distance that in some cases are surprisingly accurate. Sound travels at a limited speed (about 1100 ft./sec. instead of the 186,000 mi./sec. of light), so that the time of transmission from a sound source becomes a factor in discrimination: one slight advantage for the ear over the eye. Another is that *sound shadows* (blocking of the sound waves by an interposed object) are selective; the long waves are not blocked, short waves are, whereas with light the blocking is practically complete. Suppose therefore that a complex sound, made up of high (short-wave) tones and low (long-wave) tones, comes from the subject's left side. His left ear gets both high and low tones; but his right ear is in the sound shadow cast by the head, so there is a loss of high tones. This binaural discrepancy is a cue to which side the sound source is on. With high-pitched sounds, also, the sound shadow cast by the outer ear makes possible a discrimination of front from back.

The most important cues to direction, the ones that tend to dominate, are the relative times of arrival at the two ears, and the relative intensity. Ordinarily these two cues work together, but it is found experimentally that either is effective alone, other cues being held constant, though the time factor is the more important of the two. If a sound reaches both ears simultaneously, and with the same intensity, the source must be equally distant from them: that is, it must lie in the median plane, directly in front, above, or behind the head. If it reaches the right ear first, it must be on the right side; but with a low-pitched sound (so that the shadow of the outer ear is not effective) this gives no cue as to whether the sound source is higher or lower, forward or back. This is in fact what is found with a momentary sound, when echoes (reflections from the ground, walls, or other surfaces) are excluded. But with a continuing sound, or one that is repeated, the subject tilts his head, and at once can discriminate up from down; or turns his head to one side, and discriminates front from back. (Here is an example of the importance of response for auditory perception, not unlike the importance of eye movement for visual perceptions.)

The discrimination of the times of arrival of a sound at the two ears is astonishingly fine. The time differences involved are of the order of one or two tenths of a millisecond. The same capacity affects the perception of auditory depth. A sound made near one ear produces a binaural difference, in time of arrival, of something under a millisecond; farther away, the difference is slightly less, and this permits reliable judgments of distance. Echoes also become very important. The subject can judge the distance of a reflecting surface on the basis of the time difference between hearing a noise that he makes himself and its echo: about 2 ms for each 1 ft. distance. Many animals or birds have developed such auditory skill. The bat is the best-known example. When flying it emits very high-pitched sounds, and is guided by the echoes: so much so that it can fly among a number of obstacles without hitting any of them when the eyes are completely covered. If the ears are covered, the ability disappears.

It is the same cue that tells us when we are about to bump into something in the dark. This is sometimes a very puzzling experience; one is suddenly aware of some large object in front of one, without knowing how. It used to be thought that the trick is done by something called "facial vision," some kind of sensitivity of the skin of the face to radiations from nearby objects. Actually, the object is detected by means of the echoes of the sound of one's footsteps or of one's breathing. It is easy to show that one is dealing with auditory space perception in this case, because the ability disappears when the ears are plugged. The ability of course becomes very important in blindness. When the blind man taps his cane hard on the sidewalk he is not feeling for obstacles; he is setting up echoes from nearby objects, and the echoes tell him where he is with respect to those objects.

One does not of course perceive the echoes as separate events, estimate their time of arrival, and on the basis of the time differences in milliseconds work out the direction and distance of an obstacle, any more than we see visual depth as a result of conscious calculations about retinal disparities. There is instead an automatic transformation of the sensory stimulations into the perception of an object, as a preparation for further response. How it occurs has not been worked out, but presumably it is to be considered another example of the importance of timing in neural transmission (see Chap. 5).

Summary

This chapter differs from most discussions of perception by treating it objectively, and by giving due weight to its motor correlates. The behavioristic approach is as necessary with perception as with learning or motivation. We do not perceive our perceptual processes, we perceive environmental events: that is, a perception is itself not observable, and it must be regarded as a theoretically-known event; an inference, not a datum. The same statements apply to sensation. We may then distinguish between two theoretically-known processes, sensation as an afferent process, perception as the mediating process to which it gives rise directly.

A distinction is made further between perceiving (setting up a percept) and percept (the end product, a resetting of the switchboard). Perceiving generally involves feedback from overt motor responses, and thus has serial extent in time. The exceptions occur only with thoroughly familiar sensory patterns, and even here it appears that there is a series of events internally. Perception has a characteristically temporal organization.

Fundamentally, perception is a preparation for response, but not necessarily for a specific one. It is a change of connections in the switchboard, transient or lasting, which will modify any of an indefinitely large class of responses to subsequent stimuli. To the extent that the change of connections is lasting, it constitutes knowledge (but this term is out of place when a single specific response is involved—knowledge is a potential modification of a large class of responses).

Variability is always present in perception, even with constant sensory input. This can only mean that a given input is able to arouse different groups of mediating processes. The prime example is the ambiguous figure, but only because the change from one percept to another is dramatically clear in this case—when looked for, the variability is found elsewhere. Certain percepts can be reliably obtained with certain sensory inputs, and may seem to continue unchanged, but closer examination shows that what happens here is a persistent recurrence of a particular percept, not continuity of existence. The discussion relates these points to the problem of the figure-ground phenomenon, the perceptual constancies, the phi-phenomenon, and the perceived unity of groups.

There are two forms of perceptual generalization: series generalization, which seems inherent in the sensory process; and the generalization with patterns, which involves mediating processes and is not clearly understood at present.

The classic problem of visual space perception is how the two-dimensional retina can produce visual depth, a third dimension in the visual world. The properties of stimulation, from the object itself, are well known and traditionally classified as the primary and secondary cues to depth. More recent work adds, to these, texture gradients from the surfaces on which the object rests or with which it is in contact.

Similarly, the cues which make possible the auditory perception of direction and distance, of a sound-emitting object or sound-reflecting surface, are well known. But neither in the visual nor in the auditory case are the neural mechanisms of such perceptions understood. The sensitivity and accuracy of the ear in detecting the position of obstacles is almost incredible—when, for example, a sound is heard as coming from the left side because its vibrations reach the left ear one ten-thousandth of a second before the corresponding vibrations reach the right ear.

Notes

The background of this discussion can be found in Hebb, *Organization of Behavior,* John Wiley & Sons, 1949, and a rather similar treatment is given by Osgood (*General References,* Chap. 1, p. 19). Antidotes to Hebb and Osgood may be found in various places; see for example W. Köhler, *Gestalt Psychology,* Liveright Publishing Corp., 1929 and 1947, and *Dynamics in Psychology,* Liveright, 1940; or K. Koffka, *Principles of Gestalt Psychology,* Harcourt, Brace and Co., 1935.

Details of phi-phenomenon, contrast effects, space perception and so forth, including a number of aspects of visual and auditory perception not dealt with in the present text, may be found in any of Osgood, Stevens, or Woodworth and Schlosberg (*General References,* Chap. 1).

The experiment on tachistoscopic perception of groups of letters is by W. Heron (*Amer. J. Psychol.,* 1957, 70, 38–48); that on the simultaneous auditory perception of groups of numbers by D. E. Broadbent (*Quart. J. Exp. Psychol.,* 1956, 8, 145–152).

An excellent discussion of the problems of visual depth is found in J. J. Gibson, *Perception of the Visual World,* Houghton Mifflin Co., 1950.

Chapter 10

Problems relating to thought

I_N this chapter the main topic is man's mental capacities and the behavior they make possible, the behavior that most clearly distinguishes him from other animals. The preceding chapters provide a theoretical background for our discussion, but theory being still so inadequate the present chapter uses it more to define problems than to provide explanations. The kinds of behavior we are most concerned with are language and problem-solving, including the cooperative problem-solving known as science.

Thought and consciousness

We may begin with a general question concerning consciousness. The word needs to be used with care; for many persons it means something not part of the physical world, an attribute of an immaterial mind or soul instead of a brain activity. This might be enough reason to avoid the term entirely in scientific discussion, except that this or an equivalent term (to which the same difficulty would apply) is needed to refer to the difference between the waking, adult animal of a higher species and the same animal under anesthesia, or in concussion, or in deep sleep; and to certain other differences which seem to parallel this one. "Conscious" and "consciousness" are useful terms for designating a state of behavior, or the state of the brain which determines the behavior. The behavioral difference—between consciousness and unconsciousness—is not

200

simple, as we can see by taking some examples which also clarify our whole discussion.

Our first pair of examples show that responsiveness, by itself, is not enough to show that consciousness is present. In comparing a conscious and an unconscious animal, one might think that the only difference is that one responds to stimulation and the other does not. But this is not accurate. Reflex responses can be obtained from a man in coma, when he is considered to be unconscious. Also, the reflexes of breathing and heart action continue, or else death follows at once; some reflexes disappear, and others are altered, but the point is that the unconscious organism is not wholly unresponsive or inactive.

Secondly, vigorous reflex activity can be elicited from the after end of a spinal dog (i.e., after severing the cord at the level of the neck), which is likewise not considered to be conscious. Some persons see consciousness in any living thing, plant or animal, but such views need not concern us. Scientifically there is no justification for ascribing consciousness to sensitive plants (such as Venus's fly-trap, which makes a reflex-like response to trap the insect that alights on it), to bacteria, or to fleas or earthworms or jellyfish. These conclusions apply to any animal whose behavior is entirely reflexive, including the ants, bees and termites, the social insects whose behavior as we shall see is very remarkable but has not been shown to be more than a reflexive (or sense-dominated) adaptation to the environment.

On the other hand, it is not possible to avoid the inference of consciousness in such higher animals as the chimpanzee or rhesus monkey, or in the dog or cat, though we do not consider these latter to be quite as high in the scale of psychological complexity. None of these animals has language, so a verbal report is not necessary as a sign of consciousness. (This point is also clear when one identifies consciousness in a stranger, seen for the first time, without hearing him speak a word—a common occurrence.) The higher animals then share some feature of man's nonverbal behavior which leads us to classify them as having consciousness, and this feature is not shared by the ants and bees.

The distinction we are discussing is evidently related to the distinction between sense-dominated behavior and behavior in which thought—or complex mediating activity—takes part. We have seen that there is probably no hard-and-fast distinction between these two classes of behavior (p. 46). Accordingly, we can make a distinction between conscious higher animals and unconscious lower ones without supposing that these are two quite separate classes. We are dealing with a continuum of higher and lower species; at one end consciousness is clearly in evidence, at the other not. There is no need to try to dichotomize, to determine at just what point consciousness appears in this hierarchy (just as we can use the terms "upper" and "lower" or "East" and "West" without having to say where one begins and the other leaves off). Let us agree that the presence of consciousness is not demonstrated by reflex responsiveness alone, a conclusion which implies that mediating processes are required as a minimum; we can then go on to see what other complications are involved without treating this as an all-or-nothing question.

Similarly, consciousness in man can be impaired in various ways, and there is no good purpose to be served in trying to say just what the impairment must be before we decide that the subject is not conscious. Is the sleeper who is dreaming, but unresponsive to the world about him, conscious or not? Is a man conscious after a blow on the head, if he can talk intelligently about himself but does not know where he is or how he got there, and later cannot even recall being helped to the hospital? In either case, some of the processes normally present in the conscious subject are present now, others are absent or impaired; but these are in-between cases, and we do not need to classify them in one or the other category.

However, it is worth while paying some attention to them, because they tell us something about normal consciousness. Evidently it is not a single function but a group of functions, rather loosely associated, so that one can be decreased or abolished while another is not greatly affected. Normally, one feature of consciousness is *immediate memory* (memory for the immediate past), so that the subject remembers what he was thinking about and can reproduce much of it on request (the summation method: p. 37). He remembers what he has said and done, and does not unnecessarily repeat an action that is already complete, or bore his listeners by telling the same joke twice at the same sitting. Normally, he perceives most of what goes on around him, unlike the sleeper, though he may not give any overt sign of having done so; but if he is deep in a book or a TV program he may actually be *less* responsive to other stimuli than one who is dozing.

Evidently the state of consciousness is something that varies greatly from one time to another, even in normal subjects. This variability, in degree of responsiveness and in what the organism is responsive to, is in fact one of the marks from which we infer consciousness or the capacity for consciousness. If at times the higher animal is unresponsive to his environment (even when his eyes are open, and the EEG shows a waking pattern), at other times he prowls restlessly about or seeks ways of manipulating, and being excited by, the world about him. Further, when he is responsive, the aspects of the environment to which he responds differ greatly from time to time. That is, his interests are variable.

At times, of course, interest is determined by biologically primitive needs: at one time the animal is motivated sexually, at another time by hunger; and this degree of variability is just as characteristic of the lower as of the higher animal. But when such needs are fully met, other complex motivations appear in the higher animal (p. 174). Given activity in the arousal system, the thought process appears to be intrinsically motivated, and the complexity of behavior that emerges when no primitive need is present is an excellent index of level in the psychological hierarchy.

Finally, another index of consciousness, or of behavioral level, is an intermittent appearance of purposive and insightful behavior, to which we shall return in a moment.

A word may be said about what is called "the unconscious." This is an unsatisfactory conception, mainly for the same reason that instinct is (p. 124): it implies the existence of a separate agency fully capable of controlling behavior or of competing for control —an agency that duplicates the powers of its alter ego, the conscious mind.

In a subjective theory of behavior it is assumed that the mind can look inward and see what is going on inside itself. Sooner or later it is found, however, that there is much that cannot be observed in this way, especially if moral and emotional conflicts are involved. Hence the idea that the mind must have a separate compartment, a region where unpleasant items may conceal themselves—or, in essence, a second mind whose contents are not accessible to the first or conscious mind. But this creates worse problems than the one it solves.

The unconscious is sometimes supposed to be capable of jealousy, fear, lust and so on. It can recognize complex social situations, especially ones involving threat or competition, and make the subject act accordingly (but without his knowing the real reason). Such powers would mean that the unconscious has separate thought mechanisms, parallel to those of the conscious mind. This is the reason for saying that it is, in effect, a second mind. But the only basis for this whole approach is the initial assumption that introspection is an adequate method of study, an assumption which we already have reason to doubt (Chap. 2).

Unconscious or subconscious processes certainly exist, in the sense of mental events that affect behavior but are not retained in memory and are not reportable. The question raised here is not about their existence but whether they are—so to speak—gathered together into a separate organized entity, an unconscious mind. It is important for the student to recognize that they occur in the most ordinary circumstances, and not only where one's emotions are involved. As we shall see, for example, they play a large part in problem-solving. Unconscious processes are unreportable but in other respects they may be indistinguishable from conscious processes. There is no good reason for thinking of them as constituting an organized and separate agency.

This discussion may be summarized as follows. "Consciousness" is equivalent to "complex thought processes," and hence is not present in animals whose behavior is at a reflexive, sense-dominated level (on the other hand, verbal behavior is not a necessary requirement). It is very variable, qualitatively, in the behavior it determines: it may diminish or increase responsiveness, and may produce periods of sustained purposive behavior or periods of almost complete immobility. With this goes a great variability of motivations. An important feature of normal consciousness is immediate memory, making it possible to coordinate past experience and action with future action. Immediate memory and purpose (which involves anticipation of the future) together mean an extension of temporal integration in behavior, for longer blocks of time. (So-called instinct, in lower animals, may also produce long-term temporal integrations, but here the behavior remains under sensory dominance and there is no evidence that the animal acts purposively, or anticipates the end effects of the instinctive act: p. 125).

Insight and purpose

The meaning of *insight* will be clearest if we look at some examples from a classical series of experiments. A chimpanzee is shown food—banana—suspended above his head out of reach. In sight, but at the other side of the experimental room, is a box upon which he could stand. He jumps repeatedly for the food without success, gives this up, and paces restlessly back and forth. Suddenly he stops in front of the box, then rolls it over under the food, climbs up and seizes the food. At this point insight is said to have occurred.

In a later test the box is left outside the room, where the chimpanzee sees it as he is being led to work. It is not visible from the experimental room, but the door is left open. At first the animal stays close to the point above which the fruit is suspended, jumping for it and trying one way after another of reaching it directly. All at once he stops these efforts, stands motionless for a moment, then gallops out into the corridor and returns dragging the box, with which he secures the prize.

This sudden thinking-of-the-answer or "seeing the light" is of course well known in human problem-solving. The student should not get the impression that insight occurs only in this way, after a delay period—it must be present also when the subject sees the answer at once—but the sudden solution has a special interest because the sharp break in behavior identifies for us the moment at which a reorganization of thought processes has occurred. Like consciousness, insight is not all-or-nothing; it can be defined, essentially, as the *functioning of mediating processes in the solution of problems,* and from this point of view it is clear that some mode or degree of insight is present in all problem-solving by the higher animal. The dog shows his superiority to other animals, such as the domestic fowl, in his perception of situations which require taking an indirect route to food (*umweg* behavior, Fig. 70). The chimpanzee shows his superiority to the dog in using objects as stepping stones, as described above; it is of great interest that there is no reliable report of a dog's ever pushing a chair or a box into a position from which he could climb up to food. This is physically possible for the dog; failure to do so shows that the chimpanzee's superiority with "tools" is due to intellectual capacity and not solely because he has hands—though these are also an important factor in such behavior.

The insightful act is an excellent example of something that is not learned, but still depends on learning (p. 113). It is not learned, since it can be adequately performed on its first occurrence; it is not perfected through practice in the first place, but appears all at once in recognizable form (further practice, however, may still improve it). On the other hand, the situation must not be completely strange; the animal must have had prior experience with the component parts of the situation, or with other situations that have some similarity to it.

The chimpanzee, for example, is capable of using a stick to pull in objects that are out of reach; but he does not do so if he has never had experience in manipulating sticks. Six young chimpanzees were tested with food out of reach, and a stick lying in plain view. Only one animal used the stick to get the food; this was a female who had been frequently observed playing with sticks in the past. All six animals were then given sticks as playthings for a three-day period, and at the end of this time were tested again. Never in the intervening three days had one of them been observed to use a stick to pull anything to him—instead of using it as a rake, the stick was used to poke at other chimpanzees, or at the experimenter outside the cage—but on being retested three used the stick at once to rake in the food, and the other three did so after one false start. This was a new act, and thus insightful; but it also depended on the prior occurrence of other experience.

Similarly, dogs reared in isolation, without the normal opportunity for learning to deal with barriers, were markedly inferior to normal dogs in a situation like that of Fig. 70, as well as other "insight situations," and we have seen that experience occurring in infancy affects problem-solving in the adult rat as well (p. 126). All our evidence thus points to the conclusion that a new insight consists of a *recombination of pre-existent mediating processes,* not the sudden appearance of a wholly new process (cf. assumption 4, p. 105).

Such recombinations must be frequent in man's everyday living, and in a theoretical framework we must consider them to be original and creative. The terms "original" and "creative" as applied to human thought are commonly reserved for great intellectual and artistic achievements; but from the point of view of behavioral mechanisms one sees that

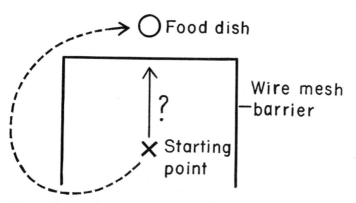

Figure 70.   The *umweg* (round-about) problem. The animal starts at the point shown, with food in sight through the wire mesh. The insightful solution is to turn *away* from the food, as shown by the broken line.

originality is a question of degree, and that in principle the housewife who thinks of a new way of serving potatoes is as truly creative as the novelist who shows us a new view of human nature. The child who imagines that her doll talks to her is being creative.

We speak of insight chiefly in the context of overcoming some obstacle or disposing of a difficulty, but we can recognize that the same kind of process is also involved in suddenly realizing, for example, that a friend is annoyed. Even in one's dreams, when one creates improbable situations, or in daydreams when one imagines how entertaining it would be if the lecturer in a large class fell off the platform, one is recombining ideas to produce what is, to a greater or less extent, a new idea. Such products of thought may be bizarre or impractical, but they share a common creativity with insight.

Purpose goes hand in hand with insight in problem-solving. Behavior is classed as purposive when it shows modifiability with circumstances in such a way as to tend to produce a constant end effect; it is behavior that is free of sensory dominance, controlled jointly by the present sensory input and by an expectancy of producing the effect which is its goal. When the situation changes, the behavior changes accordingly.

For example: the chimpanzee that has solved the problem of using a box to climb on for food is given the same problem, but no box is within reach. He goes over to the experimenter, standing nearby, and tugs at his clothing to bring him near the suspended fruit; whereupon he climbs the experimenter, and gets the reward. This is clearly a purposive action. When a dog in the *umweg* problem turns away from food, he is showing a capacity for purposive behavior in his avoidance of the barrier; because it is found that in each of a number of variants of the situation the dog immediately modifies his behavior to suit the circumstances and find the shortest route to food.

In principle, a number of examples of a given kind of behavior have to be observed before we can conclude that purpose is involved, since it is only in this way that we can demonstrate that the behavior adjusts itself to circumstance. In practice, however, one may know enough about the species—or about a particular animal—to be able to identify purpose in a single trial. Knowing that chimpanzees as a species are capable of complex insightful and purposive behavior, and that a particular chimpanzee has previously used a box to climb on, one need have no doubt about the purposiveness of the whole pattern of behavior when this animal pulls the observer over to the right place and uses *him* as a stepping stone.

In the purposive behavior of man we encounter longer unified chains of action than in any lower animal: "unified" since it is clear that the earlier links in the chain are not done for their own sake but because they make the later links possible. When a chimpanzee goes to get a stick, returns and rakes in food, getting a stick does not in itself meet the need for food, but it makes the later part of the whole action possible. In man such temporally-integrated patterns are much longer. The fisherman in need of food may spend a day or more weaving his net before he even goes near the river. He builds a shelter before he needs it, as winter approaches; and such anticipatory and purposive behavior may involve periods not only of days or weeks but even years. We customarily think of man's intellectual superiority as shown in (1) his capacity for language and related symbolisms, and (2) his capacity for solving a difficult problem as presented to him here and now. But to these, it seems, we should add also (3) a long-range anticipation of future difficulties (including some that may never arise, and some that would not arise without his help).

Communication and language

The term *communication* is used here in a broad sense, comprising three levels of behavior: (1) a reflexive or nonpurposive level, exemplified by the social insects and by the emotionally-tinged danger cries of mammals as well; (2) a purposive level, clearly evident in some subhuman mammals, which nevertheless falls short of language; and (3) language itself, which appears to be exclusively human. However, these are broad categories, and it would be unwise to think of them as sharply distinct from each other. It is not inconceivable that insects have purposive behavior. The chimpanzee, or the porpoise, or the elephant, may border on the possession of language, and conceivably on occasion may behave in a way that meets the criteria proposed below (p. 209).

1. Reflexive communication.   The social insects live in highly organized colonies, in which the behavior of one animal must be coordinated with that of others if the colony is to survive. The coordination is so good that one can hardly help thinking of it as intelligent and purposive, but as far as is known this is not so; the individual worker ant responds compulsively to stimuli from other ants, and by her behavior in turn stimulates them to respond, in such a way as to promote the life of the colony, without thought processes or any anticipation of the long-term effects of the behavior. In one wasp species the larvae in need of food protrude their heads from their cells, which stimulates the workers to provide them with food. In various species of ants, odor determines whether a worker is admissible into the colony; if an actual member is given a strange odor she is attacked and killed by other workers, but if a stranger is given the colony odor she is unmolested. In some species the nest entrance is guarded by a soldier who blocks it with his large head; when a worker approaches, to enter or leave, she strokes the head or abdomen of the guard, who then moves backward and permits her to pass. The ant is capable of learning, so this behavior may be of the

order of a conditioned rather than an unconditioned reflex, but in either case it is sensorily controlled.

In much higher species, where purposive communication occurs, there still may be many examples of an almost equally reflexive and unintelligent, or nonpurposive, level of communication—particularly in the context of fear or hostility. We shall return to these examples in the discussion of purposive communication, because they provide a contrast that makes purposiveness, when it does occur, more recognizable. Before doing so, however, we may look briefly at an extremely interesting example of communication in bees.

The worker bee which has encountered a food source at a distance from the hive is able to give the direction and distance of the food to other bees by means of the "dance" which she performs on a vertical comb in the hive, upon her return. She climbs the comb with a peculiar waggling movement, making a number of rotations in doing so. The angle of climb corresponds to the angle between the direction of the sun and that of the food source. The number of turns corresponds to the distance (a smaller number when food is farther away). Other workers follow her closely, and thereafter fly more or less directly to the food.

Such behavior has been called "the language of the bees." We have however no reason whatever for regarding this as more than a figure of speech. Though its *effect* is the same as if the bee possessed a sign language, it is not shown that any purposive element is present in it.

2. PURPOSIVE COMMUNICATION SHORT OF LANGUAGE. Now let us consider some purposive forms of communication in higher animals, together with some nonpurposive ones for comparison.

The essential distinction is whether the "sender" acts in such a way as to affect the "receiver's" behavior, and modifies the communication according to its effect on him (or lack of effect). In purposive communication the sender remains sensitive to the receiver's responses. A dog that wants to be let out may go to the door, turning his head at first and looking at his owner; if at this point the owner gets up and starts toward the door the dog simply waits, but if not after a moment or two the dog barks—the bark being gentler, more restrained, than when the dog hears a stranger outside—and if nothing happens then the barks become more vigorous. The behavior is effectively adapted toward achieving a change in another with a minimum of effort, and stops as soon as this objective is attained. A caged chimpanzee begging for food beyond his reach similarly adapts the means to the end, using begging gestures with the hands as well as vocalization. The purposive aspect of the behavior is further confirmed by the use of other means of getting the food, such as using a stick, if they are available. The individual begging act is one of a repertoire of acts, any one of which may be employed depending on circumstances.

Contrast this with the alarm call of the wild monkey that detects a human observer. This is communication, for it alerts the rest of the band so that they all flee. But there is no reason to consider it purposive, because the screaming continues after the others have received the "message," and are well out of any danger. The whole behavior fits into a picture of generalized emotional disturbance; it may have a purposive element also, but this has not been shown. The same considerations apply to the growl or bark of a dog at a strange dog, or an intruder. The dog, like the monkey, is known to be capable of purposive behavior and conceivably some of these acts also combine the purposive with the emotional—that is, the dog may growl with the intention of scaring off another dog—but again this has not been shown to be so.

3. LANGUAGE.   In man we have behavior that parallels both of the preceding classes (a cry of pain or a look of disgust may be quite reflexive, and some purposive gestures and sounds may be at no higher level of complexity than a chimpanzee's begging); but we also have a kind of behavior which, as far as we know, does not occur in any other species. This is language. It includes sign language as well as spoken and written words: and the chief problem does not concern the ability to make the sounds of human speech, since lower animals are not capable of sign language either.

What puts language on a higher level than the purposive communication of dog or chimpanzee is the *varied combination* of the same signs (words, pictures, gestures) for different purposes. The parrots and other talking birds can reproduce speech sounds very effectively—but without the slightest indication of transposing words, learned as part of one phrase or sentence, into a new order, or making new combinations of them. The phrase is "parroted," repeated as a whole without regard to circumstances and with little change from the form in which it was learned. The human child, on the other hand, uses his separate words singly or in new combinations to influence others' behavior, as well as using them in the form in which they were originally heard. We do not have to analyze long sentences to see the difference between human speech and the parrot's; the two-year-old's use of four words to form the propositions "I thirsty," "I not thirsty," "Mommy thirsty" and so on, is enough to make the point.

The criteria of language, then, are (1) that it is usually purposive communication (though a nonpurposive use is common also, as in talking to oneself), and (2) that two or more items of the behavior are combined in one way for one purpose, and recombined for other purposes. This applies as much to gesture as to speech; an animal such as the chimpanzee, which makes very effective use of begging gestures or threatening ones, purposively, seems never to be able to combine two gestures as a man does when he points to an object, for example, and then to someone to whom it should be handed.

The fundamental difference between man and chimpanzee in this respect seems to lie in man's capacity for having several sets of mediating processes at once, relatively independent of each other. The three levels of communication that have been defined may be seen as representing three stages of intellectual development. In the first there are no mediating processes at all, and the animal remains sensorily tied to his environment. In the second, mediating processes occur but (to state the general idea crudely) only one or two at a time; there is a certain detachment of thought processes from the immediate sensory environment, but not a great one, so purposive behavior and planning consequently remain rather limited. In the third, the human, stage, there is a greater fluidity of mediating processes and a greater independence from the present sensory environment.

The greater fluidity and independence make possible not only language but also a level of teamwork that is not seen in subhuman animals. This is a coordination of behavior by which two or more individuals seek a goal which they will share and which cannot be reached by them singly. It requires that the individual not only anticipate the future effects of his own actions: he must take into account also those of his partner or partners. The effectiveness of what one does is contingent on the other's doing the right thing at the right time. One chimpanzee may help another, in the sense of giving him food or (with a young animal) pulling him away from danger, but it is rarely or never that one sees two chimpanzees spontaneously make a coordinated attack on an obstacle that neither could handle alone. Such behavior is common in man, and sets him apart from other animals almost as clearly as his possession of speech. The lack of teamwork in monkey and chimpanzee may be attributed in great part to their lack of language, preventing them from agreeing on an objective in advance; but it appears that this is not the whole explanation. The same intellectual lack seems to underlie the absence both of language and of teamwork.

Problem-solving in man: laboratory studies

We know human problem-solving in two contexts: first, as it is studied in the psychological laboratory; and secondly, as it occurs in the daily life of students, scientists and citizens. Unfortunately the two are not always closely related, and there are some characteristics of real-life solutions that cannot be observed in the controlled experiment—or at any rate, have not been observed so far. To learn something about these aspects we shall turn in the following sections to a consideration of scientific thought, after looking in the present section at problem-solving as it is studied in the laboratory.

The chief limitation of the laboratory study is that it must deal, in general, with short-term solutions, ones that can be reached in a reasonable period of time; consequently the problems presented must be rather clearly defined for the subject. In real life the barrier to intellectual achievement often lies in the choice of problem, or which of its aspects to attack first, and in selecting the relevant information; and success or failure depends often on whether the thinker keeps on coming back to his problem and worrying about it for months or years. When the undergraduate enters the laboratory to act as subject, one has only an hour or so of his time. One must define the problem instead of waiting for him to find it, and put before him the necessary data and materials. As to motivation, he usually finds it advisable to please the instructor, and so keeps on working whether the problem interests him or not. But despite its limitations, laboratory study of human problem-solving has told us much about the process, especially in the light of the various records of scientific thinking and of experimental studies with infrahuman animals.

Animal studies have already shown us that thinking need not depend on language (since animals do not have language but do have fairly complex mediating processes). Human studies allow us to go further; not only do important steps of thought occur without language, they cannot be put into language after they have occurred. This may be true of quite simple problems, and of subjects highly trained (in the earlier days of psychology) in the introspective method. When the flash of insight occurs in scientific thought we have repeated testimony from the scientist that it is apt to be without warning, and without any awareness of the steps of inference immediately preceding—suddenly the answer is there, and that is all. Similarly in the laboratory: there are evidently links in the chain that are quite "unconscious"—and not unimportant ones either.

The experiments on set in arithmetical operations (p. 53), for example, concern problems which for an educated subject are about as simple as they can be. The subject is presented with a pair of digits, 2 and 6. When he has a set to add the answer 8 appears directly, or with a set to subtract the answer 4; but the set itself—clearly a decisive factor in the response—does not appear to introspection and cannot be clearly described by the subject, nor can he describe the mechanism by which the *same* pair of numbers produces different answers so promptly and, apparently, directly.

Another experiment involves a much more difficult problem, but again one in which the solution, when it is found, is simple. The subject is given the task of tying together two strings which hang down from the ceiling, just too far apart for him to be able to take hold of one and then reach the other. The solution is to take a pair of pliers—left lying about by the experimenter but in the eyes of most subjects having no bearing on the problem—tie them to the end of one of the strings, and start it swinging like a pendulum; then it becomes possible to take hold of the other string and catch the pliers when they swing close, detach the pliers, and tie the knot. When the subjects failed to see this possibility the experimenter "accidentally" brushed against one of the strings and set it swinging, whereupon a number of the subjects solved the problem promptly, but without any realization that they had been steered to the solution. For them the idea had arisen spontaneously, and they were quite unaware of a decisive factor in their thinking.

Experiments with anagrams provide still another example. The subject is given a series of anagrams such as *lecam* for *camel,* each of which can be solved by taking the letters in the order 34521. The subject is not given this rule, just a series of problems to which it applies. In the latter half of the list, however, other anagrams appear which can be solved in two ways: thus *pache,* which makes *cheap* (by following the rule) or *peach.* Few subjects find the alternative solutions, the ones that do not accord with the rule; clearly, the first half of the list develops a set to solve the problems in a particular way, and the interesting and important thing is that the subject may be quite unaware that he is following a rule.

Such sets are both advantageous and disadvantageous. A set to solve in one way blinds one to other solutions; but one's present solution may work efficiently, and it would be very inefficient indeed not to have ready-made procedures to apply to common problems. Life would hardly be possible if every time one wanted to wash one's face, for example, one had to return to first principles, examine one's ideas for possible misleading assumptions, and make sure again that the use of soap and water is a good way of removing dirt. In most of the problems of everyday life the accustomed solution is still the efficient one. But on the other hand, it is not always so; and the difficulty is to know when to stop and take a fresh look at a problem, to discard one's present method of solution and seek a better one.

Also, it is not always easy to identify one's tacit assumptions, or to change them even when one knows what they are and that it is time to make a reassessment. It can be very difficult to do in science when the assumption is a long-used, and useful, theoretical conception. Laboratory studies have shown that the more confirmations an assumption has had the less likely it is to be abandoned, even though it is not working now. In some of these experimental situations, human subjects can be incredibly blind to alternative methods and approaches when a set has been established to deal with problems in one particular way which has worked with other, apparently similar, problems in the past.

If this is true with the small artificial problems used for experimental purposes, it is much truer with the complex problems of science. Here a further obstacle may be encountered. The theoretical idea which must be given up, or changed, may affect wider matters. It was hard for the physical scientist about 1900 to deal with the problem of radioactivity, because the solution required changed assumptions, concerning the atom, which involved the whole structure of physical and chemical theory. Even when the trouble-making assumption is identified and the problem is solved, it may be difficult for someone else to accept the solution, if it affects his view of the cosmos and man's place in it; *then* one may fight to the bitter end to suppress Galileo's ideas about planetary motion, or Darwin's theory of man's origins, or Freud's view of human nature.

Discovery, invention and logic

Refusing to accept a cogent argument because one does not like it is illogical but not necessarily stupid. We tend to identify "good" thinking and intelligence with the use of logic, but some doubt about this conclusion should arise when we find intelligent people acting in an illogical way. In laboratory experiments, for example, it is not uncommon to see the subject who is baffled by the problem given him come back repeatedly to a line of attack that has failed before—even when he remembers that it has failed. This is puzzling in an intelligent subject—as long as we are thinking of problem-solving as solely a logical process. But is it? It may be recalled the airplane was invented despite mathematical proof that a heavier-than-air machine could not fly; and as we shall see shortly, there are records of other highly successful problem-solving, by the great scientists, that also departed at times from the use of logic.

The same scientists are eminently capable of logic when they choose to be (e.g., in demolishing an opponent's argument). Here, it seems, we should distinguish between two modes of thought: (1) *discovery* or invention, the attaining of new ideas, and (2) *verification*, the process of testing, clarifying and systematizing them. When an apparent absence of logical thought is observed in a competent problem-solver, it is mostly in mode (1), not (2). With this distinction, the aimless or futile moves of the baffled problem-solver become more intelligible. When the thinker is completely stuck, having tried everything he can think of, logic is of little use. What can he resort to? One possibility is to leave the problem entirely, hoping that his thought will be running in different channels when he comes back to it—this in fact is a recommended procedure, which often works;—or he may continue to react almost at random to the different elements of the situation, manipulate it this way and that hoping that sensory feedback from one of his moves will give him an idea. In such a process—which also results frequently in success—logic plays no recognizable role.

What is happening here? We assume that a new perception or new idea is a recombination of mediating processes; and that the mediating processes which occur at any moment are a joint product of the sensory input and of the immediately preceding central processes (assumption 4, p. 105, and Fig. 44). The thinker does not know in advance what combination of ideas he is looking for but must act more or less blindly, to increase

the probability that other combinations will occur besides those that have
already done so, and hope that the effective one will be among them.
Dropping the problem for a time, trying to forget it by doing other things,
can help by permitting changes in the mediating-process activity with
which the problem is approached on the next attempt; turning the problem around, looking at it from every possible aspect, juggling its component parts—even though these moves include repetitions of previous
unsuccessful ones—can increase the probability that some sensory event
will occur just at the moment when a central process is occurring which,
with that particular sensory input, adds up to the idea that is needed for
solution of the problem.

It is not implied that blind manipulation is the only source of new
ideas; what we are concerned with here is what happens after the possibilities of logically consistent analysis have been exhausted. Then it becomes, essentially, a matter of waiting for the lightning to strike. There is
repeated testimony from the great mathematicians and scientists that they
have arrived at solutions after deeply immersing themselves in the problem, thoroughly familiarizing themselves with the relevant ideas and
phenomena, trying this attack and that without success—and then, often
with little warning, the line of solution becomes evident. A new idea, a
new insight, is the adventitious occurrence of a certain combination of
mediating processes. It can be prepared for in advance, but cannot be
commanded at a particular moment; having made available the component parts of the idea (as far as he can guess what they may be) the
thinker must then, so to speak, open his mind—avoid a too narrow concentration on a particular line of thought—and wait. The element of
chance is inescapable, which means that the waiting may be for a long
time.

The role of chance (which however works only for the prepared mind)
becomes very evident in another aspect of scientific discovery. It is no-
torious that many great achievements of experimental science have been
made as a matter of accident: accident, except that it must happen to one
who can see its possibilities. An early example is the discovery of the
magnetic effects of electric current, because a compass happened to be
lying near a wire through which Oersted passed a current. Another is the
discovery of x-rays when Roentgen kept unexposed photographic film
where (as we now know) he should not have. A more modern example
is the discovery of penicillin, because Fleming had failed to keep his culture dishes clean. These are examples of great discoveries which required
great men for their making, but less earth-shaking ones made in the same
way are a common occurrence in the laboratory—in fact, they are a main
pillar of ordinary, everyday research. There are few scientists who have
not had the experience of setting out to solve problem *A* and ending up
instead with the solution to *B*, a much more interesting problem that was

not even thought of when the research began. This is serendipity, the art of finding one thing while looking for another.[1]

Another point that emerges from the scientific record is that some of the most brilliant successes do not involve any intellectually difficult ideas. Once the discovery is made, the new idea formulated, the whole affair looks obvious. Any high-school student can understand it, and we wonder how generations of brilliant men could have failed to do so. It is sometimes said that a problem well stated is half solved, and this is often (but not always) so. The true difficulty in such cases is to select the relevant facts and ideas, disregarding the rest. When this is done, the solution may be child's play. Post hoc, to us, who know what the relevant information is, the "problem" is absurdly simple; but when we put it this way we mistake the nature of the real problem, which was to select the relevant facts, to create the effective new ideas, and to get rid of the mistaken ideas of the past which were blinding the thinker.

The great scientist is not always one who thinks at a more complex level. He is great frequently because his thought somehow has avoided the complexities in which others are bogged down, because he sees the relevant issues, and—often enough with no logical justification except that in the end it works—because he has pushed apparently contradictory data to one side, leaving them to be explained later.

Two cases will illustrate these points. The student of physics today has no difficulty understanding how the mercury barometer works, and why it is that water cannot be lifted with a suction pump for more than 34 feet or so. He knows that air has weight, and can see that it must press down on the surface of a well like a gigantic plunger. If now we put a pipe into the well, and use a pump to remove the pressure from the surface of the water *inside* the pipe, the water in the pipe will rise—pushed up by the pressure outside—until the weight of water balances the weight of air outside, after which it will rise no higher. Galileo failed to find this answer; from which we may reasonably conclude, not that Galileo was stupid, but that his pupil Torricelli who did find the answer performed an intellectual feat of the first order by abandoning a principle that others were working with ("Nature abhors a vacuum") and asking whether the facts could be accounted for by the weight of the air. Once in this context, the question could be clearly and finally answered by the experiments with mercury columns (which are easier handled in a laboratory than 34-foot columns of water) that gave us the barometer.

The second case concerns the phlogiston and oxygen theories of com-

---

[1] The term serendipity is coming into common use in discussions of the scientific method but often, it seems, half-jokingly. Joke or no joke, the name is needed to refer to a main factor in fundamental research; and actually the word is well established in the English language, dating from Horace Walpole's *The Three Princes of Serendip*, 1754. The princes "were always making discoveries, by accidents and sagacity [this describes the scientific case precisely], of things they were not in quest of."

bustion. It is common to poke fun at the phlogiston theory because even when it was being used it did not comprehend certain facts which cause the oxygen theory no difficulty. Actually it was a powerful theory. It explained much that was unexplained before and introduced new order into the field. We know now that the oxygen theory produces a greater order, but at the time when Priestley and Lavoisier were arguing the matter (Priestley, though he himself had discovered oxygen, supporting the phlogiston theory) there were *also* facts that denied the oxygen theory completely. Logically, one might say, both theories should have been abandoned; in fact each scientist was confident that the contradictory evidence on his side would be explained with further work. Lavoisier was right,[2] Priestley was wrong; but here the point to note is that both men, highly capable and critical thinkers, selected the data by which to theorize and refused to accept contrary evidence.

From another point of view, of course, neither man was in the slightest degree illogical. Each was thinking in terms of a total picture of the future, when more would be known. No scientist would for a moment consider a theory really satisfactory, or "true," if he thought that the evidence would always be opposed to it; but it is a persistent characteristic of scientific thought that it deals with what is going to happen, or might happen, as well as those things that have happened already. This point will be returned to in Chapter 11, in the discussion of the statistical method by which an experimenter may treat a set of real events as a sample from a larger set of events that have not yet taken place (p. 222).

Where formal analysis and logically-formulated inference come into their own is in the testing and communication of ideas. The thought process produces ideas, as we have seen, more or less unpredictably and at random. Many of these are such that they do not survive for more than a moment or so (they are not "plausible" or "attractive"). Others continue longer, because of the kind of interaction that ensues with other ideas—the ones with which the thinker has been preoccupied during the period of preparation—and this is the point at which the powerful tools of logically consistent analysis make their contribution to thought. In short, they are the means of discovering error, and of winnowing the multifarious ideas produced in thought.

As to formal logical analyses, the use of syllogism and systematic induction, it seems likely that these are never used except in trying to pin down error in an opponent's argument or to convince skeptics of the clarity of one's own reasoning. In other words, their primary function is communication. It seems quite clear that the propositions "All men are mortal,"

---

[2] The difficulty for the oxygen theory disappeared when chemists developed methods for distinguishing between gases such as nitrogen and carbon dioxide, neither of which supports combustion, or hydrogen and carbon monoxide, both of which are inflammable. But Lavoisier died (on the guillotine) before these advances were made, and thus never knew how the obstacle would be overcome.

and "Socrates is a man," from the classic example of a syllogism, do not occur in thought as two separate processes. A neurologist finding a case of hemianopia (p. 76) would never say to himself, (1) This is hemianopia, (2) What causes it? (3) All hemianopias are caused by injury to the visual pathways, (4) This man must have an injury in his visual pathways. But he might very well do so if he had to convince a skeptic.

Similarly, scientific generalizations or laws are not arrived at by a slow process of accumulating cases and gradually formulating the idea, with increasing confidence in it as the number increases. Instead, the conclusion is likely to be formulated on the basis of one or two cases, and the remaining cases are gathered *in the light of that idea,* as a means of testing it or of convincing others of its value. As we have seen, both man and animal have a way of generalizing from one specific type of experience to others (Chap. 9); the generalization may then be supported by further experience, or alternatively may be extinguished. An example of the latter is the dog that generalized from one sound to others in Pavlov's experimental procedure but then was fed following that one sound only (p. 23f.). We may regard this as a simple experimental analogue of the procedure of the scientist who leaps to a tentative conclusion concerning a new phenomenon ("I wonder whether it could be caused by . . .?") but finds the idea not confirmed in further observations. All this implies that the generalizations of science do not arise by induction, as that term would be used in logic; but on the other hand they must be ones that survive the test of an essentially inductive method.

Summary

This chapter deals with the problems of consciousness, purposive behavior and planning, language, and complex problem-solving: in short, the "higher mental processes" which, actually, have been touched on repeatedly in earlier chapters but which are considered here primarily from the point of view of understanding human thought. Emphasis is given to scientific thought, not because it is really different from the thought of artist, business man or soldier but mostly because it is relatively pure problem-solving and because we have available a far more complete record of its progress (including the failures).

Consciousness is a complex and variable mediating-process activity, its manifestations in behavior ranging from immobility (as in attentive listening) to extreme activity (as in a tennis match); from aimless wandering about ("just looking for something to do") to long-term temporal organization ("don't bother me, I have an exam next week"). It is not an all-or-none condition, and a blow on the head for example may have after-effects which abolish or minimize one of its usually-present attributes (immediate memory) without greatly affecting others. Thus it is not possible to attempt any sharp dichotomy of conscious from unconscious states in man, or between unconscious lower animals and conscious higher ones.

Insight and purpose are important properties of consciousness in problem-solving situations. The occurrence of a particular insight may be easily identified from behavior when there is first failure, then sudden success; but obviously it must occur also when the solution is seen at once, or when it is achieved through a series of smaller steps with no very noticeable break in the over-all pattern of behavior. Purpose is closely related. It involves an expectancy of reaching a goal, and of the effects of intermediate actions as helping to reach it; the behavior at each step is jointly controlled by the expectancy (a mediating process) and perception of the present state of affairs. Thus the behavior changes with each change in the situation, in such a way as to tend toward a constant end effect.

The criteria of purposive behavior allow us to distinguish between the reflexive communications of the social insects, and a higher level of purposive communication—the latter is an action done with the purpose of affecting another's behavior. (The reflexive, nonideational, communication can also be seen in higher animals, including man, for example in the vocalizations of fear or rage—not all our communication is purposive.) Language is a still more complex phenomenon; its essence is in the purposive combination and recombination of two or more communicating ("symbolic") acts: words, gestures, marks on paper, or the like. This gives us three classes of communication: reflexive actions affecting others, the simpler purposive communication, and language.

Studies of human problem-solving in the laboratory have certain practical limitations, but are complemented by study of the scientific record. The laboratory data especially show that thought is not an equivalent of internal speech, and that much of the thought process is quite unconscious—not directly known to the subject himself, not reportable to others. A large part of it is made up of set, including the prior assumptions with which the subject approaches a problem, or ones he generates during the first exploratory period in working with it. These sets may be advantageous or disadvantageous. A large part of the difficulty of a scientific problem may be in realizing that it is time to change an assumption. In retrospect, after the change is made, the problem may look easy.

There are two modes of scientific thought, the discovery or invention of ideas, and the testing of ideas. The first is not primarily a logical process; new ideas occur adventitiously, in large numbers, many of them bizarre and ineffective, which must then be screened by the second mode, by systematic testing in thought or in the laboratory. The second mode is logical and consistent in its operations, but *formal* logical analysis seems to be used only for the purposes of communication and persuasion.

Notes

An excellent account of human thought and problem-solving appears in Woodworth and Schlosberg; see also R. Leeper, Chap. 19 in Stevens (*General References,* Chap. 1, p. 19). A detailed and thus somewhat difficult account is G. Humphrey, *Thinking,* Methuen & Co., 1951: especially valuable for its synthesis of the classical literature with modern experiment, both animal and human.

On the effects of experience upon insight: the work with young chimpanzees is by H. G. Birch (*J. Comp. Psychol.,* 1945, 38, 367–383); with dogs reared in isolation, by W. R. Thompson and W. Heron, *Canad. J. Psychol.,* 1954, 8, 17–31).

A more detailed presentation of the treatment of language and cooperation in this chapter is given by Hebb and Thompson, in Lindzey's *Handbook of Social Psychology* (Chap. 1 *Notes*). The study of communication in the bee is by K. von Frisch, reported in a very readable little book *Bees: Their Vision, Chemical Senses and Language,* Cornell University Press, 1950. References for the laboratory studies of human problem-solving can be found in Woodworth and Schlosberg.

Two stimulating accounts of scientific problem-solving are: J. B. Conant, *On Understanding Science,* Yale University Press, 1947 (also paperbound in Mentor Books); and J. Hadamard, *The Psychology of Invention in the Mathematical Field,* Princeton University Press, 1945 (also paperbound in Dover Books).

Chapter 11

Statistical thinking

A_{LL} scientific measurement is subject to error, and it is important to be able to estimate the probable extent of such error. Also, when predicting a specific event on the basis of preceding observations, and when drawing conclusions about a general class of phenomena from experience with a limited number of them, one is not dealing in certainties but in probabilities. To evaluate such probabilities we use statistics, which makes statistics an essential part of the scientific method.

The difference between biological and physical science is not that one is inexact, the other exact, but in degree of exactness, this being related to the number of variables which must be dealt with simultaneously and the extent to which they can be controlled. In general the biological sciences must deal with larger errors than the physical sciences; but this is not uniformly true, as the student will see if he considers the accuracy of meteorological prediction or if he comprehends the meaning of the fact that the structural engineer considers it necessary very often to use a safety factor of two or three hundred per cent. The statistical principles of dealing with error in measurement, or in prediction and generalization, are the same whether the errors are large or small. Statistics is not a means of confusing issues that would otherwise be clear, nor a substitute for obtaining clear answers, but a means of checking and controlling hasty conclusions by providing an estimate of the error to which a conclusion is subject.

Statistical method has been highly developed mathematically, and is usually presented to the student in such terms. Essentially, however, it is a way of thinking, which very often involves no computations nor any use of formulas. It has two functions: the description of empirical data, permitting one to see a mass of facts as a whole; and secondly, provision of the rules of inference and generalization, from a limited set of observations to a larger universe of which one has observed only a part. It is sometimes said that science is not interested in the unique event. This is certainly not true. If the sun turned a mottled green for 30 seconds, just once, then returned to its usual sunny disposition and remained so with no sign of further upset, we can imagine whether this would have any interest for astronomers or not. But it is true that the scientist is inveterately concerned with general classes of events, with regularities in repeated observations, and the unique event may be considered of interest because it implies the existence of a class of *possible* events.

The scientist persistently generalizes from the seen to the unseen. When he draws a conclusion from an experiment his statement concerns more than the specific objects or events that were part of the experiment. He observes that 43 specific chicks, fed a particular drug, grow faster on the average than 43 other specific chicks not fed the drug; he reports this as a fact, but his conclusion is the inference that *all* such chicks grow faster under certain conditions. (As we shall see shortly, what he says is, "The difference between the means is statistically significant"; and this statement distinguishes between the fact of a faster average growth for his particular chicks—this is a fact, there is no argument about it—and the inference about the growth of all such chicks in such conditions. When a difference is found to be "significant," it implies a generalized conclusion.) When I measure the rate of learning of laboratory rats in a particular set of circumstances, my concern is not primarily with those rats in particular, but with the way in which rats in general, or mammals or vertebrates in general, learn.

This inference from the particular to the general is of course not a scientific prerogative but a fundamental feature of human thought, and so too is the other (the descriptive) function of statistics. In this book, consequently, statistical thinking is of interest in two ways: so that the student can understand how it is made more precise and controlled; and also, as a feature of human thought that has intrinsic interest psychologically, something from which we can learn about the thought process.

If for example the student has come to the conclusion that men are taller than women, not restricting his statement to the specific men and women that he has seen personally, he has made a statistical inference. If he has ever taken an average, he has made a statistical description. If he has even, without any adding up of quantities and dividing by the number of cases, observed that the average day in July is warmer than the average day in June, or has estimated how high the temperature may go in August, he has made a statistical summary from his own past experience (which is necessarily limited), and has gone on to generalize, with an implied prediction about what is going to happen next year and the year after.

Statistical conclusions without computation

If the present chapter is not an example of statistics without tears, it may be that less tears will be shed than usually. A good deal of analysis of data can be done by simply arranging them in an orderly way (especially by graphical means). The object here is to show the student how to think statistically, and perhaps he will succeed better than if he were given an elaborate set of mechanical computations to carry out, which may sometimes act as a substitute for understanding.

First, two conceptions about which it is quite important to be clear. The scientist works with a *sample* from which he draws conclusions about a *population* or *universe*. The sample is a sample set of the items making up the population. It is one's collection of facts or observations, the empirical data available to work with, their number of course being finite and often rather small. The population is not necessarily a population of persons or animals—this is another scientific figure of speech—but is usually events or properties of objects or events; in an experimental science a population is characteristically hypothetical and indefinitely large. The sample is a set of properties or events that have actually been observed; the population or universe includes all the properties or events in this class (i.e., of the same kind) that could have been observed in the past or that may conceivably be observed in the future. To illustrate:

An astrophysicist investigating shooting stars wants to know what they are composed of. He manages to find, let us say, fifty meteorites and determines their composition. This is his sample. The population in which he is interested however will include future meteorites and past ones which were not recovered. He may go on to draw conclusions about the bodies in space that hit other planets, thus going even farther beyond his facts—but of course quite legitimately.

A psychologist breeds rats for maze-learning ability, mating with each other those that do well and those that do poorly. After several generations of such selection he finds that the descendants of the good learners always do better than descendants of the poor learners. He has tested perhaps 20 rats of the sixth generation in each of the bright and dull strains. He has therefore a sample of 20 animals from each of two infinitely large populations: namely, rats with heredities determined in certain ways. Apart from his two samples, these populations do not exist in actuality, for no one else has bred animals in this way. But this does not prevent him from concluding that future samples will show the same difference that he has found. This means that he is talking about learning ability in two indefinitely large, hypothetical populations of *all rats that will be, or might be, obtained by the breeding operations that he has carried out.* No one really cares, scientifically, about the maze learning of a particular rat, apart from the implications it has for larger questions. The question here concerns the relation of heredity to the learning ability, or intelligence, of rats in general and of mammals, including man, in general. Drawing such conclusions about hypothetical populations, making such generalizations, is certainly subject to error; but we must generalize, and there are statistical methods for evaluating the inevitable error.

The first step in all this is to describe the sample. Consider for example the error scores that were made by 31 rats in a simple maze problem: 27 9 13 32 23 16 18 21 15 24 23 19 19 4 29 22 33 7 30 17 26 17 10 22 17 16 36 27 22 12 26. Each number gives the total errors for an individual rat. The properties of the sample become easier to see merely by rearranging in order: 4 7 9 10 12 13 15 16 16 17 17 17 18 19 19 21 22 22 22 23 23 24 26 26 27 27 29 30 32 33 36. The highest and lowest values, or the range of values, are evident at a glance, and the *median* value, 21, can be found by counting to the mid-point in the series from either end (if there were an even number of scores the median would be half-way between the two middle scores). The distribution of values becomes clearer from the next step, which is to group the scores by larger steps as shown in Table 2, or to represent the same grouping as in Fig. 71. With this change some detail is lost—one no longer sees what the lower limit of error is, for example; it may be anywhere from 0 to 4, whereas in the raw data it was 4. But we now see clearly the bunching of scores near the middle, we see that the distribution of scores is approximately symmetrical, and we can estimate the *mean* directly. The mean is the "average" of elementary arithmetic, the sum of the quantities divided by their number. (Technically, there are several averages, of which the arithmetic mean is one.) By inspection, the mean is a little above the

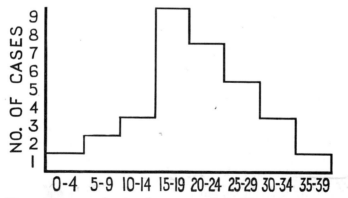

Figure 71. Histogram showing the errors made by 31 rats in a maze test (Table 2). One rat made errors in the 0–4 range, 2 rats made errors in the 5–9 range, and so on.

Table 2.   Frequency distribution of error scores by 31 rats in a maze test

Interval	Frequency
0–4	1
5–9	2
10–14	3
15–19	9
20–24	7
25–29	5
30–34	3
35–39	1

dividing line between 15–19 and 20–24—that is, above 19.5. (By actual computation from the raw scores it is 20.4.)

There are two values here of primary interest: the central tendency, and the degree of dispersion or variability. The central tendency is the single average, the representative value which, if you must report a single value, best stands for the whole set of values concerned. "Best" here differs according to circumstances, but for most psychological experiments the mean or (less often) the median is used. As soon as we have this central value, however, the next step is to ask how much the single cases differ from it. How variable are the values in the sample? Here also there are several ways in which the answer may be given, but we shall consider only two: the *range* and the *standard deviation,* or SD.

"Range" is easy, determined simply by inspection of the highest and lowest values. Often it gives a sufficient description of the degree of variability. In an experiment comparing the intelligence of dogs and rats, for example, the score for rats ranged from 5 to 20, for dogs 24 to 27, in a test in which 27 was a perfect score. For the purposes of the experiment in question no further analysis was needed: the superiority of the dogs was evident.

However, range is apt to be unsatisfactory as an index of the amount of variability, because it is determined by the two most extreme cases only and does not tell us much about the less extreme ones. In the experiment referred to, for example, one exceptionally stupid dog might have made a score of 12: then the range for dogs would be 12 to 27, and this fact would not tell one that almost all dogs make scores over 20. A more stable index—less capable of being deflected by one individual subject—is provided by the standard deviation. To find the SD one must do some computing (it is the square root of the average of the squares of deviations from the mean), but this is not necessary in order to understand how the value is used.

It is generally used in conjunction with what mathematicians call the *normal probability curve*. Distributions which are approximately symmetrical and bell-shaped, as in Fig. 72, and which as the number of cases increases come closer and closer to the smooth curve of Fig. 73, are frequently found with biological measures such as men's heights or weights. The smooth curve applies only to an infinitely large population, an idealized conception. A finite number of cases, even as large a number as that presented in Fig. 72, can only approximate it; and when

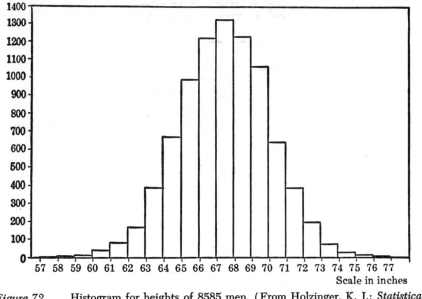

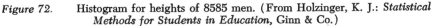

Figure 72.   Histogram for heights of 8585 men. (From Holzinger, K. J.: *Statistical Methods for Students in Education*, Ginn & Co.)

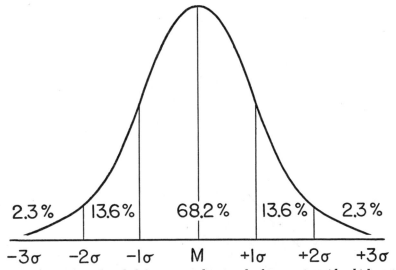

Figure 73.   Normal probability curve, showing the frequencies with which certain deviations from the mean occur. "σ" = SD, or standard deviation; 68.2% of all cases fall within one SD of the mean, 95.4% within 2 SD (68.2 plus 13.6 plus 13.6), and so forth.

we have a small number, as in Fig. 71, the irregularities loom large. But Fig. 71 is about as close to the smooth curve as we could expect for a sample of this size, and we can assume that it is a sample from an infinitely large population to which the normal probability curve, the idealized distribution of Fig. 73, applies.

In that case, the standard deviation has certain quantitative properties shown in the figure. About two-thirds (68 per cent) of all values will fall within 1 SD of the mean value; one-sixth fall more than 1 SD below, one-sixth more than 1 SD above the mean. About 2.3 per cent fall more than 2 SD above (or below) the mean, and 0.1 per cent more than 3 SD's above.

For example: consider adult IQ's on a particular test with a mean of 100 (which is what the mean IQ is supposed to be) and a SD of 15 (approximately what is given by existing tests). If these values hold for the general population, normally distributed, we know without being given any further information that about a sixth of the population have IQ's above 115, or that a man with an IQ of 135 is in approximately the top 2 per cent of the population. If it is found that all students who do well in college have IQ's above 115 (which has been reported, though the precise value is somewhat arbitrary), it is implied that no more than one-sixth of the population could do well in college, as things stand at present. It is usually considered that IQ 70 is the dividing line between those who can assume control of their own lives and those who cannot (between "normal" and "mentally defective"). Since intelligence tests are subject to error, a test score should not be the sole basis of judging such a question in the individual case; but statistically, for the general population, it is implied by this definition that about 2.3 per cent of the population are mental defectives.

Now let us look more closely at the inference from sample to population. Suppose that we want to know how tall the average male college student is. Having searched out and measured 20 of these rare creatures, we find their mean height to be 69.8 in. Is this the value we are looking for? We know that men differ in height, so we cannot just measure one, or two or three. We need a large group; is 20 large enough? We track down 20 more and measure them, and this time we get a mean of 70.3 in. Three more groups of 20 give means of 70.1, 67.7 and 71.6. *The means of samples are variable too.* We pool the five groups and get a mean for the 100 men: 69.9. But another group of 100 would give us still another mean. The larger the samples the less variable their means will be, but the variability will not disappear. We cannot get a final, precise answer, and we must try another approach.

We first get as large a sample as is practical. The mean of this sample is the best estimate of the mean of the universe from which the sample is drawn. In the example just discussed, our best estimate of the mean height of all college men is 69.9 in. Next we determine the variability of values in the sample, and from it estimate the variability in the universe.

Now we can look at our estimates critically, and ask how far off they are likely to be. We can ask, for example: could the true value be as low as 69.5 in? We have a sample of 100 heights with a mean value of 69.9; is it probable that such a sample could be drawn at random from a population with a mean of 69.5? Mathematically, it is possible to determine exactly how often this would happen. It turns out to be, let us say, once in 25 times. The probability that the true value is as low as 69.5 therefore is only one in 25, or 4 per cent; it can be concluded with reasonable certainty that the true value is higher than this. Could the true value be 69.6, if it is not 69.5? The probability of this degree of error in our estimate can also be determined. We cannot ever say what the true value *is;* but we can determine the probability that it differs from the estimate by a specified value, or that it lies within a specified range. With these fictitious data we might be able to say, for example, that there is a 50 per cent probability that the true value lies between 69.7 and 70.1; a 90 per cent probability that it lies between 69.6 and 70.2; and so on.

Now for scientific purposes it is customary to emphasize two levels of probability in asking such questions: the 5 per cent and 1 per cent levels. In the example just used, we may say that the mean obtained differs *significantly* from 69.5 *at the 5 per cent level.* In other words: the difference can be given some weight, since a chance difference as great as this would be found less than 5 per cent of the time. (The student must remember, however, that the chance difference at this level of significance does occur—once in 20 experimental determinations.) For a higher degree of confidence the 1 per cent level is adopted, with a 1-in-100 chance of being wrong. When one encounters the statement that a difference is "significant" it signifies, by common convention, that the probability is at least 19 to 1 against this being due to the operations of chance in obtaining our sample; "highly significant" may be considered to mean that the probability is 99 to 1 against. Alternatively, one may say that a difference is "significant at the 5 per cent level," or at the 1 per cent level.

Summarizing: we can never say what, precisely, is the true value of the mean of the universe from which a sample is drawn. But we can, with the proper computations, determine the probability that it differs from our *estimate* by more than any given amount. Also, we can state limits within which it must lie, with a probability of 20 to 1 or 100 to 1—or if we wish, 1000 to 1.

No one can do more. Improved methods of measurement and larger samples cut down the size of probable error but do not abolish it. They decrease the uncertainty range within which the true value lies, but do not decrease it to zero.

Restating matters, with some further (improbable) examples

Statistics asks the student to think in a new way about the meaning of averages and related matters. He is used to thinking that we know—or could determine—the *exact* value for the height of the average man, or the income of the average family; is this not the sort of thing the census does for us? If it is impractical to do it for all men, considering some of the out-of-way places in the world, why should it be impossible to obtain a precise value for the mean height of all adult male Americans, or Indonesians, or Swedes? But as we shall see in a moment, precision in this sense is chimerical. The scientific use of statistics really does ask for a new way of thinking, which though inherently simple is at first hard to achieve. It is unlikely that the preceding pages have fully conveyed this point of view, so the purpose of the present section is to restate it with some bizarre examples that may help to make it intelligible.

Let us see why it is chimerical to ask for an exact figure for the mean height of American male adults. First, there is the fact that *every* measurement has its probable error. Next, any biological population is not static but changing. A number of American males die daily, and a number reach the 21st birthday that marks adult status. If we are really to have a precise figure for the whole population and not a sample (however large), we must fix on some date and hour—say 12 noon, July 1, in the year following the decision to undertake the project—and with the aid of 10 or 12 million assistants we get everyone measured within a few minutes of the hour, including all those on their sickbeds, aloft in airplanes, at sea or abroad.

Now, assuming that we could succeed in this improbable undertaking, we must recognize that the mean we obtain will be out of date by July 2; in fact, well before the necessary computations could be completed. The net result of all this labor would therefore be, at best, a precise value for the population at a particular time in the past, not the present. To apply it to the present at once involves an element of estimation. We cannot treat census figures for this or any other aspects of the average man as precise factual values, independent of inference; they are estimates—from very large samples it is true and with correspondingly small deviations from the "true" value—but still estimates that are subject to error. For most purposes we will thus be better off if we recognize this fact in the first place, and frankly use a sampling-and-inference method.

Now another improbable example, which may help in understanding the logic of this method. Let us suppose that an explorer who has penetrated to some fastness in the mountains of Mexico, where no one has been before as far as he knows, discovers and traps a single specimen of an elephant 10 inches high at the shoulder. He has seen no others, nor heard of any. What information has he about the species, the population from which his sample of one has been drawn? His best estimate of the mean height of the species is 10 inches; but having only one in his sample he has no basis for estimating variability and thus no basis for saying how far off his guess about the average height might be.

Even with a single specimen, however, he is bound to have formed some idea of the size of other members of the species, and there are some conclusions that can be drawn quite logically. He can rule out the hypothesis, for example, that the mean of the population is 40 in., the standard deviation 12. This situation is shown roughly by the larger curve, diagram A, Fig. 74. He can also rule out the hypothesis that the mean is 15, SD 2 (smaller curve, diagram A). Both hypotheses imply that the first animal he happened to encounter is one of the very smallest—2½ SD's away from the mean. The probability that this would happen is well below the 5 per cent level. Similarly, he can rule out the hypothesis that the mean height is 6 in., standard deviation 1.5 in. (diagram B, Fig. 74). Many hypotheses cannot be ruled out, but some can be.

His most probable hypothesis is represented by one of the curves of diagram *C:* some distribution centered about a mean of 10 in. The different curves in diagram *C* are meant to show that, with a single specimen, nothing is known about variability and so the SD may be large (considerable spread in the curve) or small (little spread). As *D* shows, these curves may be shifted somewhat to left or right and still represent tenable hypotheses, as long as the given sample value, 10 in., remains in the central part of the curve.

When 4 more animals are captured, giving values of 9.6, 9.7, 9.8, 10.0, and 10.1 in., an estimate of variability can be made—it is small—and now the distance becomes smaller by which the curve can be shifted to left or right and still represent a tenable hypothesis. The point for the student to get from this example is that we can quite freely form hypotheses about the population, after seeing a sample from it, but must then proceed to test them rigorously. The elaborate machinery of statistics, the formulas and computations omitted in this book, make it possible to state precisely what the probability would be of getting a known sample from any given hypothetical population. If the probability is low we disregard that hypothesis (but cannot rule it out absolutely and finally, for the very improbable sometimes happens).

However, this process cannot pick out, from among those hypothetical populations which might reasonably have produced our sample, *the* one correct hypothesis. The larger the sample, the more we can narrow the zone within which probable answers lie, but we are always left with

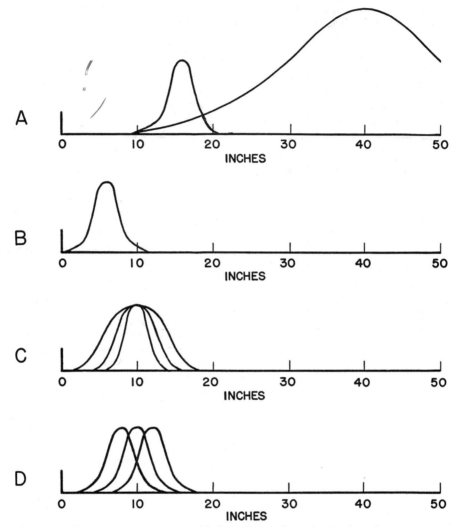

Figure 74.   Representing possible hypotheses about the heights of a new species of pygmy elephants, given a sample of one, 10 in. high. Diagram *A:* two hypotheses, (1) that the mean for the species is 40 in., SD 12 in. (larger curve, to the right); and (2) that the mean is 15 in., SD 2 in. (smaller curve). *B:* mean 6, SD 1.5, and so forth; see text.

an uncertainty range, even if small. This is represented in principle by diagram *D*, Fig. 74.

To be epigrammatic, science does not work with absolute truth but with a probable error. Its goal is to reduce error to a minimum, only. The scientist *thinks* in terms of truth when he sets up a hypothesis for testing, for what he says in effect is: Let us suppose that the true mean has such-and-such a value; if so, what would be found in a sample? But the result, the only conclusion that can be justified, is that the "true" value has a thus-and-so probability of lying within such-and-such a range of possible values.

Comparing two values

Now a different but related case: the comparison of values and the determination of significant differences between samples.

Take first a familiar case, the comparison of the heights of men and women. Suppose that we have two samples, 100 in each, of the heights of college men and women. The two means are 69.9 and 65.4 in. Are men taller than women? That is, if we had the mean of all men's heights would it differ from the mean of all women's?

We attack the question by saying, Assume that the heights of men and women are *not* different. This is the *null hypothesis*. It amounts to assuming that the two samples of heights come from the same population. Now we can ask, What is the probability that we would draw from the same population two samples like these, with means that differ as much? We know that any two samples from the same population will give different means, just by chance; is that what has happened in this case? But the answer here might well be that two such different samples could come from the same population less than one in a thousand times; it is thus very unlikely that the null hypothesis is true. We therefore reject it. This in turn means that we conclude that men and women differ in height. The usual way of reporting such a result is to say that "the difference between the means is significant" (or in this case, of course, very highly significant).

This method of analysis might be applied in an experiment as follows. We want to know whether the frontal part of the brain is more important for maze learning than the occipital part. We remove equal amounts of brain tissue, on the average, for two groups of rats. Those with frontal damage make, let us say, a mean of 42.1 errors; those with occipital damage, 55.7 errors. Our two samples are certainly different, but is the difference significant? We apply the null hypothesis, assume that there is no difference in the means of *all* rats with such frontal lesions and *all* with such occipital lesions, and see how often two such samples would be drawn from a single population. The variability in our two groups is great, indicating a wide "spread" in the curve representing the parent population (Fig. 74), and this implies that the uncertainty range is rather great. As a result, computation shows that our two samples might be obtained from a single population about 20 times in 100. The difference is far from the 5 per cent level of significance, so we cannot reject the null hypothesis. We have not yet established the proposition that occipital damage is worse than frontal damage in its effect on maze running.

The student should keep in mind, however, that the odds still favor the proposition; by increasing the size of the samples, and thus decreasing the uncertainty range—the amount by which the means may vary—a further experiment might find a significant difference after all.

In the preceding examples we have dealt with measurements and normally distributed values. One is not limited to mensurability, and normal distributions, in statistical thinking. Suppose we are interested in the relation of wildness to heredity in rats. We bring up 20 rats from an albino laboratory strain and 20 from a wild gray strain, all separated from the mother at weaning and brought up singly in identical cages. Heroically, the experimenter reaches into each cage when the occupant has reached 70 days of age, and picks up the animal once. He counts the bites received: 1 bite from the albinos, 13 from the grays. There are methods of computation (e.g., Chi-square, which need not be described here) that make it possible to determine that this result is highly improbable on the assumption that biting rats are equally likely to occur with either heredity. The result is therefore highly significant. We reject the null hypothesis (that there is no difference in the frequency of biters in the two universes of all hypothetical albinos, and all hypothetical grays, brought up in this particular way). Rejecting the null hypothesis is equivalent to concluding that there is a relation between heredity and wildness. Here we treat biting as an index of wildness, but the procedure does not measure wildness in the individual animal, and we have no idea whether it is normally distributed.

The control group

The experiment just considered brings us to the use of the control group. In the physical sciences it may often be possible to hold constant all but one of the factors that might affect the outcome of an experiment; this one, the "independent variable," is changed systematically, and the experimenter observes the effects in the "dependent variable." In a study of the pressure of the atmosphere, for example, the independent variable may be height above sea level; the dependent variable is the height of a column of mercury in a barometric tube. Other influences that might affect the outcome are eliminated or kept constant: temperature, contaminating substances in the mercury, movement of the surrounding air, and so forth. In the biological sciences one can only approach this ideal procedure; and only too often fundamental questions have gone unanswered because it was not possible to get anywhere near it. In psychological research there are two great difficulties which frequently demand the use of control groups as a substitute for the ideal procedure.

One is that making a psychological test usually changes the subject; a later test does not give the same result because of *practice effect*—the subject as we say "remembers" the first test. The second difficulty is that we are dealing with extraordinarily complex material; after we have used up our first sample of the material (the first subject or group of subjects) we cannot get a second that is identical with the first, because animals and men differ in many ways which we cannot identify before beginning an experiment.

Suppose for example that we want to find out whether removing the frontal lobes of a monkey's brain affects his ability to learn a visual discrimination. In an ideal procedure we would measure his learning ability, remove the frontal lobes, and measure his learning ability again. But in reality the second measurement is disturbed by memory of the first. We must measure learning ability by the number of trials, or the number of errors made, in achieving the discrimination. In the second measurement there will almost certainly be a practice effect, and we do not know how great. Next best, in a slightly less ideal world, we would obtain two monkeys identical in all respects; we would remove the frontal lobes from one, have both learn the task in identical conditions, and see how much faster the normal monkey learned, compared to the one operated on. But in practice we cannot find two identical subjects, animal or human. (Identical twins are identical with respect to heredity, but it is impossible that everything that has happened since birth which might affect them psychologically is exactly the same. Also, of course, there are not many of them.) Thus we are driven to the comparison of two *groups*, large enough, we hope, that the kind of individual differences that may occur will average out; if the original learning capacity of two subjects is not identical, the average for two groups is likely to differ much less, and the probable degree of difference can be dealt with statistically.

The ideal cases referred to, however, should be kept in mind, for they tell us what we are trying to achieve by the use of the control group. In the frontal-lobe question referred to, what we would like to do is measure the learning ability of the same monkey with and without his frontal lobes, the second measurement not being affected by the first. This is impractical. So is the hope of finding two identical monkeys; but it is not impractical to find two groups which, if they are large enough, will be much more similar, as groups, than two individual monkeys. Our choice of a control group, then, is a matter of choosing animals which are as like the animals in the experimental group as possible, in every way that affects visual learning.

The experiment may then proceed in one of two ways. First, we can operate on one group, and test both. We compare the mean scores of the operates and of the normal control subjects, and see whether they differ significantly. Statistics at this point enables us to evaluate the probability that the difference we have found is due simply to accidental differences in our two groups, treating them as two samples in the way already described. The second procedure would be to test both groups, operate on one, test both groups again, and see whether the increases in score by the normals (due to practice effect) are significantly greater than the increases by the operated (though the experiment might come out with a still clearer result, the normals all showing increases and the operates all showing losses).

The principle is clear: make your control group like the experimental group in every way that would affect the outcome of the experiment, except for the one variable in which you are interested. The pitfalls and gins besetting the path of the investigator on this point mainly consist of not recognizing a variable that affects the results. If one is picking rats out of a colony cage, and puts the first 10 into the experimental group, the second 10 into the control group, one overlooks the possibility that the most easily-caught animals, or the ones that come to the front of the cage and allow themselves to be picked up, are tamer than the others; and this difference is likely to affect any experimental result. The easiest solution is to put no. 1 into the first group, no. 2 into the second, no. 3 into the first, and so on. (There are also more sophisticated ways of doing this by the use of random numbers assigned to the animals, which we need not go into.)

Again, in clinical investigations one does not have the choice of one's "experimental" group, and one perforce must try to find a similar control group. This is usually difficult. The clinical group (corresponding to the experimental group of the laboratory) generally includes people of all sorts of occupation, rural as well as urban, educated and uneducated, old and young. It is difficult indeed to persuade a group of similar persons, who are not ill and have no reason to take tests, to give up the time to act as subjects—especially since they are apt to view any psychological test with suspicion. But if one wants to know whether removal of the human frontal lobe affects intelligence, and if the clinical group with frontal lobe operation has a mean age of 40 and a mean of 8 years' schooling, for example, one must make one's comparisons with a group that is similar in these respects, for intelligence-test scores vary with amount of schooling and with advancing age.

Correlations

Correlation is the degree of relation between two variables. A *coefficient of correlation* is a quantitative statement thereof. It is even more time-consuming to compute than the quantitative values we have been dealing with so far, but—once more—the student's aim here should be to understand instead of memorizing a formula and methods of computation.

Correlation coefficients range from plus 1 to minus 1; plus 1 represents a perfect relation between the two variables, high values accompanying high values, intermediate values accompanying intermediate values, and so on. Minus 1 *also* represents a perfect relation, though it is reversed: the highest score on X goes with the lowest one on Y, next highest on X with the next lowest on Y, and so on. The relation is perfect in this sense. Once you knew what a man got on test X you would also know what he got, or will get, on Y. Finally, a correlation of zero means no relation at all; here a high score on the first test might go with a high, a medium, or a low score on the second.

To see better what is meant, consider Fig. 75. Tests A and B (first of the three diagrams) have a zero correlation. Knowing what a man has made on test A tells us nothing about what he will make on test B. Now consider tests P and Q (second diagram). These two are perfectly and positively related (perhaps we may note that such perfection simply does not occur in psychology). If we know a child's score on P we do not have to give Q; the two tests correlate 1.00, so the second score can be determined as soon as the first is known. Similarly with tests X and Y, though now the relation is negative; if a subject makes a poor score on X we can predict, without further testing, that he will make a good score on Y.

These, however, are only the extreme cases. One thing the student needs to know is the degree of relation, roughly, that is represented by such correlation coefficients as .30, .50, .70, .90. In general, one may say that the relation is not nearly as close as one of these figures makes it sound. The first, .30, represents a barely discernible relation. A correlation of .70 is not 70 per cent correspondence, or agreement 7 times out of 10, but 49 per cent; a correlation of .90 represents 81 per cent correspondence. In psychology, because we must often deal with coefficients below .60, it is common to speak of one above this value as representing "a high correlation." But this is misleading, and it would be better to reserve the term for coefficients above .90.

All this has more meaning for the student if expressed graphically. Figure 76 shows a plot of two sets of scores, on parallel forms of the

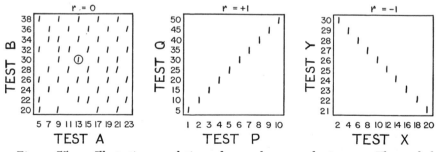

Figures 75.   Illustrating correlations of zero, plus one and minus one. The symbol *r* is a particular index of correlation (the Pearson product-moment coefficient). Each mark represents a single subject's scores on the two tests being correlated. In the first diagram, for example, the encircled mark is for a subject who made 12 on the first test (test *A*) and 31 on the second (*B*).

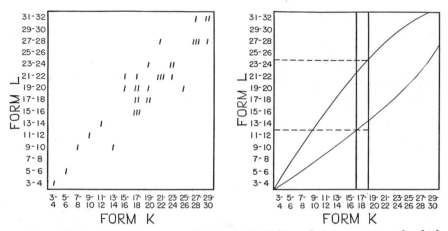

Figure 76.   Illustrating a correlation of .93 (left) and the accuracy with which prediction of a second score (on form L of the test) can be made from a first (on form K on the same test). Even with as high a correlation as this, the accuracy is not great; on the right is shown the roughly-drawn "envelope" enclosing the entries. The vertical lines enclose the entries which represent scores of 17 or 18 on form K; the width of the envelope at this point determines how much variability may be expected in the scores on form L—roughly, from 13 to 24.

same test, in which the correlation is .93. It is reasonable to speak of this as a high correlation, but let us see how close the correspondence really is. The vertical lines in the second diagram of Fig. 76, on each side of the 17–18 value on the baseline, contain the entries for all subjects who made 17 or 18 on the first form of the test. On the second test, these subjects made scores ranging from the 15–16 bracket to the 21–22 bracket. (From the raw data it could be seen that one man who made 18 on the first test made 15 on the second; another who made 18 on the first made 22 instead, on the second.) Evidently no very close prediction of the second score is possible, despite the correlation of .93.

Figure 77 shows a somewhat lower correlation, .72. A comparison of Figs. 76 and 77 shows clearly that the thickness of the diagonal band made by the entries on such a correlation plot is the essential factor in predicting the second score from the first. With a high correlation we have a thin band; when the vertical lines are drawn, as in Fig. 76, only a short segment from the diagonal band is enclosed, which means that the amount of variation in the second test is small—and prediction is good. When the correlation is lower, the band is broader and prediction is poor. In the perfect case, the correlation in the second diagram of Fig. 75, the band would have no width whatever (all the points plotted fall on a single straight line), and prediction is perfect.

This graphical analysis is of course rough, and there are much more exact ways of dealing with the predictions that can be made, and their degree of error. But it is still true here, as elsewhere, that a good deal can be learned about complex data by simple inspection, and there is no other way that is as good for conveying the fundamental meaning of a correlation coefficient, high or low.

With a correlation, it is clear that we are always dealing with a causal connection. However, the connection may be very indirect, and a correlation, in and of itself, does not tell us what causes what. If A and B are correlated, A may cause B, B may cause A, both may be caused by an outside factor C, or there may be a mixture of these relations. It is known, for example, that intelligence-test scores are correlated with years of schooling—but we cannot leap to the conclusion that one's IQ is determined by one's education. The relation may be just the opposite—those who have not the intelligence to do well in school tend to leave earlier than others, which means that intelligence affects amount of schooling. A more important factor may be that intelligent parents tend (1) to have intelligent children, and (2) to encourage their children to keep on at school. In this case, the parent is the outside factor, C, that determines the level both of A (intelligence) and of B (schooling); A and B could thus be correlated without one's causing the other.

Intelligence in the growing child (mental age, not IQ: see Chapter 12) is known, for example, to be correlated with length of the big toe. This old joke might well be remembered by the student; the statement is quite true, for as a child grows his capacity for solving problems increases at the same time that his bones are growing in length, and the two therefore show a significant correlation. This may help the student to see that, though a correlation shows a causal relation *somewhere*, it does not necessarily mean that one of the two things correlated causes the other.

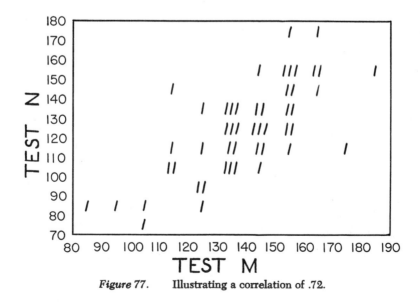

Figure 77.   **Illustrating a correlation of .72.**

Summary

Statistics is a fundamental feature of the scientific method; it is concerned with evaluating the errors which must occur in any measurement, or in generalizing from known data (a sample) to the larger class of values or events to which the data belong (a population or universe). The elaborate mathematical methods of statistics increase the exactness with which the estimate of error is made, but they are not the essence of the matter; graphical methods, and simple inspection, are often sufficient for a particular problem in which results are relatively clear-cut. (Some scientists say they make no use of statistics; what they really mean is that inspection is sufficient for their purposes, without formal computations.)

The first step of analysis is a description of the available data, the sample. Two values are of primary importance: a measure of central tendency, and a measure of dispersion. Central tendency is a single representative value, an average; there are several averages, of which the most important is the (arithmetic) mean. Dispersion is the extent to which individual cases deviate from the average; one index of it is the range, but a more useful one is the standard deviation, or SD. This is particularly so when we are dealing with the "normal probability distribution," the symmetrical bell-shaped curve frequently found with biological data.

Given the mean and the SD, we can then ask how probable it is that our sample has come from any given hypothetical population. If the probability is low, we reject the conclusion that the sample has come from that population. For scientific purposes, it is customary to work with two levels of "significance" (i.e., of probability) in drawing such conclusions: the 5 per cent level (when it is reasonably sure that the sample has not come from that population) and the 1 per cent level (still surer).

To determine whether an experimental treatment of some sort has had an effect on a group of subjects, we use essentially the same method. We have an experimental group and a control group, the latter treated in exactly the same way as the experimental group except for the one treatment in whose effects we are interested. What we ask is whether the two samples, the data from the two groups, could have come from the same population. That is, we make the null hypothesis: we assume that the treatment did *not* have an effect. (The difference between our two groups may have occurred by chance, since any two samples from the same population are likely to differ.) Statistics allows us to determine just how probable such a result would be—how often we would get, from the same population, two samples as different as these two. If the probability is below 5 per cent, we reject the null hypothesis: that is, we conclude that the treatment did have an effect. The chance of being wrong in this conclusion, of course, is 1/20; if we wish to be more certain to avoid a wrong conclusion, we may use the 1 per cent level instead.

Correlation is the degree of relation between two variables; a coefficient of correlation is a quantitative measure of the relation, ranging from plus 1 to minus 1. Graphical analysis is very useful here as well, especially since calculating the coefficient may be very laborious.

When two variables are correlated, there is a casual relation, but from the correlation alone one cannot determine what causes what: A may cause B, B may cause A, or they may share a common cause, C.

Notes

Further details on the statistical method and its use in psychology are provided in a number of books on "psychological statistics" or "the design of experiments." To find one suitable for his purposes, the student should consult his instructor.

Chapter 12

Problems of measurement

Tнıs chapter deals with the methods of measurement that are used in psychology. It does not try to cover the whole field, even in an elementary way, but attempts to provide examples that will show what the principal problems are and what kinds of solution have been found for them. Special attention is given to the measurement of intelligence in the latter part of the chapter, both because of its intrinsic importance and because of the light it casts on methods.

It is common in science to use one thing as a quantitative index of another; some measurements, that is, are less direct than others. An example is the measurement of temperature by the length of a thread of mercury within a glass tube. Another is the use of certain magnetic effects in the neighborhood of a piece of wire to measure the amount of electrical current flowing through it. Another is the measurement of time by counting the oscillations of a pendulum, or a balanced wheel attached to a spring, by means of a complex device called a clock.

Now it might be thought at first that direct measurements are better than indirect. This does not follow; the direct method of measurement may have larger errors. The measurement of temperature by use of a common thermometer is more direct than the use of a thermocouple, which involves several steps of inference, but the latter provides more precise data (still more direct than the thermometer, and still less precise, is the method of putting one's hand on an object and saying how hot it is). What we want is to find an indicator A which can be reliably read—

and which comes as near as possible to being perfectly correlated with *B*, the thing in which we are really interested. A thermometer is a very good measure of temperature: it is highly reliable, which means that with repeated testing the same results are obtained, with a very small error range; and valid, which means that its readings are closely related to temperature, as determined in other ways, and consistent with theoretical conceptions.

Reliability and *validity* are fundamental conceptions in psychological measurement. Reliability, roughly, is the accuracy with which a test measures whatever it is that it measures; more precisely, it is the consistency of repeated measurements. Validity is the extent to which it measures what we want it to measure. Reliability is customarily determined in psychology by the correlation between two separate measurements. Theoretically, validity is the correlation of the test with a perfect measure of what we are trying to get at: correlation with a perfect measure of intelligence, or mathematical aptitude, or musical appreciation. In practice, we have no perfect measures; and so we have no good way of determining validity quantitatively. We can make rough estimates, however, and the conception itself is a most important one.

To increase reliability and validity is an important objective in all psychological measurement. We shall return repeatedly to these two conceptions, but in the meantime we may illustrate the problems to which they refer by considering the question of how an instructor is to measure the students' comprehension and mastery of a college course.

Traditionally, the essay examination was used for this purpose. It is a relatively direct measure and has a fair degree of validity. It is however known to be not very reliable; when two examiners mark the same set of papers the correlation between the two sets of marks in a large class is not apt to be above .60, and as we have seen this is not a high correlation. The correlation would be still lower between two different examinations set on the same subject-matter.

Reliability can be increased by the use of objective examinations; but unless validity is also kept in mind, we may get results that are even farther from our goal of measuring *comprehension*. For example, the objective questions may simply test memory for the exact words of the textbook; a student who has worked hard to understand it, and has intelligently worked out its implications, might make a poor mark; another who has simply memorized, with little attempt at rational understanding, might make a good one. Devising objective examinations that do not sacrifice validity in this sense is not easy, even after one has been in the business for some time. For the inexperienced examiner it can be very laborious. The experienced examiner has a stock of questions from past years to use as a guide, or even to use again together with new ones; and he is more likely to hit on a satisfactory wording for a question at first try. What we are concerned with here however is not the discomforts that examiners must undergo, but the principles of mental measurement, which will be illustrated best if we see how one might go about developing an objective examination from the ground up.

In practice, one might proceed as follows. First one would devise the best questions one could, in rather large numbers, since some of them will turn out to be unsatisfactory. Next, one needs some way of sorting out the class, roughly, into good, fair and poor students. If the class has had to prepare a term paper or do laboratory work, from which an independent evaluation of the students is available, nothing more is necessary, and the final paper may consist of the objective questions only. If not, the paper may include some essay questions. From the term paper or essay questions one then finds a group with good comprehension of the course work, and a group with poor comprehension. Finally, one examines each objective question to see whether the more capable group did better with it than the less capable, and discards all questions for which this is not true—a procedure known as "item analysis."

In this method, one cannot be sure that the "high" group contains all the best students, and only the best; nor that the "low" group is made up only of the poorest. Essay questions, or term papers, have not sufficient reliability to determine this (if they had, one would probably not go to all the labor of making an objective examination—which is easier to mark, but far harder to prepare, than an essay examination). But the essay questions are reliable enough to discriminate between groups, and allow one to pick out two groups which differ greatly in level of ability. On the average, the group of high scorers on the essay section of the paper will be much better students than the low scorers.

For each objective question (or "item"), one determines the number of correct answers by each group. If for example 47 out of 50 in the high group answer a question correctly, and 14 out of 50 in the low group, the question is evidently valid. But on another question, one may find 35 correct in the high group, 34 in the low group; this one clearly does not discriminate sufficiently, and should be excluded from the examination because it increases the amount of chance error. Worse still, one may find a question which gives: high group 22, low group 28. In fact, whenever an item analysis of this kind is done with an objective test one finds such questions, which are clearly invalid and are better left out of the final reckoning. Having thrown these out, one then proceeds to rescore the shortened examination for all students. This gives the final mark.

It does not matter how logically justifiable a question may be; if in fact it confuses the better student or misleads him into looking for subtleties that are not there, but fails to confuse the student who perhaps does not know enough to be misled, the question is a poor one. As we shall see later, the whole success of intelligence tests rests on asking, What questions or problems *are* handled better by the intelligent person? and rigorously refusing to construct a test with questions that an intelligent person "should" answer—in the opinion of the maker of the test. The same thing applies to course examinations, at least apart from the small advanced course, where the student has got far enough with the subject so that he and the examiner really know that they are talking the same language. In the introductory course particularly, an examiner never knows certainly how a question will be read (or misread) by the student, or how difficult a question is, until it has been tried out on the class.

To summarize what has been said so far: the direct measure or estimate of the quality in which we are interested may lack reliability or accuracy. To improve reliability we use some less direct measure, but must then take precautions to see that validity is preserved as far as possible.

Sensory limens

The problem of validity does not arise in the determination of sensory limens, generally speaking; what we do is measure, by established physical methods, some property of a stimulus (such as energy, frequency or extent) which produces a given response—rather than measuring the degree of response. However, errors of method are possible that can invalidate the determination of a limen, and the question of validity enters in this sense.

The first and main precaution is to see that the subject has no supplementary clues, no other source of information about variation in the stimulus except the one on which he is being tested. Otherwise, even if the subject is honest and cooperative, his judgment will be affected and we do not get a valid result. If we are testing a subject's ability to discriminate between different weights, by having him compare a 10-oz. weight with a 9-oz. and an 11-oz. weight, we must not allow him to see that the 11-oz. weight is larger than the 10-oz. or the 9-oz. one; standard procedure here is to use identical cardboard boxes containing lead shot (packed in cotton wool to prevent auditory cues), so that the total weight is 9 oz., or 10 oz., and so on, in a series of boxes that are otherwise indistinguishable.

If we are trying to discover how far apart two stimulated points on the skin must be, in order to be recognized as two and not one (the "two-point limen"), we must not allow the subject to see the two points of the dividers as they are applied to the skin; and the two points must touch the skin at the same time or else, feeling two separate stimulations, one after another, the subject would know that he was being stimulated by the two points whether he perceived them as being in different spots on the skin or not. If we are trying to determine how faint a light the subject can see, there must not be the click of a switch to tell him when the light is on or off. If one is trying to determine a limen for pain, by slowly increasing the amount of electric current passed through an area of skin until the subject reports pain, one must not let the subject see the rheostat

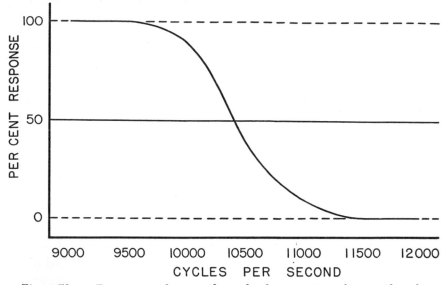

Figure 78.   Determining the upper limen for the perception of tones. The subject never hears 11,500 cycles as a tone; he always hears 9,500 as a tone. Considering the frequency which is heard on 50 per cent of the trials, the limen is about 10,500; but we might take the 75 per cent point instead (about 10,000), or even the 100 per cent point (9,500), depending on the circumstances in which the limen is to be used.

scale by which the current strength is determined; for subjects have a liking for consistency, and if a man knows that he reported pain last time when the needle got to 1.7 on the scale he is likely to do so this time when it gets to that point, whether he really feels pain or not. This is so even when the subject means to be honest; suggestion can be a very distorting factor in such determinations.

Next, it is always essential to make a number of determinations if one wishes to be exact. The reliability of the individual determination is not great, but the mean of a number of determinations is of course much more reliable. We treat these as a sample from an infinitely large population of such determinations, and, as we saw in Chapter 11, the probable degree of discrepancy between the mean of the population and the sample mean gets smaller as the sample gets larger. Also, making a number of independent determinations allows us to determine how variable they are and whether the probable error is large or small.

A further consideration: the limen is not a single point, above which the stimulus is always effective, below which it is never effective. When careful determinations are made, a range of uncertainty is always found. This may be illustrated in the determination of the upper limen for hearing a tone. Hearing for high-pitched tones is a characteristic that varies with age, youthful subjects being able to hear tones of about 14,000 cycles per second, while older subjects can go only to perhaps 9,000 even though they are not deaf in the usual sense of the term. Let us suppose that we are dealing with a man in his thirties. By means of an oscillator we produce a pure tone increasing steadily from 7,000 or 8,000 cycles per second until the subject reports that he does not hear a tone. We do this repeatedly and get an average value of, let us say, 10,650 cycles. Now we start from above and move down from 14,000 cycles until the subject reports a tone. The average of this second set of determinations, however, is not at the same point, but at 10,200.

What is the limen? 10,650 or 10,200? One way of dealing with this situation is just to take an average of the two values. Another way, more elaborate but in principle much the same, is illustrated in Fig. 78. We stimulate repeatedly with tones of 9,000, 9,500, 10,000, 10,500, 11,000, 11,500 and 12,000, *in random order;* and record the number of times each is heard as a tone. We find that tones up to 9,500 are always heard, and tones of 11,500 and up are never heard. We draw the curve for all frequencies, as in the figure, and the point where this curve crosses the horizontal line representing 50 per cent response we may say is "the" limen: with frequencies below this point, the chances are in favor of obtaining a response; above, against it. However, the limen may be defined instead as the point at which 75 per cent response is obtained instead of 50 per cent, or 90 or 99 per cent, depending on the purpose to which the determination is to be put.

Quantifying memory

Our next examples are taken from the field of memory, in which measurement is also relatively direct. We do however encounter the problem of the selection of units of quantification, and the fact that each measurement is likely to modify the memory we are measuring.

The problem of units of measurement offers little difficulty with certain artificial material, such as nonsense syllables or mazes; one simply counts the number of syllables the subject can recall, or the number of blind alleys he enters, obtaining a success score or an error score. It is more difficult to quantify memory of a complex experience such as reading a novel or, still more difficult, memory of childhood or the events of a summer holiday. To attack such a problem one would use a sampling method, and one would immediately encounter a problem of validity: are the items on which one has chosen to question the subject representative of the whole experience? It is for reasons such as this that psychologists have devised a number of artificial learning tasks to study the course both of learning and of forgetting.

The second problem, arising from the fact that testing a subject's memory changes it for future tests, must be handled in general by the use of groups. When one wishes to know the rate of forgetting of nonsense syllables, instead of testing the same group repeatedly one must establish a number of comparable groups and test the first at one minute (for example) after learning is complete, a second group two minutes after, a third five minutes after, and so on; for merely testing the first group at one minute may serve to remind them of syllables they had forgotten, and reinforces the memory of those they do recall.

The three main methods of testing memory are: *recall* or *reproduction; recognition,* or selective response to an object seen before as distinct from those not seen; and the method of *savings,* based on the rate of relearning. The first of these, recall, is what one usually thinks of when one speaks of memory—the facts you can write down in an examination are the facts you remember, others you say have been "forgotten." But the fact that cannot be recalled may still be recognized. In multiple-choice examinations, the student may be offered a number of statements from which to select the correct one. Here it is the recognition rather than the recall method that is made use of.

For our present purposes, however, the savings method is of most interest as a method of psychological measurement. A subject has been trained, let us say, to repeat a list of nonsense syllables. After some days, we test him by the method of recall, and find that he cannot "remember" any of the syllables (or perhaps can remember one or two). Has he then lost all, or nearly all, of what he acquired in learning the syllables? We now test him in another way, by seeing how many repetitions of the list are needed before he can again repeat it perfectly; and we find that he only needs half as many repetitions as on first learning. From one point of view, it would therefore be much more accurate to say that, instead of having forgotten nearly completely, he had only forgotten half of what he had learned, even though he may not have been able to repeat a single syllable.

Intelligence and its measurement

We can turn now to the example par excellence of psychological measurement, the first great demonstration of the practical value of psychological methods outside the academic field and the one that best illustrates the possibilities and the difficulties of quantifying complex variables in behavior: the measurement of intellectual capacity. Our discussion will not be restricted to method alone. In order to see what the problems are, one must consider something of the nature of intelligence, and the theoretical limitations on the meaning of this term. Only thus will we be able to see the limitations on the results of measurement.

In a sense, what happened early in the century was that Binet, the great French psychologist from whose work modern intelligence tests derive, learned how to measure something without any very clear idea as to what it was he was measuring. His method was extremely successful. By allowing us to quantify, it has resulted in greatly changing our ideas about intelligence, and shown us the nature of the problem more clearly.

Let us clarify our terms before going on. "Intelligence" at best is not very precise, but even so it happens to be used in two quite different senses: (A) it is what one is born with, the innate quality of brain function quite apart from the question of what knowledge or skill the subject may acquire by experience; and (B) it is the average level of comprehension, problem-solving, or intellectual function in general, in the half-grown or fully-grown subject.

We may then define *intelligence A* as an innate potential for the development of intellectual functions. *Intelligence B* is the average level of that development, at some later date. Intelligence A cannot be tested, B can, though a rough estimate of A is possible in certain circumstances. The student should recognize that A and B are not two different things, entirely separate: on the contrary, A enters into and is a necessary feature of B. What we are distinguishing here are two different ways in which the word intelligence is used.

Let us now look at the methods used to measure intelligence B, coming back later to its relation with intelligence A.

The first point is that these methods are empirically justified, not theoretically, though theory may subsequently catch up. For example, one might devise a measure of intelligence by saying, Intelligence is the capacity to solve problems, so we will get a collection of puzzles for our test. This would be a logically theoretical approach. Or one might say, Intelligence is the capacity to adapt to the environment, so we will test our subjects by putting them into strange situations; or, It is the capacity to learn, so we will measure their ability to memorize lists of nonsense syllables. And so on. But these theoretical approaches do not work. Binet tried a different one. In effect he asked, What do bright subjects[1] do that dull ones do not? and when he found things that distinguished the bright from the dull in this way he put them into his

---

[1] Here of course the question of validity enters, as troublesome as ever. Until we have a test of intelligence, how can we tell which subjects are bright and which dull? What Binet actually did was assume that older children are better problem-solvers, have a more developed intelligence, than younger ones—on the average. Some five-year-olds are better than some six-year-olds, but as a group six-year-olds surpass five-year-olds. Binet then used test items on which scores increased with age in growing children, and discarded others.

This method cannot be used with adults, and the great American psychologist Thorndike proposed another approach. Let us say that intelligence is the quality in which a group of geniuses, such as Newton, Einstein, Leonardo, Aristotle, Pasteur and so on, differs most from the occupants of a home for the mentally deficient. This defines our two groups for choosing test items. It is not very practical as it stands, because most of our geniuses are dead; but one can modify it in practice as follows. In any society there are people who are known to be skilful, ingenious, good learners and so on, and others who are known to be the opposite, on the basis of years of observation by others. These judgments are none too reliable in the individual case, but it is hardly to be doubted that if we set up two groups in this way one would be on the average much better than the other. We could then validate our test items.

The ultimate validation, the real evidence that such procedures do in fact work effectively, is found in later experience with the test. The validity of Binet's method was established gradually, over a period of years; it was found, in fact, by many different workers in different countries, to be the best predictor of level of performance in varying occupations.

test. Everything that did not he kept out, whether it "should" be a good test or not. This is an empirical procedure.

For example, one would not think that seeing the point of a rather bad joke could be used to detect the level of a child's intelligence, though —after we find that this is in fact so—one can see in retrospect that it may not be unreasonable. One would not think that such tasks as copying a simple diagram from memory, discriminating between a neatly drawn and an untidily drawn face, or stringing beads (alternating square ones with round ones), would function in this way. Yet these tasks do in fact discriminate between levels of intelligence in young children. It was Binet's brilliant achievement to discover that such tasks serve the purpose where others, a priori more plausible as tests of intelligence, do not.

The essence of the matter is in applying the item-analysis procedure described in the first part of this chapter. To construct a new intelligence test the first requirement is a group of bright subjects and a group of dull subjects. Then, with each task or problem that one proposes to put into the test, one looks to see how it functions. If the bright do well and the dull do badly on a particular problem, one can keep it in the test; if not one cannot, no matter how ingenious and promising it seemed when one thought it up.

Applying this criterion has produced some rather surprising results. The best test material, in general, does not consist of new tasks that seem to challenge one's problem-solving capacities, but of familiar or near-familiar ones. These can be called Binet-type tasks. They include such things as giving the name of the sovereign or president who was in office before the present one, completing analogies like "Boy is to girl as man is to——," explaining in what respect an airplane is like a balloon, recognizing an absurdity in a picture or supplying a missing part (such as drawing in the fingers on a hand), or drawing a simple diagram from memory.

Most of these are related to past experience; they really ask, How much has the subject learned, without any special training, about his environment? What sort of problems has he solved for himself in his observation of common phenomena and of social relations? Even in the last example, memory for a diagram, success depends on the subject's noticing that the diagram consists (for example) of a square rather than a rectangle, plus a diagonal rather than a vertical line which passes through the midpoint of the base; whether he notes such detail or not, and reproduces it, is to a great extent determined by his earlier perceptions of the everyday environment. The Binet-type test essentially samples the subject's level of *past* observation and thought.

An excellent example is the fact that about the best single index of intelligence—if one has to use a single kind of material—is the subject's score on a vocabulary test. One would not have guessed this a priori; but having found that it is so, one can see that the more observant subject, the better learner, the subject who has developed more concepts (ready for words to be attached to them), might be expected to have a larger vocabulary.

The words in the test must not be technical words, of course. The essence of the method is to sample experiences that are open as far as possible to all members of the culture in which the test is to be used, and to avoid specialized fields (including higher education). Another principle of great importance is closely related. A rating of intelligence should be based not on a single kind of material, but on a variety of materials, because the subject for some reason may not have had adequate exposure to one particular kind; varying the test materials makes the score more representative of all aspects of the subject's ability. Thus he might have a relatively poor vocabulary and still make a high score on the whole test.

This brings us to the next point. In varying the test material one should use nonverbal as well as verbal tests. The nonverbal test is usually (though not necessarily) more puzzle-like than the verbal, and has a special value in rating intelligence. As we have seen, the Binet-type test item asks the subject to reproduce some of his past thinking or learning, and characteristically it seems obvious and easy to the subject who can do it at all. Why is this picture funny? What is the meaning of the proverb, "Once bitten, twice shy"? What is the capital of Italy?

The puzzle-like item makes a more active demand on the subject, appears to him to require effort and thought. It may consist of arranging a series of pictures so as to tell a story, or putting blocks together to form a certain pattern, or tracing a path through a printed maze without making any error. Thus we may think of the Binet-type item as sampling the subject's *past* problem-solving, the puzzle-like item as requiring problem-solving of him here and now.

The difference between them permits a certain kind of diagnosis. If something has happened to impair the subject's mental processes, so that his present level of intellectual function is lower than in the past, the Binet-type test should show a higher level than the puzzle-like test. This in fact is what is observed in cases of mental illness; after brain damage (provided the subject's language capacity is not interfered with, as in aphasia: p. 84f.); and in old age. If no deterioration of mental capacity has occurred, the two kinds of test should show about the same level of ability.

Such diagnosis does not have a very high reliability, because normal subjects differ in past experience and thus often show some difference between Binet-type and puzzle-like tests even though no deterioration has occurred. But in general, it is not a good sign when a subject shows a higher verbal score than a nonverbal, since the verbal tests now in use are mostly Binet-type, the nonverbal mostly puzzle-like; it is suggestive at least that some disturbance of mental functioning is present. On the other hand, when a patient is found after a bout of mental illness or after a brain operation to have as high a score on nonverbal tests as on verbal, this is a strong indication that he has made a good recovery.

The meaning of the IQ

The result of an intelligence test may be given simply as a score. If a test gives a mean score of 72 for the population and an SD of 20, the subject who gets 65 or 80 is in the middle ranges, one who gets a score of less than 52 is in the bottom sixth of the population, and so on.

Usually, however, the result is given as an *intelligence quotient* (IQ). To see how this is obtained we must consider first the *mental age*, or MA. The child who makes the same score as the mean for 6-year-olds has an MA of 6; if he falls halfway between the means for 8 years and 9 years, an MA of 8.5; and so on. The IQ then is 100 times the quotient MA/CA (CA being chronological age). With an MA of 6, CA 4, the child has an IQ of 150; MA 6, CA 6, IQ 100; MA 6, CA 8, IQ 75. The IQ may thus be regarded as indicating the rate of intellectual development during childhood. A high IQ means that the child is ahead of his age group, a low one that he is behind.

At maturity the situation is rather different, because intelligence-test performance does not continue to rise after the age of 15 or thereabouts (the exact age is not known, and probably differs according to IQ). Thus the subject cannot have an MA over 15, strictly speaking, and if we continued to divide MA by CA the IQ would fall steadily, and rapidly, as the subject got beyond the chronological age of 15. However, this situation can be avoided by (1) taking 15 as the CA for all adults in calculating IQ, and (2) working out a set of artificial MA's that go beyond 15, arranging these so that the mean IQ for adults continues to be 100 and the SD 15 (p. 226).

In the adult subject, therefore, the IQ can be considered to represent the estimated rate of intellectual development during childhood, assuming that those who developed to the highest level had the fastest rate of development and vice versa—an assumption for which there is a good deal of evidence. But the essential significance of the IQ at any age is to give us a ranking of the subject with respect to the general population. For any given IQ we can determine in what fraction of the population the subject falls with respect to intelligence B.

We have already seen that a man may make a higher score on one kind of test material than another, and that the score depends in part on what kinds of past experience he has had. Whether intelligence A is unitary or not we do not know, but it is clear that intelligence B is made up of a number of separate abilities. It is not a unitary thing or process or problem-solving power. *Factor analysis* is a complex mathematical method of analyzing test scores which shows that we are dealing with at least seven or eight separate components, or factors, in measurement of intelligence. We do not know precisely how these are to be weighted (that is, which are more important, or how much more important) when they are combined in an intelligence test. "Intelligence" therefore is a rough working conception—a very valuable one, as a sort of estimate of the average level of intellectual function—but a first approximation only. For more exact analysis the separate factors, or different forms of problem-solving, must be treated separately. This is especially important in dealing with the patient who has had a brain operation, or the subject whose environment during the period of growth (up to the age of 15 years or so) is different from that of other members of the culture in which he now is.

Also, the IQ itself is not an exact measure. The tests from which it is calculated have reliabilities of the order of .90 to .94, and this means that there may be a considerable difference in score when a subject is retested (cf. Fig. 76). Fortunately, the error of measurement is least with the low IQ. The person who gets an IQ of 125 on one test might get 118, perhaps, or 130, on a second test, but at this level nobody's future is likely to be determined finally by the precise value of his IQ. But a low IQ may determine whether the subject is to be classed as feeble-minded or not, or whether he is fit to go to school; and here the probable error is small. An IQ of 56 on one test means that a subject might get 55 or 57, or even 60 (though this would be infrequent), on a second, so that a good deal of weight can be given to such a result.

The student is reminded, however, that the validity of the test depends on the subject's having had adequate exposure to the culture in which he is living, and it is often hard to be sure of this. A final decision as to the future of the subject should never rest on a test result alone. Dogmatism does not become a psychologist, even in the field of mental measurement.

The *constancy of the IQ* is another point on which dogmatism is out of order. It was thought earlier that heredity alone, or almost alone, determined the IQ. Therefore, if an IQ could be determined at the age of 2 years (which it can) one would know what the IQ would be for the rest of the subject's life (since his heredity of course does not change). We now know however that the IQ, though constant in the adult, is not constant during the period of growth. As we have seen (Chap. 6), intelligence *B* and the IQ are joint products of heredity and environmental processes. The potential of intelligence *A* needs environmental stimulation to develop into intelligence *B*. The effects of such stimulation during the growth period are in great degree permanent, for good or ill, so that the level of intelligence *B* which is achieved by the age of 15 or thereabouts will last. A subject may have a good intelligence *A* and be reared in a stimulating environment, producing a good intelligence B; thereafter he will always have that level of intelligence (unless he becomes a victim of disease, malnutrition or injury that affects brain function). But the same subject, if he is reared instead in an inadequate environment, will have a low intelligence B; and manipulation of his environment after the age of 15 will not significantly raise it.

From these considerations it is clear that the level of intelligence B, which we can measure, does not necessarily reflect the level of intelligence A, and hence that we cannot really measure A. B reflects A if we can assume an adequate environment for the full development of A's potential. If the environment is good and B is low, A must have been low also; but a low IQ obtained by a subject reared in an inadequate (or doubtfully adequate) environment leaves a question as to whether the result is due to a low intelligence A or not.

Unfortunately we have no very good knowledge of what kind of environmental stimulation is necessary to the full development of intelligence B and the IQ. One may guess that an exposure to ideas, through conversation or books, is a prerequisite; one may guess also that the exposure need not be prolonged, that relatively infrequent stimulation occurring at fortunate times will have disproportionately great effects, by setting up an active seeking out of further stimulation. Some of the most profoundly intelligent men have come from what seem, at least on the surface, very limited backgrounds.

These men are evidence of the existence of great differences in intelligence A (though not as conclusive as when a man of low intelligence comes from a good environment). The point here, however, is that we have no good way of assessing the role of the cultural environment quantitatively, and thus no basis for measuring intelligence A when there is any doubt of the adequacy of the environment during growth. It is rarely, among subjects of low IQ, that such doubts would not be justified; and we cannot conclude therefore that all, or even most, such subjects have as poor a native endowment as the test seems to imply. A low test score does not necessarily mean a poor heredity.

A closely related point: it is a well-established principle in psychology that no valid comparison can be made of innate intelligence between members of different cultures. The classical case is the comparison of Negro and white in the United States. Negroes in general were found during the first world war to have lower IQ's than whites in general; but it was easily shown that they also had, as a group, much less exposure to the test materials by which the IQ was established. This means in short that though we can validly compare specific components of *intelligence B,* in subjects of diverse backgrounds, we have no basis for comparing their innate intellectual potentials, or their children's. The measurement of intelligence fundamentally consists of ranking the subjects of a particular culture with respect to their levels of intellectual development. It does not give an absolute measure of what they might have been capable of in an optimal environment.

Summary

Reliability and validity are fundamental aims in measurement. Reliability means consistency of test scores (a second measurement of the same thing should give the same result); but the reliability of most psychological measurements, unfortunately, is not high. Validity cannot really be got at directly, in practice; ideally, it is the correlation of one's measure with a perfect measure of the thing one is interested in.

The problems that are involved are illustrated in the comparison of objective with essay examinations: the objective examination is capable of higher reliability, but at the risk of sacrificing validity: it may not measure what one wants it to. There are special precautions one can take. These involve the use of two criterion groups, one high in ability, one low. The scores they make on individual test items permit one to see which are invalid, and reject such items from the test. The same kind of procedure is fundamental to the construction of an intelligence test.

The measurement of limens is usually considered to mark the beginning of experimental psychology as a separate discipline from philosophy, which took place about 1860. When the routine precautions are taken to prevent the subject from making his judgment by means of extraneous cues, no problem of validity arises in these measurements; but the reliability of a single determination is apt to be low, and repeated testing is necessary to minimize quantitative error.

A special problem arises in the measurement of memory; the act of measurement changes the thing one is measuring. Thus, to follow the decline of memory with time, separate groups must be tested, one for each different interval. There are three kinds of memory test: recall, recognition and "savings."

The chief emphasis in this chapter is given to the measurement of intelligence, partly because of its intrinsic importance, partly because it illustrates the problems of measuring a complex entity or group of entities. The main problem was solved when Binet abandoned logically meaningful definitions of intelligence a priori, and instead asked what differences of response could be found between a more intelligent child and a less intelligent one. No item is included because intelligent persons *should* do well with it; only ones on which they *do* do well. The most valid items, the ones which are most closely related to a wide range of intellectual functioning, are based on problem-solving and thinking the subject has done in the past. These are mostly verbal tests. However, it is important to include with them some test items which come closer to problem-solving here and now, many of which are nonverbal. Comparison of results on the two kinds of items then may give some sign when intellectual deterioration is going on, for the "past-experience" items should show a higher score than the "present problem-solving" items. This is not always a valid index, however.

The IQ is primarily a rate of intellectual development during childhood (the MA refers to the level of development). The IQ at maturity does not refer to a present rate of development, since the one we are dealing with ends about the age of 15 years; but those who develop at a faster rate in childhood end up at higher levels, so the IQ at maturity is interpreted simply as giving a comparison of intellectual level with other members of the culture. The "constancy of the IQ" holds only at maturity; during growth the IQ is subject to the influence of cultural experience.

"Intelligence" is used to refer both to (A) one's innate intellectual potential, and (B) the extent to which that potential is realized in later life. These two meanings are separated as "intelligence A" and "intelligence B." It is well established that intelligence A cannot be validly compared in two persons with significantly different past experiences, since experience affects test performance. Comparisons of intelligence B are somewhat less open to criticism, as long as the false inference is not drawn that differences are necessarily due to hereditary endowment (i.e., to intelligence A).

Notes

For the general problems of measurement in psychology, see Chapter 1 (Stevens) in Stevens' *Handbook;* the special problems of measuring limens and memory are also discussed in various chapters of the *Handbook* as well as in Osgood, and Woodworth and Schlosberg (*General References,* Chap. 1).

On the nature of intelligence, its decline with various pathological conditions (including age over 25), and its measurement, see D. Wechsler, *Measurement of Adult Intelligence,* Williams and Wilkins Co., 1944. A more detailed presentation of the point of view of the present chapter will be found in Chap. 11 of Hebb, *Organization of Behavior,* John Wiley & Sons, 1949.

Chapter 13

Psychology and the
scientific method

Let us now cast up our accounts, return to the problems
raised in Chapter 1 and see how they look in the perspective of the
chapters that have followed. It was proposed that psychology deals with
behavior, and that behavior consists only of muscle activity and glandular
secretion. On the face of it, this is far removed from what many students
are interested in when they enroll for a course in psychology. It has been
seen, however, that understanding behavior does have its complexities,
and that such an approach need not shut us off from a consideration of
mental processes—even quite subtle ones.

The systematic application of objective scientific method has changed
the countenance of academic or "pure" psychology completely in the
past half century.[1] The changes have been taken mostly for granted in
the preceding chapters. We may now consider them more closely, first
with regard to the relation to applied psychology, and secondly with
regard to the contribution or otherwise of quantitative methods and
neurological ideas, both of which may seem foreign to the true concerns
of psychology.

[1] Since (1) 1912, when Gestalt psychology began as a reaction against both the old-
fashioned introspective brand of psychology, and the newer S-R brand of Thorndike;
and (2) 1913, when Watson formally launched the behaviorist movement (see below).
By 1950, psychology as a unified body of knowledge could very nearly be described as
a synthesis of these two movements.

The several faces of psychology

Psychology, as defined, comprises a number of different kinds of enterprise, so different that they may seem to have nothing in common. One psychologist is engaged in vocational guidance; he spends his day talking to high school students, studying their academic records and their test scores and from these, in principle, showing the student how to clarify his own ideas about his future training and occupation. Another spends his day studying delayed reaction in goldfish or the navigation of bats. Other psychologists are assisting in the diagnosis of neurotic patients, doing research on the childhood experiences that contribute to neurosis, or taking part in a combined research on the effects of tranquillizers. But all such disparate activities have this in common, that the methods derive from the same fundamental training in the procedures and conceptions of academic psychology, and that the worker is either putting the conceptions to practical use or trying to improve on them (or both).

The effective application of method still requires a general background in academic theory. It is this background that psychologists share—together with the fact that most psychologists are interested in advancing *both* theory and application. The man whose main work is some form of counselling, for example, may seize every free hour to get on with a theoretical analysis of data he has obtained from his clients' test scores; the man whose primary work is pure research is excited when he sees some practical consequence of his own work, or that of a colleague, published in the *Psychological Review* or the *Journal of Comparative and Physiological Psychology* (than which none is purer).

The same psychologist thus wears two hats, applied and theoretical or professional and academic. It is this that may make difficulty in distinguishing between psychology (1) as a profession and (2) as a science. Nevertheless, the distinction can be made if we do not try to find some great gulf between the two aspects; and making it helps us to understand the difficulty some students have with the introductory course in psychology. Psychology has mostly been popularized in its professional aspect, and the student may have enrolled with the expectation of finding out how to get over shyness and lack of confidence, or some other difficulty of his own, or how to go out at once and start benefiting society. It then comes as a shock to find that he needs first to master basic facts and theory, before beginning to practice the profession. Every competent wearer of the professional hat has first fitted on, and become at home with, the academic one. Without that academic background, he is not a psychologist, no matter how eager he may be to help mankind.

There is a similar hurdle to be passed by the neophyte scientist, the student who wants to make discoveries and add to knowledge. He too may have picked up false expectations, from popularizations of the scientific method; looking forward to dramatic disclosures about the human mind, he is offered instead a plodding discussion of limens, conditioning, reaction times and reflexes. But if he can survive the apprenticeship he will find that the excitement is still there.

At the very heart of the scientific method is a preference for simple procedures, for reducing the complex problem to a number of simpler ones; this makes for a better control of independent variables (Chap. 11) and helps in identifying the a priori assumptions that may need to be changed before the problem is solved (Chap. 10). At first sight, and especially to the beginner, some of the value and interest in the problem may be lost in so doing. But this is at first sight only; the maneuvers do not evade battle but seek the vulnerable flank of the problem; and there is no more exciting event in science than the simple little experiment, trivial in itself, that points up a mistaken assumption of the past and shows a new way of dealing with larger problems.

Often we must approach the important questions by indirection. If statistical analyses seem dull to most students, if tests of a dog's intelligence interest no one but the pet lover, the impact of such methods on our understanding of human behavior is far from dull. Science has been well described as an intellectual adventure; it is unfortunate that before the student can reach the adventurous and exciting part he must do some work, but the reward for work is there. At present psychology is in a period of rapid development affecting the most diverse questions—from learning sets to the selection of foremen, from the "maternal instinct" to brain-washing—and in each case the development can be clearly traced to some feature of scientific method in "pure" psychology; and in each case, solving one problem tends to make two grow in its place, so there will be plenty left for the future scientist to do.

The effects of quantification

The history of experimental (as contrasted with armchair) psychology could almost be written as the history of the development of quantitative methods. As late as 1850 it seems to have been generally considered that the study of mind was by its nature a matter for the philosopher, with no possibility of experimental analysis. By 1875 this opinion had vanished, or was rapidly vanishing; and what had made the difference was the appearance of two forms of measurement, of the strength of sensation, and of reaction time. Neither originated in the work of psychologists; the work on sensation began with the interest of Weber, a physiologist, in skin sensitivity, and that on reaction times in the astronomer Bessel's concern with certain errors of time estimation in recording the exact moment at which a star reached a certain point in the heavens. Neither measurement has now the fundamental significance for psychology which at first it seemed to have. Nevertheless, these events turned psychology into a quantitative experimental study at the same time that they led, if tortuously, to more fruitful problems.

Fechner, who may be said to be the first experimental psychologist (he was also a physicist), extended Weber's observations and generalized the results in what is known as the Weber-Fechner law. This says (roughly) that the strength of a sensation increases as the logarithm of the strength of the stimulus. The law has had to be radically modified; the relation of sensation to stimulus is nothing like as simple as this; but the important point is that sensation was considered to be a mental event, and so a mental event had been measured for the first time (accurately or not). The impact on the armchair analyzers was tremendous.

The study of reaction times may be seen in the same light. At first it appeared to be an avenue of direct attack on higher mental processes. It was found for example that simple reaction time (a single stimulus and a single response to be made) was quicker than reaction time requiring a discrimination (e.g., press the left button for a red light, the right button for a green light). Was it not possible then to subtract (1) simple reaction time from (2) the time needed for reaction plus discrimination, and thus measure precisely the duration of a mental process, discrimination? Unfortunately, it turned out that the attitude of making the choice affected the whole process of reaction, rather than being a separate event in time, and this form of analysis had to be abandoned. But in the course of such work the problems of set and attention began to show up—reaction time depends on set, and varies according to whether the subject attends to the impending stimulus event or to the response to be made to it—and, though it took a long time to get these latter problems clarified, merely getting them formulated in experimental terms was a big step forward in the analysis of behavior.

In this atmosphere of experimentation and measurement two other events of long-lasting significance occurred. In 1885 Ebbinghaus reported his studies of learning and memory, which were directly inspired by Fechner's measurement of sensation. It was thought at the time that learning was a process too subtle and involved to be dealt with experimentally, much less measured. There may be difficulty of this sort with some of the complex learning of everyday life, as we have seen (p. 245), but the difficulty was completely avoided by Ebbinghaus's invention of nonsense syllables. They provided definite units for measuring retention, and minimized confusing effects from other, earlier, learning. The results in general were so clear-cut that eventually other workers were emboldened to apply the methods to more complex and meaningful material.

The second event was Binet's 1905 publication of an effective method of quantifying intelligence in school children.

Between them, these two events determined in large part the shape of psychology at the present day. Jointly, they made possible an experimental educational psychology. The method of measuring intelligence was promptly extended to deal with special abilities (mechanical aptitude, for example, or musical appreciation), and its success stimulated the ingenuity of other investigators to devise methods of measuring such things as neurotic tendency, vocational interest, masculinity versus feminity, or the authoritarian (i.e., anti-democratic) attitude, or the attitude toward God. Applied psychology—educational, clinical, counselling, industrial—and the study of personality alike are inherently a realm of quantitative procedures.

In theoretical and academic psychology, the learning problem and its ramifications are central. Ebbinghaus's work with man was followed by Thorndike's with animals, in which he encountered at once the question of thought processes (is the cat's learning an acquisition of S-R connections only, or is it also affected by ideas?) and the nature of motivation and reinforcement (in the law of effect). These are theoretical problems that we are still struggling with. They were first clearly recognized as a result of the methods of quantifying learning and performance, and work on these problems still depends on such methods to a very great extent.

The student must not gain the impression that this is a complete picture of modern psychology. Far from it. Together with the emphasis on learning theory (represented after 1935 by Hull) went a powerful opposing reaction by the *Gestalt* group (including Köhler) and later Lashley and Tolman. The view taken was essentially that the problems of perception and thought could not be dealt with in Thorndike's or Watson's terms: a point that we shall return to in a moment. The critique, by experimental methods, added immeasurably to our knowledge of behavior. Modern psychology, in fact, constitutes a rapidly developing and intricate pattern, and cannot well be defined in terms of one component only; but the quantitative thread can be found running all through it, with a greater importance as the intricacy of the pattern increases.

Neurologizing and theory

It was Thorndike in 1898 who really posed the problem of the thought process in an effective way, by denying that it existed in his cats, and doubting that it did in monkeys. Watson, the founder of behaviorism (p. 3), drove the point home in 1913 by denying the existence of ideas, images, purpose—any of the supposed components of thought—even in man. The earlier chapters of the present text, in the discussion of mediating processes, have tried to show that this was an erroneous position; and yet to formulate it clearly, in the context of definite experimental procedures, was one of the great clarifications of psychology. Thorndike and Watson produced for the first time an intelligible theory of behavior, one that showed others how to go about attacking it experimentally and how to broaden psychology in so doing.

It is important to understand this point. A man who constructs a theory is certainly trying to hit on the truth, but the function of theory is better seen, perhaps, if we regard it as a sophisticated statement of ignorance: "sophisticated," because the ignorance is put in a form that shows us how to go about decreasing it. The function of theory is to guide us to new observations and better experiments. If it does this it is good, whether it is "true" or not. (In our present state of knowledge it is hardly likely that any theory will do justice to the complexities of mental function. It has already been seen that we do not yet understand the behavior of the laboratory rat, let alone man's. Good theory leads to its own destruction by making better theory possible; since a new theory is generally a qualification or extension or restructuring of older ones, not something entirely unrelated, progress is made by successive approximations.)

In this light we can see better what Thorndike did. He was preceded by others—Lloyd Morgan and Romanes especially—who had made a considerable clarification of the issues in animal learning. Undoubtedly they contributed to his success. But it was he who made the bold stroke of saying that his cats learned to get out of puzzle boxes without any benefit of "understanding" (i.e., mediating processes). He described learning solely in terms of S-R connections, and his law of effect, attempting to say when connections would be strengthened or weakened by the repetition of an act, was the first formulation of an essential problem (p. 136).

By current standards these formulations were none too satisfactory in experimental terms, but they were a great advance on what had gone before, and their implications were clear enough to be understood and strongly objected to by those who had ideas about a richer mental life— even in cats. The answer was Hobhouse's brilliant experiments of 1901, repeated by Köhler in 1917. These were the original experiments on insight (Chap. 10). Köhler's analysis particularly is another landmark in psychology; it was straight to the point, and it left no doubt of the existence of complications in behavior that were not accounted for by Thorndike's approach.

What the complications meant, however, was not so clear. Animals think—but what does "think" mean? Just what is the behavioral significance of such a statement? The clearest answer was provided by Hunter's delayed-reaction procedure in 1913 (p. 54): a simple and precise attack on the problem. Neural conduction is rapid; if behavior is determined only by S-R connections, a stimulus must have its effect promptly or not at all. Hunter argued therefore that the ability to make a delayed response would be a sign of ideation. As we have seen, this is still a fundamental approach to the problem.

EARLY NEUROLOGIZING.   Much that is puzzling about the early discussions becomes clearer when we realize that the neurological information and ideas available for psychological use were primitive compared to what is available today.

Watson in particular was engaged in making psychology into a completely objective study, a biological science in which no immaterial mind or soul would have anything to do with the control of behavior. The means of doing so was to explain behavior strictly in terms of neural activities, and this meant the S-R formula. The nervous system was thought of by the physiologists as a collection of paths running from receptor to effector, some longer and less direct (e.g., via the cortex), but all one-way streets; the closed or re-entrant pathways that pervade the CNS had been described by the great Spanish anatomist Ramón y Cajal but were forgotten. Consequently, a delay in transmission seemed impossible to Watson. The delayed responses reported by Hunter, he thought, must be due to the muscular interplay described in the motor theory of thought (p. 58). It seemed that the only alternative to the S-R formula was mysticism.

Similarly, set or attention could not be understood. The differences of functioning in divergent and parallel paths, the importance of summation at the synapse, the arousal system, the continuous activity of neural cells as shown by the electroencephalogram—none of these were known of. Aspects of behavior that now present no special difficulty, because we can see at least a possibility of explaining them (Chap. 5), seemed wholly mysterious.

In short, the psychological evidence was in conflict with physiological theory. When theory is well established, in such a situation, one tends to reexamine the evidence carefully, to see whether perhaps it has been misinterpreted, or is open to other interpretations. Here is where Thorndike, Watson and Hunter come in. Alternatively, if one is convinced that theory is wrong, one may seek further and more convincing evidence to oppose it. This is what Hobhouse and Köhler did, and later Lashley, in a powerful series of experiments in the twenties which left no doubt that existing neurological ideas of learning would have to be modified.

From all this it can be seen that psychology in its historical period (arbitrarily considered here to be up to 1930) inherently involved neurophysiological conceptions, just as it was inherently quantitative in method. Few psychologists were using the *procedures* of physiology (i.e., they did not operate on the brain, or stimulate nerve tissue directly), but they made active use of physiological ideas. But with this there was also a vigorous skepticism about the accuracy or the sufficiency of such explanations, for the more closely behavior was examined the greater became the difficulty of accounting for it in terms of existing physiological knowledge.

This is our inheritance, from which we can hardly detach ourselves. On the one hand our most fundamental conceptions relate to the nervous system (hardly surprising, since behavior is after all under neural control). The reflex and conditioned reflex, part and parcel of psychology, are neurological conceptions, and so in origin is the S-R formula; attention and set became experimental problems only in the light of knowledge of the speed of transmission of nerve impulses; and similar considerations were at the bottom of the motor theory of thought. But on the other hand, the facts of behavior are just as stubborn as the facts of neural function, and persistently suggest qualifications in neurological theory. Eventually a satisfactory theory must include all the facts; we have seen, particularly in Chapters 7 to 10, that many aspects of behavior are still not explained in neurological terms, and the psychologist must maintain his skepticism toward what others tell him about what the brain can or cannot do, as the basis of behavior—a skepticism that is fully justified historically by the occasions on which psychological analysis anticipated physiological discovery.

The student may be surprised to find no mention of Pavlov's contribution in this account. Pavlov turned to neurophysiology about 1900, but had no influence on the development of psychological ideas until about 1918, when Watson adopted the conditioned-reflex terminology. By that time the psychological pattern was set. But the two lines of development were remarkably similar, and coalescence was prompt. By 1930 the CR was an integral part of psychology.

Further limits on neurologizing: psychological constructs

What has been said is this. Until neurological theory is much more adequate, the psychologist has to take it with a grain of salt. But we must go further. It seems that some aspects of behavior can never be dealt with in neurological terms alone. We turn next to the necessary limitations of neurologizing, and the use of psychological constructs: conceptions for dealing with behavior that do not derive from anatomy or physiology.

The essential point is that the simplest behavior of the whole animal involves a fantastic number of firings in individual neurons and muscle cells, as the animal moves for example out of the starting box in a maze, or as the student reads a line of this text. There is no possible way of keeping track of more than a few of these cells, and little prospect that it will become possible to do so in the future. To describe mental activity in such terms would be like describing a storm by listing every rain drop and every tiny movement of air.

We must have units on a larger scale for the description. To deal with the storm, the meteorologist speaks of showers or inches of rainfall instead of counting raindrops, the advancing cold front (extending over hundreds of miles), and so forth. For our problem, we can use neurological constructs such as a volley of impulses, the level of firing in the arousal system, or the occurrence of widespread summation in the cortex. But the intricacies of brain function are such that this still does not take us far enough, and we reach a point at which the use of psychological conceptions, on a still larger scale of complexity, becomes inevitable.

To discuss what goes on inside a rat's head as he runs the maze, for example, we use such terms as "hunger drive," "expectancy of food," "stimulus trace" and "the stimuli of the choice point." Such constructs have little direct reference to neural function. They were invented and subsequently refined in the context of studying behavior, and their use does not require any detailed knowledge of what is happening in the CNS. Of our psychological constructs, some are ancient and now have little value: "instinct" and "will" for example. Some older ones are not very precise, but still useful ("memory" or "intelligence"), some can be used quite precisely ("attention" or "after-image"); and some are wholly modern ("mediating process," "drive").

But now we come to the problem. How can some of our conceptions be psychological, some neurological? What is the working relation between the two?

The situation is that we have two ways of knowing about the workings of man's mind, one from examining the brain, one from observing behavior. We cannot afford to give up either (the problem is too great for us to neglect any possible clue to its solution). There is bound to be some difficulty about coordinating the two but this is something for research to handle. The situation is not peculiar to psychology, and there need be no logical inconsistency in using both large-scale and small-scale conceptions in the same set of ideas. (For example, the meteorologist can logically discuss both the formation of a snowflake and the behavior of a cold front.) Working out the relation between neurological and psychological conceptions, to avoid inconsistencies, has increased our knowledge both of brain function and of behavior.

This can be seen in the case of "ideation" or "mediating process." An essential part of the problem of thinking was first clarified when Hunter, following Thorndike, cast it in neurological terms: in short, the problem of "holding" (Chap. 3). Hunter's delayed-response experiment then showed that the existing neurological theory was wrong in some respects; it made no provision for holding, yet holding could be demonstrated experimentally. This in turn drew attention to the closed or circular paths in the CNS, as an explanation: a line of thought which was a corrective for earlier neurological theory.

But when an attempt was made to work this out in detail, it appeared that a number of individual neural loops might have to work together, in a cell-assembly, to account for the psychological facts. To form a cell-assembly might take a considerable time, requiring many sensory stimulations during the period of early infancy. Perception and thought would, in that case, depend on exposure to a normally-varied sensory environment during infancy. Alternatively, perception and thought might be innately organized. From this kind of question arose the experiments on early experience and "Factor IV" (p. 123) which add extensively to our knowledge of behavior, whether one is interested in the original neurological question or not.

It can be seen that "cell-assembly" and "mediating process" are two names for the same thing; yet there is a difference in meaning and in use. The cell-assembly idea is a hypothesis, in neurological terms, concerning the way in which a mediating process would function. It is a bridging conception, relating the mediating process—known from behavior—to brain function. Physiological psychology makes hypotheses about the nature of psychological constructs, on the assumption that the hypotheses may have clarifying value; but it does *not* try to get rid of all psychological constructs.

Psychology cannot become a branch of physiology. We cannot escape the need of large-scale units of analysis, nor the need of the special methods of behavioral study on which such analysis is based. Some of the most important aspects of brain function, that is, can only be known and studied by psychological methods.

It seems on occasion to be thought that the neurological entity is somehow more substantial, more "real," than psychological entities: that the study of nerve impulses is a more scientific affair than the study of anxiety or motivation. This is entirely mistaken. It may be that the "probable error" of a psychological conception is apt to be larger than that of the neural conceptions of anatomy and physiology, just as the probable error in psychological measurement is larger than in the physical sciences; this would hardly be surprising, in view of the complexity of the problems dealt with. Our conceptions, that is, may need more revision and sharpening. But they are not less related to reality. The wood is as real as the trees, a shower of rain as much an entity as the drops that compose it. There must be different levels of analysis in natural science, from the microscopic (or submicroscopic) to the large-scale macroscopic. At any given level, "reality" consists of the unanalyzed units whose existence is taken for granted as the basis for analyzing the next higher level of complexity. Otherwise we should have to deny the reality of the raindrop as well as of the shower; for the drop is "only" a group of molecules, and such reasoning would lead us to the ultimate conclusion that the only fit objects for scientific discourse are the subatomic particles of nuclear physics—this page would not exist as an entity, nor the student who is now reading it.

In these days when the peculiar notions of physics and chemistry have been validated in everyone's mind by such things as hydrogen bombs and sputniks, when such products of science as penicillin, cortisone and vitamin B_{12} have become commonplace, it is easy to forget how wild the speculation was that lay behind some of these developments, and how opposed to common sense. It is an implausible idea, to say the least, that energy is a form of mass, or vice versa; Newton found the Royal Society openly skeptical of the preposterous proposition that white light is simply a mixture of the colors of the rainbow; no good defense can be offered for the idea that the sun does not rise or set, that instead the earth is revolving and carrying us through space at speeds up to a thousand miles an hour. There is no defense for these ideas, that is, except that they work, and have led us to new understanding and new knowledge.

If then in psychology the student encounters ideas that clearly contradict common sense, this may be a sign not that the ideas are bad but that psychology is following in the grand traditions of science. We have hardly begun to understand the human mind; if the ideas with which we are working at this stage seem implausible, it can only be expected that they will become more so as the study of behavior progresses. With good fortune psychology may hope eventually to achieve that degree of implausibility—and fertility—that now characterizes the longer established sciences. .

Summary

Use of objective scientific methods in the present century has led academic psychology into some unexpected lines of enquiry, involving the development of elaborate quantitative methods and a considerable emphasis on the nervous system. Either or both may be a formidable deterrent to the student. What relevance have these for the study of the mind (or of behavior)?

Those whose interest lies in helping others find much more congenial topics in applied psychology. Yet the applications grew directly out of an interaction with academic psychology, and their use still depends on a mastery of academic conceptions. Fundamentally, applied and academic psychology are two facets of the same broadly-defined endeavor, the study of the more complex aspects of behavior.

Quantitative methods made modern psychology possible. Experimental psychology appeared first in the measurement of limens and reaction time, then broadened with the inclusion of human learning (Ebbinghaus and his nonsense syllables) and later animal learning (Thorndike and his cats). Paradoxically, the central problem presented by human thought was first clearly formulated (Watson, Hunter) in the context of studying learning in cats and monkeys; not so paradoxically, the formulation in terms of a very narrow theory led to a reaction (Hobhouse, Köhler) that broadened our knowledge of behavior and the methods available for its study.

The first quantifications assumed the truth of certain conceptions from neurology which we know now were grossly inadequate. Historically, psychology has been obliged to take two attitudes toward neural anatomy and physiology: (1) such knowledge is obviously important and has had great value for psychological purposes; (2) it has definite limitations and must be utilized with caution.

Though we must get as much value from neurologizing as we can, it will never be possible to substitute neurology for psychology. The complexity of the events controlling behavior is too great to be analyzed in terms of nerve impulses or the detailed relations between specific structures of the CNS. We must use larger-scale psychological conceptions as well as the smaller-scale neurological ones: constructs such as "fear" or "interests" or "learning capacity" which originate in trying to understand behavior rather than as inferences from known facts of neural

function. It is essential to work out the connection, hypothetically, between the two kinds of conception, and doing so is a corrective for both;
but we cannot expect in the foreseeable future that the purely psychological conception will become unnecessary.

Also, there is no inconsistency in a combined use of both kinds. A
geologist uses both photomicrographs and aerial survey photographs—
small-scale and large-scale analysis—in his study of rock formations. Conceptions of crystalline structure and of lava flow are coordinated by his
research, but with no expectation that his conclusions will ultimately be
reduced solely to one or to the other level of analysis.

Experimental and theoretical psychology is developing slowly, and we
are still concerned with problems that Thorndike raised in 1898 (and
some that were raised still earlier); but we deal with them now on a
very different footing, with a far clearer understanding of the enormous
complexities involved in the operations of the human mind and a much
better realization of what we do not know as well as what we do.

Some of the results of this process may be antithetical to common sense:
the idea, for example, that one can study another's mental processes by
objective methods better than one's own, introspectively. But the great
successes of the scientific method in other fields have flouted common
sense even more openly; the real test is not common sense, but whether
the ideas in question lead us to a better comprehension and control of
behavior.

Notes

For the way in which psychological ideas have developed, see E. G.
Boring, *History of Experimental Psychology*, 2nd ed., Appleton-Century-
Crofts, 1950; or G. Murphy, *Historical Introduction to Modern Psy-
chology*, rev. ed., Harcourt, Brace, 1949.

Lashley's experimental critique of early S-R theory can be found in
his book, *Brain Mechanisms and Intelligence*, University of Chicago
Press, 1929: a classic in the combination of physiological and psychological methods. He concluded that the cortex acts as a whole ("mass
action"), without differentiation except for the several sensory areas and
the motor area. The evidence was not entirely conclusive (cf. Morgan,
Chap. 20 in Stevens, *General References*, Chap. 1, p. 19), and some
more recent work seems clearly opposed (H. C. Lansdell, *J. Comp.
Physiol. Psychol.*, 1953, 46, 461–464; C. J. Smith, *J. Comp. Physiol.
Psychol.*, in press); but Lashley's work decisively refuted earlier theories,
and represents a turning point in the development of psychological
ideas.

On the uses and limitations of theory, see Conant (Chap. 10 *Notes*,
p. 219). The effect of neurological ideas on psychology has been discussed elsewhere (Hebb, *J. Personal.*, 1951, 20, 39–55; *Psychol. Rev.*,
1955, 62, 243–254).

Index